Learning to Listen: Life and a very nervous dog

Learning to listen

Life and a very nervous dog

Anne M. Scriven

Kennedy & Boyd

Kennedy & Boyd
an imprint of
Zeticula Ltd
The Roan,
Kilkerran,
KA19 8LS
Scotland.

http://www.kennedyandboyd.co.uk
admin@kennedyandboyd.co.uk

First published in 2013
Reprinted 2014
Copyright © Anne M. Scriven 2013
Cover photographs © Sam Scriven@me.com 2013

ISBN 978-1-84921-139-0

For my dancer with dogs — they are so lucky you exist.

What needs to be said.

As this is as near a true story as is possible, and as I would like to keep living where I live, I have changed, where strategic, some of the names of the real people and some of their dogs. They will now have a jolly time working out who is who and hopefully getting it wrong. By contrast, Sally and Jenna told me they are C21st girls and are willing to embrace the Celeb culture so I have retained their names. Sally also says that should this book go to film she doesn't want 'that wuss Lassie character' playing her as 'she's a total *looser*'. Further to this, Colum would like to be played by Viggo Mortensen, I would like to be played by Meg Ryan and Sam by Joseph Gordon-Levitt – even though they would have to work hard on their Scottish accents. Jen says she'll play herself as she's heard actors get to eat Danish pastries.

Oodles of thanks must go to my menfolk. To Sam, for putting up with parents who take on a daft project and see it as an honourable quest when it is so obviously insane. And to Colum, my partner of over two decades, without whom life would be more conventional but distinctly beige.

And finally, this is an account of how a complete pair of rookies took on a crazed rescue dog. It is not a text book or suggested programme for working with such dogs. All references to the Amichien Bonding method of Dog Listening, as founded by Jan Fennell, are but personal – and perhaps incorrect or shifting – understandings. Should you need help with your own dog you can do no better than contact this excellent foundation at www.janfennellthedoglistener.com or, for those lucky enough to reside in the west of Scotland, http://doggychillin.tumblr.com.

Anne M Scriven

2013

And so it begins.

It is an unusually warm day in April and the town hall clock is striking noon. We are sitting on the old wooden bench in our back garden. The sun is massaging our wintered bones, the coffee in our mugs is hot and delicious, our newly established bee-and-butterfly patch is delighting my senses, sections of the weekend newspapers have been perused and lie scattered at our feet, our pretty red-and-white Collie has been walked and is dozing on the soft green grass. We have no hurry to be anywhere. Life is most pleasant. The rest of Easter Monday lies before us to do with exactly as we like.

I stretch out my arms and legs in appreciation of the ease of the moment and say to my husband, who is idly watching the gentle sway of the lime trees, "Do you want to do anything much today? Go for a bike ride? Visit someone? Or just stay here?"

He replies to the effect that it would be good to do something with our holiday. I fall quiet for a moment and then hear myself say "We could go to the SSPCA and see if they have a dog for us. What d'you think?"

Colum is already on his feet gathering up the newspapers and coffee cups. "C'mon then," he says.

Within twenty minutes we are hurtling towards the SSPCA Rescue Centre. Our nineteen-year-old son, Sam, has also come along. For a few weeks he and I have been amusing ourselves by checking out the dogs on offer on the websites of various rescue centres. We are both drawn to the scampish-looking ones – those with lopsided ears who look inquisitively at the world. I also like the fun Labradors, but recognise that smaller dogs are more portable and eat less. I also like Collies, the soft silky-coated type, like our Jenna. A black-and-white version of her would be fine. I grew up with Collies; we have cared for a pure Lab and a Collie-cross over the last years so we believe ourselves to be quite knowledgeable about these breeds. Or maybe a cute terrier would be an entertaining change. We know a pint-size Border Terrier called Pablo. He's a smashing wee chap. Sam thinks so too.

Colum says he doesn't mind too much but, if push came to shove, his vote would go for a black Lab. What we are agreed on is that a girl would suit us best. Means we don't need to worry about all those testosterone related issues we remember from our lovable rascal lads whom we never had the heart to neuter. And we would not have to accuse ourselves of trying to replace our beloved Joe and Jack who died a few months ago. And Jenna could lie about in peace without having to guard her rear end. So, girls it is.

I feel quite excited. Something of the fizz I get from searching out bargains in charity shops is rising in my veins. But this shopping experience is of course far more honourable. And it's ticking the recycling box too. And the family budget box. It's surely then a win-win situation. I imagine returning home some time later and a furry ball of canine energy jumping out of our Berlingo van and romping gleefully into our Dogs-R-Welcome home. Wonder what the furry ball's name will be? I suppose we will know when we find her.

We turn into the drive leading up to the rescue centre. It's green and leafy. I'm surprised. People had told us this was a sad place. Looks ok to me. None of us have been here before. We have never had a rescue dog or been in any animal rescue centre. We all comment that it has a pleasant driveway and nice location. Hell of a noisy place though. We can hear the dogs barking the moment we open the car doors.

We go into the reception area. I wonder if there is a standard format for requesting a dog but if there is I don't know it, so I just say to the officer behind the desk that we are thinking of rehoming a dog. She tells us in an automatic tone to go and look round the cages and come back and ask about any dog we see. We do exactly that. Again I feel a buzz of retail therapy/ jumble sale rummage simmer inside of me.

There are pathways around lines of large concrete cages. Most of the cages contain dogs. There are lots of Staffies. Lots of hoarse Staffies, still resolutely barking, despite having exhausted their throats. I'm definite on the fact that we don't want a Staffie. Apart from Cleo, a cherished pet of a neighbour, I don't know any Staffies and feel rather nervous around them. I know if treated well they make terrific loyal pets and are sometimes called 'Nannie dogs' because of their ability to guard infant children, but a Staffie that comes from a rescue centre probably hasn't known too much kindness and I'd rather not deal with the legacy of that. No, we are definitely Labrador, Retriever or Collie people with the option on a Terrier.

Some of the dogs have fouled their cages. Dogs will never do that unless really stressed or desperate. To be expected, I suppose, but my heart goes out to them. We spot a beautiful white Golden Retriever. Looks like a girl. Maybe three or four years old. My pulse quickens. Some other people are also looking at her. We skip back to the reception. The other family gets there first and asks about her. Darn. The officer asks us to fill in a registration form while we wait to see if the family fit to the Retriever. Another officer comes in to quiz the family. He says the Retriever apparently has issues with men. The family decide she is not for them. The officer asks me which dog we are interested in. I say I am also interested in the Retriever but I live with two adult men.

"Can you lose the men?" asks the officer.

"Em, no," I say. "They bring in the money."

"Pity," says the officer. "I think she would be happy with you."

The family before us are now asking about puppies. My ears prick up. I also ask.

The officer dealing with us says "You have to be certain you want a puppy. Once you see the puppies you can't go back to see the dogs – no offence, but there are issues of cross infection and all that."

I ask what breed the puppies are.

"Mixed breeds," she says.

I hear "cross breeds" and have visions of Staffies crossed with Pitbulls and decide they are not for us. "Ach no, we've done the puppy thing," I say "we're really looking for an older dog."

So we leave. We walk down the path towards the car, all feeling disappointed.

"Mum," says Sam. "There's a row of cages we haven't looked at."

And so there is. Four cages which we have completely overlooked. Colum has gone off to the Gents, so Sam and I wander past the cages. In D2 is a youngish black and white dog lying on the ground.

"Oh, Sam," I say "it's a Collie."

Eighteen months on from this scene and I still wonder what curious mix of naivety, mistaken confidence and compassion was at work in our heads while we peered into the large concrete cage at the dog who whumped her tail at our show of interest. There have been so many times that, had I been able to turn the clock back, I would not have walked down that row, would not have looked into the cage, would not have had my heart lurch at the sight of the unwanted Collie and would not therefore made one of the daftest, most ignorant, decisions in my life. But we didn't do that. Instead, we intercepted Colum on his way to the car (why, oh why, did we?) and gabbled something incomprehensible about the Collie, and almost ran up to the office. The gods sat back, chortling.

Surprised to see us back, the officer on desk duty nevertheless listens to our excited queries about the Collie and scrolls through their data base for the dog's background. Her scant history is that she was picked up in the city centre as a stray, taken to the Rescue Centre, rehomed, brought back, then we arrived. At least, that's what the first officer tells us.

It sounds workable to us. We ask if we can let our own dog, Jenna, whom we have left in the back of our van, meet the Collie before we make a decision. They say that's fine and we all go to the small exercise field behind the rows of cages.

We go in first with Jen and let her off lead. She sniffs about a bit then looks at us expectantly.

"Wait till you see your new pal,' I say.

Two officers come in with the Collie. She spies Jenna and immediately lowers herself into a submissive posture. This is good. Our Jen can be a bit feisty. She likes to be boss. This could work. Jen ignores her as is befitting to an older dog. The officer gets out a coloured rubber ball and throws it. The Collie darts after it, brings it back and then drops it near Jen.

"Oh, that's lovely," I say. "She wants her to play."

Jen grabs the ball in her mouth, and stretches out to have a good chew of it. The officer throws another ball for the Collie. She brings this one back too.

"Your dog seems calm and well adjusted," says the officer, "she'll help the new dog settle in."

We agree. There doesn't seem to be any serious issues between the dogs. That's fine then. One of the officers says we should make our way to the office and they will bring the Collie back to her cage until we're ready to take her home. We leave them in the field.

Just as we are completing the paperwork, an officer notes the records showing the Collie has actually been rehomed twice. A little warning bell rings somewhere deep in my head but the bit of my brain which gets a high from impulse buys stifles it. The divine force of care-for-stupid people tries again. We have forgotten to bring some ID. The dog can't be released until we show some. Do we take this as an opportunity to pause and reflect on our actions? No. We switch into mental mode and Colum hurtles off home to get the required documents.

Just before he gets into the car I say "Do you think she is right for us?"

He pauses for a nano second and says "I trust your intuition."

I feel a lurch in the bottom of my stomach. I ignore it. I like what Colum is saying. It makes me feel good.

I stay at the Centre, finish the paperwork and sit outside in the sun. A young volunteer brings me a cup of tea. I think that is charming. Now I wonder that I didn't hear champagne corks popping in the office as they celebrated the successful duping of a complete mug. I sip my tea and text a friend to let them know about the new addition to our family.

"We r rehoming a rescue Collie. Approx 2 yrs old. Female. No issues."

The friend texts back. "Good one. Your lives were too quiet."

I smile at her humour and continue to soak up the sun.

Half an hour later we sign the release forms and pay the suggested donation. "Why was she brought back twice?" I casually ask.

"Too boisterous," the officer reads off the screen.

We smile smugly. We are dog people of eleven years standing. We can handle lively dogs. You just have to understand them. We already have a

Collie. We know the breed. We will be fine. We load the new dog into the back seat of our van. I sit next to her in case she is nervous and we drive away.

It's still wonderfully warm when we get home, and, being clued-up dog people, we take the new dog and Jenna to the back garden. The new dog can sniff around here and stretch her limbs, get to know Jenna a bit better and chill out before we bring her in the house. She was a bit restless in the van but generally ok. And she didn't widdle from nervous tension but she could probably do with a pee opportunity now.

Colum takes both dogs down to our garden. We live in an old Victorian house which was converted lots of years ago into two big flats. We have the top flat but it has its own front door. At the rescue centre we were asked if we lived in a house or flat. Technically our house is a flat but we have always called it a house. So I ticked the 'House' box. And we were asked if we had a secure private garden. Our garden is reached by going round the side of our building, down a chuckie path, down some steps, past our neighbour's garden and into ours. On one side there is a hedge, on another three huge lime trees and a wooden fence which screens us from the railway line a few metres away. The third side has a high wooden fence and the fourth a more flimsy, but aesthetic, woven fence which Colum is slowly crafting. Jenna has never tried to find an escape route so I had ticked the 'Yes' box to the secure garden question. We are all parched, the Rescue Centre is a bit of an assault on the senses and it's hours since we had anything to eat. I go inside to make a pot of tea and get some slices of my tasty lemon-and-poppy-seed cake which I had made yesterday. I carry the tray down to the garden curious to see how the new dog is settling in.

Jenna is the only being in the garden. I hear my name shouted and look over the woven fence to see Colum some hundred yards away louping over a neighbour's garden.

"What happened?" I call.

"She got out!" he shouts. He sounds anxious.

I put the mugs of tea on the makeshift table we have constructed from slates and a milk crate but put the cake higher up on the closed lid of the compost bin. I see the new dog head up through a neighbour's garden towards the front of the houses and the street. I run out of our garden, up the paths and out into the street.

The new dog is a hundred yards or so away. She is shaking and one of her legs seems to have blood on it. Colum appears.

"I think she's cut her paw," he says "she leapt off that high wall a few gardens along."

"Dear God," I think. I call the dog. "C'mon girl! Biscuit! Good girl!"

My call feels completely inadequate. I have no name for the dog. The Centre said they had called her "Molly" but we could rename her. We don't think it suits her but any port in a storm.

"Molly! Here girl! C'mon! Biscuit!"

Nothing doing. 'Molly' stands quivering well away from us. Any move towards her results in her backing further away.

"We have to get her confidence," says Colum.

"I'll get a ball," I reply and rush back to the house. Rummage in the over-stuffed dog stuff basket. Where is it? God, we need to sort this out. Too much chewed rubbish. I find a ball and rush back up the steps to the street then slow down. I begin to walk across the street ignoring 'Molly' who is still standing a few hundred yards away. I toss the ball into the air. I get to the other side of the street – thanking God we live in a quietish cul-de-sac – and take a sneak look out of the corner of my eye. 'Molly' has come closer. Good. On the right track. I sit down on the kerbstone and toss the ball up and up again. 'Molly' comes to within a yard of me. I keep tossing the ball. She stands and watches me. I turn to look at her and say "C'mon Molly, want the ball?"

She backs right away again. Damn. Colum is watching all of this. I call to him "Let's toss the ball between us". We stand in the middle of our street and play ball. 'Molly' watches these strange people – as no doubt do the neighbours.

"Edge back towards our house and see if she follows," I say. We do so and get as far as the end of our path with 'Molly' following – her curiosity getting the better of her fear. We get near our front door. I pull the gate open. 'Molly' darts off back up towards the street and into another garden. Colum belts down the back of the house in the hope of locating her. I run up into the street and along the road watching for a black and white shape. I see a neighbour.

"Jean! Have you seen a wee black-and-white Collie?"

"Black and white? I thought Jenna was red and white?"

"Yes, she is, but we have just rehomed another dog and she got out of the garden and she won't come and she's already hurt herself and it's the stupidest thing we've ever done!"

Jean looks at me with high amusement. "When did you get her?"

"This afternoon."

"This afternoon! That's nothing. Wait till you have grand-children then you'll know all about it."

The Scots pragmatism pulls me up short, gives me a slap on the chops. Yes. Calm down. It's not really the end of our world as we know it. I hear Colum calling.

"Quick Anne get into Suzie's garden and I'll come the other side and we might be able to trap Molly."

We do so. It works. Colum clips her lead on. We go home. All three of us have shaky legs. The tea is cold in the garden but Jenna has enjoyed the cake.

And it continues.

Sometime later, pots of fresh tea sunk, we talk over what happened.

"Well, they did say to us not to let her off," says Colum. "Now we know why. Guess that's why they didn't let us wait in the field while they got her back on the lead. It might have put us off. Crafty. Very crafty."

"It's to be expected," I reason. "She must have had a rubbish time of it in that Centre. That exercise field really isn't that big and all that constant barking must have driven her nuts. Collies are sensitive. And she doesn't know us yet. She's probably just really confused."

We decide to bath her. Her foot needs cleaning. It has stopped bleeding which is a good sign but we think a bath might soothe her. This goes quite well. I feed her bits of ginger nuts as Colum lifts her into the warm water. We've bathed dogs many times and know all about showing them the cloth and the soap, etc, and no sudden movements. But the rinse with the shower head, even though held really close to her skin so to minimise the noise, still freaks her and she makes a break for it. Colum manages to grab her and keep her in the bathroom. He towels her off. It seems to be the carpal pad on her right foot that is cut. Colum dries it off carefully. We let her out the bathroom. She belts around the hall, up the stairs, back down, up again, back down, round the rug, into the kitchen, then does it all again.

Jenna watches her bemused.

'Molly' is really thin. Too thin. We decide to give her some grub. The Rescue Centre said they had to rely on donated food so it changed all the time. We're Pedigree people. We give her a couple of handfuls of the dry kibble and give Jenna a biscuit as it isn't time for her real dinner yet. 'Molly' tries desperately to eat the kibble in one mouthful. She galumphs the food, shaking all the time.

"I suppose she didn't know where her next meal was coming from," says Colum.

"Poor thing. Food might be a bit of an issue for her."

We take the dogs out – 'Molly' firmly on her lead, Jenna trotting happily beside us. We go up to the hill that rises up from the cycle track at the end of our street. This is a wide circular hill with nothing on it – no swings, roundabouts, putting green or other human-centred amusements; just trees, grass and a great view over the Clyde valley – and a goodish stroll can be had around it. I worry that 'Molly' will catch cold if she has just been bathed. Colum pooh-poohs this fear. Feeling the still warm sun on my skin, I concede he is probably right.

'Molly' strains on her lead. I am holding it as we think she responds better to my voice. We start to go up the hill. 'Molly' finds a stick and goes into a frantic dance of pleasure. I find it hard to hold her. We manage to persuade her to leave the stick and trot up to the top of the hill. We sit down, looking at the view. It is a thinking space. Local mythology has it that the local saint meditated here. Whatever the historical correctness we have found lots of apparent problems somehow diminish after a good sit on the hill.

"We need a name for her," says Colum. "Molly isn't right."

I agree. All of our other dogs, for reasons known to fate alone, have had names beginning with a "J" but we can't think of a girl's name that we all like that begins with a "J" and that we are all happy shouting in the street. We do a few circuits of the hill, 'Molly' still pulling like mad, and go home.

We discuss names. Sam thinks 'Jazz' is a good name and would be in line with our naming tradition. I don't like the name. I quite like 'Lizzie' but the men don't. Sam suggests 'Clem' – beautiful name but too close to 'Jen' and we think this would be confusing for the dogs. Sam, having said his say, retires to his room to tell his Facebook friends about the new dog.

I pour Colum and me a glass of wine and put on a CD by Kate Rusby. We believe in soothing music for dogs and Kate has a lovely gritty earthy tone that eases around tired senses. Our other dogs have been brought up on Classic FM although I have a fantasy that they change the frequency to Radio 1 when we are out of the house. Kate is singing an old ballad called "Awkward Annie". I sing along to it, then look at 'Molly' and find myself singing the paraphrase "...she is our dear old...Sally!"

"Hey, how about 'Sally'?" I ask.

Colum tries it out around his mind and says "Yeh, ok, good name, it's fine, don't mind shouting that in the street."

Sam appears back in the kitchen looking for some munchies. I tell him the decision. He says he doesn't like it. Colum says "Well, it was Mum who paid for the dog, so she gets to name her."

"And it will be us who look after her long after you've left home," says I, although house prices being what they are I think that Sam may be with us for a long time yet.

I squat down next to the new dog. She hasn't yet sat down without persuasion and has got nowhere near lying down.

"Sally," I say. "How do you like that name?"

'Sally' looks at me quizzically but doesn't seem to make any real objection. So Sally it is.

We have some dinner. It's now mid evening. Where did the day go? We give the dogs their 'proper' dinner. Me holding on to Sally until Jen has her food put down first. We must stick to respecting the older dog status. Sally jumps and strains against my hand. I finally let her go and she belts her food down in the same frantic manner as earlier. Colum stands between the dogs realising that Sally is going to finish first and may challenge Jen for hers. Jen eats steadily and politely. In comparison to Sal – as we are already calling her – Jen comes across as a little lady in a tableclothed restaurant delicately wiping her lips with a napkin. Jen finally finishes. Sally leaps on her bowl and checks it is empty. Jen trots out of the kitchen. Sal follows. We hear scrabbling noises in the living room. Colum looks in.

"Come and see this," he calls.

I follow him and peer in. Sally is down in a play bow on one side of the coffee table and Jen is watching her from the other. Jen gives a wee jump then runs round the table towards Sally. Sally wags her tail and bounds to the other side. Jen follows also wagging her tail. Sally lifts a paw and taps Jen. Jen responds by lunging at Sally and grabbing her round the neck. They tussle. They are playing.

Colum and I stand at the door watching. Our other dogs never played together. Our Lab, Jack, declared himself the boss over Joe, our gentle

Collie-cross. All toys were declared Jack's and Jack's only. And, further to that, Joe was not allowed to join in games with us. That was how the dogs had decreed it and by and large we accepted it. Sometimes we held onto Jack's collar so Joe could get a turn of the ball or frisbee or a chase round the dining room table, but Jack knew he was the boss and allowed this to happen only on sufferance. And Joe seemed to accept it. So to now have two dogs who seem to want to play together was a complete novelty to us. We stood at the door like two proud parents watching their children. Things were looking good.

Some twenty minutes later it goes quiet in the sitting room. I smell something rather 'unsavoury' as my mother would say. I peer in to find a steaming pile of pooh deposited on the old Afghan rug. "Oh heck," I say "Where's the disinfectant?" I'm not really annoyed though. I mean it's quite understandable. New home. New name. New neighbourhood. New food. Bit too much newness for a dog's bowels to hold. We get out the poop scoop and disinfectant; open a window and light some incense.

"Maybe we should do their last walk," Colum says.

"Good thinking," I say "but make sure her collar is firmly on."

I put Sally on her new lead which I had bought at the Rescue Centre and we head out the door.

Ah. Different situation. The dog at the end of my lead is lunging upwards and gaining a good height. Deep hoarse barking emanates from her. She flips and tosses like a young horse and it takes all my strength to hold her.

"Wonder if she smells the cats next door?" I gasp.

"Could be," says Colum watching Sally. I hold onto the lead tightly still believing that she will respond better to me.

"Calm Sally. Now, calm...Sally...calm. Calm...I said caaaalm! ...Good girl. Goooood girl...No. No. No...Nooooo Sally! No! No! Calm. Calm. Calm!...OH, FOR FUCK SAKE SALLY!"

The expletive slips out of me as we edge near to the hill. The hill is home to a number of foxes, whom our Jenna tries to visit whenever she can even if this means a quick trot along the nearby railway line. We had learned with her that the last walk was a lead walk and, although she tugged a bit, in comparison to the berserk behaviour Sally was now exhibiting, Jenna is a model of restraint and decorum. My hand is being rubbed raw by the chain on the lead. It isn't a choker chain but I have wound my hand round the chain part as well as the cord handle in an attempt to keep control. And it isn't working. I manage to walk about two steps then have to pause and try to rein-in this crazy dog. Taking pity on me, Colum takes over. Sally doesn't seem to notice the change of driver. We stagger round the hill and back along the path. Jen remains composed and dutifully does her pees and poohs.

"Well, at least *she*'s ok," Colum says "Wish I could say the same for this one. Woah Sally! ...No! Sally. Calm Sally! ...Sally! Sally!...Streuth!'

We make it back to the house and dry off the dogs – Sally, like the neighbours' curtains, still twitching – and shoo them upstairs to our living area.

"Phew!" says Colum. "That was a challenge. We're going to have to work on reassuring her."

The dogs decide that it's time for another play session but we think otherwise. Closing over the doors to the sitting room and dining room, turning down lights we try to set a peaceful atmosphere. Sally is still breathing quickly. She gulps down half a bowlful of water in the kitchen then runs out into the hallway.

"We need to calm her down," I say.

Colum sends Jenna up to her sleeping area outside of our bedroom – we are both of the opinion that the sleeping area of each dog is sacrosanct and, as the older and more established dog, Jen has a continued right to her own space. Sally bounds up and down the stairs trying to get in to where Jen is. Colum brings Sal downstairs then sits down on the floor beside the dog basket we had prepared for her. I put on some soothing classics thing and turn off as many lights as possible. I notice that Colum had settled down on the floor in the company of *The Dog Listener* by our dog guru, Jan Fennell. The philosophy of this woman and her revolutionary method has done us proud in the past and all of our dogs have settled to become quiet contented beings – or so we thought – and we have much to thank her for. I see that Colum has turned to the chapter on rescue dogs.

Day the First

Get up at 6.50am. We walk the dogs early so Colum can help out before he escapes to work. I am already seeing it as an 'escape' not a necessity. Sally has been utterly silent through the night. Amazing. She had slept in what we considered the day basket of Jenna. Ok, so maybe a dominance tactic or maybe she just needed to smell the scent of another dog. Whatever, it worked. And the morning walk works too – to a certain extent.

I have always fed Jen after her morning romp with her dog pals up the hill and she then settles down for a good sleep while I get a few hours' work done at my desk. Ever since Jen came to us from a local family, who had loved her but found it impossible to find adequate time for a dog's needs, I can't remember her having 'an accident' in the house. She has been sick a few times but has had the house training bit down to perfection. But Sally. Different dog. This morning another ominous smell emits from the sitting room – or perhaps that should now be 'the shitting room'. The disinfectant is again employed. And the window. And the incense. Maybe we need to feed her before we walk her; otherwise I am going to have to schedule in another walk and that will impact on my precious writing time. Meanwhile I clear the mess up. Colum goes off to work and Sam to college.

I call Jenna to her basket and Sally to hers. Jen settles like the fantastically good girl she is – our appreciation of Jen is steadily growing – but Sally is restless. I call her back to her basket, get her to sit and then pull out her front legs so she will lie down. She stays in the position for two seconds then sits up again. I repeat it. Same result. Time is moving on. I have words to compose. I sit at my desk. Sal persuades Jen to get out of her basket and come and play. I call Jen and she goes back to her basket. Sal does it again. I correct Jen again. Realising Sal thinks this a tolerably amusing game; I decide to supervise at closer quarters. A friend had recently given me a large travel rug with a waterproof backing. He had thought to use it himself but didn't like the fact that there were dog hairs on it which couldn't be washed out. Perfect for our needs then. I roll this out on the laminate floor beside my desk. Call Jen who comes, sniffed at the new-to-us rug, finds it ok, and lies down on it. Bless her. Call Sal. She looks at the rug, at me, at Jen. She seems to say "Now why would I want to rest on that when there's all this zip in my bones?" But Jen wants her morning sleep and has closed her eyes. Double bless her. Sally sighs and lies down. Not on the designated rug but under the dining room table keeping one eye firmly on Jen. I turn on my laptop and ignore them.

I'm the kind of writer who likes tea almost on tap. I believe T. S. Eliot was the same. But the dogs are sleeping – well, one of them is – and a fragile peace reigns. The kitchen and the kettle seem a long way away. I stick it out for an hour as I work on entangling a glitch in a short story which I had recently sketched out. But when 10.30am flickers in the corner of my laptop I give in. I just have to have some tea. Have to have. The creative juices don't flow without it.

I ease myself up out of my chair and begin to tiptoe across to the door. Our son is now a strapping young man; I had thought I had long ago left the days of moving without a modicum of sound from one room to the next when, as a fractious baby, Sam had finally shut his eyelids for ten minutes. But here I was again. Shimmying across the floor, hardly breathing. I make it for about four steps. Sal opens her eyes and bounds up. "Damn!" I think and walk in my usual tread out of the room.

Half an hour later, tea drunk, dogs played, settled, played, settled, Sal is still determinedly restless. I put her in the hall keeping Jen with me and shut the door. She demurs a bit then goes quiet. I do a mental check on doors and accessible rooms. Can't think of any that are open apart from the kitchen and that room is dog proof. Get on with my work. Some time passes. I don't notice. Colum appears home for lunch.

"How did it go?" he asks.

"Fine. Good," I reply.

"Excellent," he says with a smile on his face.

In the afternoon I take Sal to register at our vet. There really isn't any huge rush for this. The SSPCA had checked her over and she apparently had no health problems. But I just want her registered with our vets anyway. Seems the responsible thing to do. We can walk to our vets' surgery along the cycle track. We do this and get there with minimum fuss. Sal is checked over by a vet who likes Collies. The vet says Sal is too thin. I say I can see that but we are working on it. I buy some vastly expensive flea treatment because the vet thinks it a good idea and we go home. Good job done.

As we walk back along the cycle track I think about the first time I visited our vet the morning after the arrival of our Collie-cross pup, Joe. Joe was a great wee thing – although at five and a half weeks was far too young to leave his mum. We didn't know that and the farmer didn't tell us. So the poor wee lad had to adapt very quickly to life with humans and was a slightly worried dog all his life. Gentle, beautiful, but worried. We brought him home from a local farm in my cycle basket with some old towels wrapped around him. We hadn't exactly thought through what we would need for a pup. We had no food ready. No proper basket. Sam did have a bowl, a collar and lead though – all given to him on his recent tenth birthday by his Aunty Clare, who was in cahoots with him that his parents should honour their promise that if we ever moved to a big enough house we would get a dog. We had moved from our tiny flat to our current big Victorian conversion a couple of months previous to this and Sam hadn't forgotten our promise. So, one cold January evening, we called the local vet who told us that a local farm had a litter of pups and gave us the address.

We first saw Joe curled up in his cosy hay-strewn stall with his mum and his brother and sisters. With the cows mooing in the other stalls, the moonlight evening, and the smells of sleeping animals it was all picture-book stuff. Joe's brother jumped up at us. 'We've been calling him Bob,' said the farmer's wife, 'after Bob the Builder because he's so big and stocky.'

'Do you like him, Sam?' I asked.

'No,' said Sam. 'I like his wee brother better.'

Joe, as Sam named him, was half Bob's size and when Sam picked him up softly licked his hand. Each recognises its own. Sam has always been a gentle person uninterested in the loud and brash. This wee pup suited his nature; it was a good choice. As I learned more about dogs, I often wondered why the farmer didn't say that we could have Joe but would need to leave him with his mum for another few weeks. Maybe he was as much in the dark about care of pups as we were. Whatever the reasons we lifted Joe away from his worried mother who began circling and whining in anxiety. Poor lass. How stupid humans are sometimes.

It was quite late in the evening when we got home. I found a cardboard box and filled it with the old towels. I had read somewhere that you should leave a radio on for the first night so that the pup thinks it is not alone and also put a hot water bottle in the pup's bed. We did all of that. And we gave him some scraps of bread mixed in milk for his supper in the full belief that that would be comfort food for him. We shut all the doors to the other rooms. Left Joe in his new bed in the hall and took ourselves to our own beds. He cried all night. Colum or myself, I can't remember who, went to check on him after he had cried for an hour. I had again read somewhere that you must be strict about ignoring them for the first night or so or the dog would rule the roost. But it was hard. The poor wee thing sounded so sad. I tossed and turned for most of the night as did Colum.

Bleary eyed in the morning, Colum turned to me and said 'This is the worst thing we have ever done.'

Colum's parents were coming to stay for a few days that afternoon – always an opportunity for potted stress – and we wondered how much sleep they would get, as Joe's basket was right outside their door. To his great delight I kept Sam off school for the day as I just couldn't think how to get the house ready for visitors, look after a puppy and take said puppy to the vet all on my own. Later that morning I walked into the vet's surgery, not knowing this was to be the first of many many visits over the years, put Joe down on the consulting table and said "What do I do?"

"What do you mean?"

"What do I do to keep him alive?"

"Have you never had dogs before?"

"Em, well, yes, no, not really. It was a long time ago. And my dad did it all. I can't remember anything."

"Well, it's quite simple. Just get a good puppy food..."

"Such as?"

"Any of the standard brands."

"Such as?"

"Er…Pedigree…"

"Right. How much exactly and how often?"

The vet's soul must have sighed as he watched me scribble down any snippets of valuable information he could give me on feeding, exercising, toileting. At least Joe was now registered with them. We'd done that right at any rate.

An hour later, my mind bulging with puppy care detail, we drove off stopping at the supermarket to buy bags of dry puppy food, and at the chemist to buy ear-plugs for our visitors. And so our family journey with dogs began.

That memory belongs to eleven years ago. Lots and lots of learning has gone on since. And today I confidently ask the vet about Jen's penchant for sheep chasing while we also discuss Sally. I enjoy the chat and leave the practice feeling peaceful. I decide to capitalise on Sally's quiet mood and instead of returning directly to the house I walk past it to the far end of our road.

A friend and neighbour has asked if I would water his precious newly-sown vegetables while he is away visiting his daughter in London. Donal's garden with its glorious herbaceous border, soft green grass, carefully pruned trees, and vegetable and fruit plots is always a balm to the soul. As the day is again beautiful and warm with a light breeze, it seems a good idea to extend Sally's exercise with a few turns around this lovely space. We arrive and make our way to the tree, in the middle of the garden, under which are a wrought iron bench and small table. All is quiet, the late spring flowers toss their heads in the sunshine, delicate scents tickle my nose, and the grass is downy and deep green. Sally eases herself down below the seat. I lift my legs onto the wee table, tilt my hat to block out the glinting sun, and sit back on the bench. This is good but I keep a good hold of the lead in case of unexpected change. Sally, however, seems quite relaxed and is stretched out on her side at my feet. Yes, this is what owning a dog is all about. At one with them. Quiet. Peace-filled. It would be more perfect if I had thought to bring a flask of tea and some bics, but I will remember next time. Maybe I will come tomorrow and bring a book. Sal and I, and maybe Jenna too, can chill here. I envision myself telling friends of the 'Therapy Hour' I gave Sally, chuffed with myself for thinking of it.

We sit there for a half hour or so. It is blissful and deeply peaceful but I really need a cup of tea. I try to stay in the moment. My higher self says pompously that all my needs are met but my lower self says "Stuff that, I need tea!" So I get up, Sally springs up ready, so she wasn't as deeply relaxed as I had thought, but it's early days. Early days.

When Colum gets home from work I tell him of the tranquil hour and the vet visit. He gives me lots of praise and I feel I have cracked this rehoming thing. Just takes a bit of thought. A bit of calm. That's it really.

Then the evening walk happens. Complete repeat of the evening of Day One. We come out of the house around 9pm. Sally goes ballistic. Colum takes her. He struggles up the hill and back along the top path doing lots of soothing but holding on to her lead for dear life. Jen gives Sally a wide berth but apart from that seems unconcerned. More curtains twitch. We made it home stressed and despairing. Colum reads more of the dog training book.

Day the Second

Day Two. Since when did I count days? Morning walk is again fractious. Colum and I both tired. The new routine is getting to us, especially me as I am now getting up an hour earlier to feed and help walk the dogs. We are still trying to get a hold – that's figuratively speaking – of Sally's bowel needs. Seems best to feed her first thing in the morning then get her out of the house as quickly as poss. Jenna looks at us with bleary eyes when we put her breakfast down at 7am – she was used to a 9am run and then food around 10.30. But times change, girl. Times change. She eats it anyway because otherwise Sally will pounce on it.

Outside I notice that I am shying away from taking Sally's lead and am happy to let Colum assume the alpha male role. A paid-up feminist all my adult life, but there some jobs where I am more than happy to admit that male strength is a necessary requirement. And anyway, I am *choosing* not to take the lead. I value my arm sockets too much.

We talk about Sally as we proceed up the hill and round the top of it. We don't seem to have stopped talking about Sally since Monday 3pm but we seem to need to lance our confused thoughts. Colum is being positive.

"Well, what is good is that you're actually getting down to your writing earlier in the day. That's quite amazing really. We have Sally to thank for that."

And 'tis true. My routine had been such that I would take Jen up the hill at 9am, meet another couple of dog people, walk and blether with them about shoes and ships and sealing wax, come home, feed Jen, put on washing, tidy the kitchen, warm up my laptop, make tea and finally settle into some work around 11am. Now, the dogs are fed, walked, we have breakfasted, tidied up, sorted washing and settled the dogs by 9am or 9.30 latest. Funny that. Makes me think of Virginia Woolf who apparently got up early because she wanted to learn Greek. Well, it takes all sorts. But the other thing is that as I am trying to instill a respect for routine and quiet in the house while I tap away at my desk, I have minimised my movement around the house. Where I would once have meandered around the rooms doing non-writing stuff, I now make myself sit at my desk and only take one mid-morning break. If I don't do this Sally bounds up, dances in front of Jenna begging her to get up for yet another chase around the coffee table. She doesn't yet seem to respond to "Sally. Sally. Sit. Sit. Sit…Down. Calm now. Calm now." She only flumps down when Jen yawns and blanks her. Great girl Jenna. Brilliant dog. So wise. I try, when praising her, not to verbalise "Why did we ever want more than you?" but it pushes into my mind nevertheless.

The major difference in the two dogs can best be illustrated by the fact that Jenna doesn't like raised voices – a legacy perhaps from her first family – and there has been many a time when we've had to explain to her concerned wee face that raised voices don't necessarily correlate to anger. 'It's just dramatic emphasis' we say to her; being the intelligent lass she is, she licks our hands and trots off quite happily – probably to read up on the origins and subtleties of dramatic emphasis as opposed to irony. Meanwhile, with Sally, I see that we are going to have to work on the basic rudiments of 'Sit!'

The gods however must have overheard my private and somewhat biased beliefs and, in the spirit of fair play, thought they would remind me that Jen was her own dog too. That afternoon I take Jen and Sal along the road again. The memory of that zen-like session in Donal's garden still fresh in my mind. Jen would like it, too, I think. I will be Anne the Dog Soother, Anne the Harmonizer, Anne-the-Woman-in-Tune-with-the-Spirits-of-Dogs. By the end of the afternoon I was more like Anne the Demented. Ah dear. It went like this ....

We all proceed happily along the road. Jenna running ahead, Sally on the lead. We get roughly three quarters of the way there when a young fox chooses her moment to jump out and shout *"Na na, Na na na!"* at Jen and Sal. Jen belts after her. Sal, of course, goes mental. I focus my energy on Sal with a mix of soothing phrases and "No Sally! No! No!" depending on what height her franticness was taking her. The vet had told me a tip, which was when speaking to a dog you should always give a command. Don't just say

"Jenna!" or "Sally!" but tell them what you want them to do. So, here's me in the middle of the road, holding onto a crazed dog, who if she could-just-get-off-this-damned-lead-would-show-that-damned-fox-a-thing-or-five, and also trying to factor in the vet's advice and give off intermittent shouts of "Come Jenna! Jenna come!" She doesn't appear. I decide the game is up and think the best thing I could do is get home.

I keep Sally on the tightest of leads talking to her constantly. Actually I am talking to myself. My legs are shaking and I am saying "Calm now. Calm." Sal begins to calm and I begin to breathe. It is then I notice a man, standing about twenty feet away, watching me. I am about to say some passing casual remark like "Who would have a dog, eh?" when he speaks.

"Have you lost a dog?" he asks.

I was going to quip that no, I hadn't lost one but just didn't know where she was, but for some reason just say "Yes, a fox freaked both my dogs and you see this one is a rescue dog and …"

But he doesn't let me finish. Empathy for dogs or dog owners is not on his life agenda.

"Well, I am really annoyed. My kids are not even old enough to know what a dog is and yours is in my house traumatising them."

I want to say 'Don't talk tosh man,' but actually say "Oh, don't worry, she's really good with kids." Big mistake, it's the opening he has been waiting for and I handed it to him on a plate.

"My kids don't know that!" he says triumphantly.

Now, why is it that non-dog people think that they are the originators of that statement? They are so damned smug when they say it. It's as if they're saying "I'm now going to say something that you can't argue with because I am completely in the right and you are completely in the wrong, and if you don't agree I will call the police." It's a totally loaded statement and carries a welter of dog hate with it. Now, I have a hot temper. The blood of the Celt is strong in me. The accent of this chap was that of a southern Englishman. I have married an Englishman who is my soul partner. My mum grew up in Essex. I have zillions of lovely relatives south of the border. But right at that moment the inheritance of my west highland, Glaswegian and Irish ancestry reared its head and I feel a rise of pure anger surge through me.

My first impulse is to yell "Don't you dare presume to tell me that I am in the wrong. You, you Englishman you! I am on my home turf. If you don't like it, then go away!" But, praise God in her highest heaven, I don't. It isn't the racism of my intent that stops me (although it should do) but the fact that I have, on the lead, Sally, who is still panting and pulling. If I let rip with my quelling schoolteacherish lexis which lies dormant most of the time but comes out of my mouth like an Old Testament flood when called on, there will be a total showdown with this self-righteous eedjit. And it will escalate and it will not be good. Instead I opt for the tack of "Oh my goodness. I am *sooo* sorry. I can only apologise," tactical response.

Perhaps he really wanted the Old Testament eye-for-eye bit because the chap deflates his shoulders a bit and says "I've jammed your dog in my garden and, as I say, I will not have my kids traumatised."

I follow him up the chuckie-stone driveway. Jenna is behind a four-foot wooden fence. He opens the gate just as I am saying "Don't open it! Wait till I get there," but being the non-dog person he so is, he opens it. Fortunately Jenna must have had enough of her fox fun and trots over to me. I quickly clip on her lead and say to the chap. "It's a poor excuse but, you see, dogs know this house. Are you new here?"

Oops, oops, wrong question. He bristles. "No, I'm not new."

I rush on to smooth his ridiculously ruffled feathers.

"Well, you see, I knew the previous owners who were friends of ours and they had a Wolfhound. So this driveway must still smell of dog. And dogs were always welcome here."

Realising that I have knowledge of the place and therefore have some slight standing, he hesitates but then comes back with the self-important "Well, this is my property and I will not have dogs coming in here."

I opt again for the gracious genteel lady bit and say "I will do my level best for it not to happen again," although just how the hell I was going to do that was beyond me.

"Goodbye," I say. And with our tails held high, Jen, Sal and I walked away.

I keep it all together for a couple of hours after this. I even frame a letter to the chap apologising for the 'intrusion' of Jen, but offering to take her back along for his children to meet her in a controlled and safe manner. I say I am a resident of long-standing and often walk my dogs along there and it was silly and needless of us to be at odds with each other. "The world is too full of strife for us to be at loggerheads," I write. I will show him. I will claim the moral high ground. I won't stoop to public argument and discord, I will show him that I a woman who behaves with dignity and is, in effect, a modern day Gandhi. I re-write the letter three times. Each time tweaking it to read with more gravitas and command. It does something to vent my frustration.

My cool patrician mood lasts until Colum gets home and asks me how my afternoon had gone. I begin telling him then start to cry.

"I can't do this, this is just too hard. I now have people shouting at me. And it wasn't even really Sal's fault, but that bloody fox. And I live here, and now I can't walk to the other end of the road because of that chap and his stupid open gates. Everything is just horrible!" and promptly use up five tissues while Colum turns his brushed up Sal-soothing techniques on me.

"Sounds like you did exactly the right thing. There's no reasoning with people like that. You should have said to him. 'Well my dog doesn't know your kids are dog-phobic'. Cheek. Jenna of all dogs! He probably did the thing of jumping up and flapping his arms and spun his own kids into panic mode. What a way to teach children about dogs. The guy obviously hasn't a clue. And why was his garden gate open anyway if he has pre-school children around? Wait till I tell the neighbours, they will laugh. Wee Cammy over there, 2 years of age and he loves Jen. And wee Charlie next door, 4 years old, she would take Jen home if she could."

I was still blubbering but lapping up the sympathy. "Well, I'm staying away from there for a bit. If I go along to Donal's, I'm going sans dog," I sniff.

"That's fair enough," says Colum wisely agreeing with anything I said as he put on the kettle.

I go out for a run in the evening with my women's group. I talk about anything other than dogs. See people walking their dog. Their one dog. Feel envious. What the hell were we thinking? We should never have got another dog. This was so not thought through. But the run does me good.

I get home and rip up the excellently worded letter. Stuff him. He can sort out his dog phobia himself.

Day the Third

Feels all a bit of haze. Sal fixating on dust particles in the kitchen, in the dining room, on the top landing, in the garden. I clean up a twice poohed carpet. Mental evening walk. Why, oh why did we do this? There is an oppressive weight on me. When I think of Sally my mind fills with a cloud of black.

Day the Fourth

I want to return Sal. I am not enjoying her. Not in the slightest.

Sam is not on board either. "She doesn't suit us, mum," he says.

At lunchtime Colum phones the SSPCA. He paints a fairly positive picture, as is his cup-half-full nature, but says we are wondering if Sally has mental health issues. *If? If?* SSPCA says it is still early days. Tell us to give "a sharp tug on the lead when she misbehaves," and to call back at end of next week if still having major problems. It's not what I want to hear; I feel like throwing a major hissy fit, but content myself with battering some washing into the machine, almost breaking the dial as I turn it round. I need to get out of here.

After lunch I walk over the track to the local shops. I like this row of shops. The Post Office is here, and a charity shop with tempting bargains, a useful Co-op and a friendly pet store. It feels akin to a healthy village high street, lacking a duck pond and graceful willows, Miss Marple and a bicycling policeman, but in this dark age of soul-less shopping malls, it's nice all the same. And I'm here without dogs. Thinking about them, but free from their physical presence.

I go into the pet store and buy a tie-up, a halti and two filled bones. Some of me resents buying anything dog related. I would prefer the SSPCA van drove up and I could pitch Sally into it. I tell the kind woman in the shop of our new arrival. I really want to wail and fling the huge black weight, that is the dog and us having the dog, onto her counter and beg her to find a home for our nutty mut. I feel as if she really isn't getting the enormity of our situation as she gives me a controlled dose of sympathy and shows me how to use the halti. She has probably seen the panic in my eyes and glided on to 'keep customer calm and carry on' praxis. I expect I'm not the only traumatised dog owner she must have to deal with – but surely I am the most in need. Surely? But she patiently demonstrates the halti and assures me it will help. I clutch it like a life jacket in a raging sea. How things change. In all our eleven years owning dogs we have never resorted to such a device. But needs must. It's this or my sanity.

Both my purse and my heart are lighter as I stroll over to the bakery and teashop. I sip tea and eat a pineapple cake. It's overly sweet and gluey but I enjoy it. And I enjoy sitting there, being out, not coping with dogs. I go into the Co-op and buy a bottle of fairly-traded red wine (because I am a good an ethical person even if demented), some salad ingredients, croissants and marmalade. My insides need pampering. It has been a hard few days. I meander around the second-hand shop and buy a Joanna Trollope novel. An aga-saga is perfect for the stressed mind. I take space and feel like me again. I don't give a fig how the dogs are doing. I stay out for two hours. Feel so much better.

Later, after we have eaten the salad and drunk some of the wine, Colum and I watch some of *Marley and Me*. We laugh hysterically as Marley does his thing and Owen Wilson and Jennifer Aniston try to cope. Why is it though that Jennifer Aniston's hair always looks great despite her character's stress level? And how do they manage to get their apartment back into order when Marley keeps trashing it? Guess that's where the make-up artists, prop people and camera crew come in. Fiction is so much easier than reality.

We try the halti on Sally on our evening walk. She is quieter but Colum still has to hold her. I don't want to.

Day the Fifth

It's Saturday, and Colum is home. Life is so much easier. I go for a run, eat a large and long breakfast then cycle down to the second-hand bookshop. I need a copy of *Othello* as I had prematurely given away all my Shakespeare when I left my university teaching job, thinking that I really didn't need the English bard in my life anymore. But, as fortune would have it, I am now tutoring a young lass who has *Othello* listed as required reading for Higher English. I haven't read the play for years – all I can remember is that it's the one where the noble Moor husband strangles the wife. Nice.

As I cycle, I muse on why schools insist on hierarchising tragedy over comedy. They have this daft notion that a study of pain is good for the young. Fortunately the young have their own way of dealing with gloom. Such as the time I tried to pitch *Macbeth* to a class of young lads in my first teaching post in the north-east highlands. These lads knew fine that they were only biding their time until they would be out working on the fishing boats, their family's farm, or small businesses. School was but a mere amusement and great fun was to be had with this very new naive teacher, who was only four or five years their senior, recently arrived from the lowlands and who failed to appreciate that the works of Shakespeare were a complete anathema to their culture. I diligently gave out speaking parts to as many lads as possible and then asked the first one to commence. He stood up to much applause from his comrades and proceeded to speak the first witch's line in his best Mickey Mouse accent. The second witch's response came hot on the heels from the first lad's side-kick and proclaimed in a Donald Duck speak. And so it continued. The class were in hysterics.

"Miss, this stuff is brilliant!" said one as he guffawed his way through Scenes One and Two.

"Right, lads, shut the books," I said. "I think we had better do something else."

"Aw, Miss, this is a great laugh," said a lad who had delighted us with his Disney 'What's up, Doc?' voice.

"Maybe so", I said, "but somehow I don't think Willie meant it to be."
But perhaps the lads had it right.

I wonder as I lock my bike on a railing next to the bookshop door, if the
Monty Python team had perhaps done an adaption of Othello that could liven
up my next tutoring session.

If they did, the bookshop don't have it, so I opt instead for a school study
copy of *Othello* with useful explanatory notes. I know the staff in the shop as
I sometimes do a stint in the shop when help is needed.

They ask how I am doing and I say something like "Well, we rehomed a
dog this week…," to which the owner replies "Just how many dogs do you
need?" That's actually a bloody good question and one which I so wish I had
asked myself six days ago.

But things are not so bad. Really. Earlier Colum had taken Sally up the
hill with Jen and met other dogs. He had let Sally off lead and she had a great
run. A kind neighbour who owns a floppy docile Weimaraner let Colum
entice Sal into his enclosed garden and they managed to get her back on lead
eventually. So, for the moment, Sal is well exercised. Things are returning
to normal. Why is it then that my stomach clenches when the bookshop staff
continue to quiz me as to the arrival of the new dog?

The ride home along the cycle track does something to calm my insides,
which then tense again an hour later as we watch Sam's basketball team
down at the local leisure complex. His team batter out a hard-won victory.
We are all jubilant. Sam goes off to celebrate with his team mates. Colum and
I watch the rest of *Marley and Me*. I cry when Jennifer Aniston's character
says something about having given up so much of what makes her her and
feeling bad for even saying it, and cry again when Marley dies.

Day the Sixth

I go with Colum up the glen. The glen is a fifteen-minute drive away and has been the delight and solace of all our dogs. Jen adores coming here and particularly loves getting a swim in one of the pools at the end of the walk. As she plunges in, doing her ladylike swim, flipping her wee paws daintily to each side as she skims after floating sticks, we let Sally off lead. We are hopeful that she might swim with Jen. She leaps away from us. Comes back to look at Jen, but doesn't go in the water. After ten minutes of unsuccessfully persuading her to go in the water, we make our way back to the car in the parking area. Fortunately the area is quiet. It takes us an hour to lure Sally back into the van. Treats and encouragements don't do anything. It is now steadily raining. I'm feeling shivery with the damp. This isn't fun.

We find the old chewed frisbee in the van and start throwing it into the boot. We make it into a game and have to stop ourselves from doing rugby dives on Sally when she gets near the van. Colum edges nearer with each throw then finally manages to get both the frisbee and Sally in the boot at the same time. We are both thoroughly wet.

We stop at the supermarket for a hot drink. We discuss the useless back garden fence and if we can afford to replace it. I vote we dip into our paltry savings. Either that or Sally will have to go back to the rescue centre (yeh!). She obviously has a phobia against coming back on the lead. We need somewhere to exercise her until she trusts us.

We go to B&Q, price fence posts and strong wire fencing. We then go to a garden centre and spot another kind of fence post which could be battered and not cemented in – a method which might save uprooting my nice shrubs. We buy by ten posts. Hurrah for our old Berlingo ... she carries the posts with great ease. My eldest brother offers to come and help Colum secure the garden. Hurrah for eldest brothers.

Day the Seventh

I still have a feeling of treading on egg-shells. At yoga class this evening our teacher takes us through the 'Life Lessons mantras': Be patient. Slow down. Gather and sow love. Laugh at yourself. Celebrate. Am aware I am sore in need of this teaching. I lie on the floor at relaxation thinking of Sally. What is it that she has to teach us? I feel at peace as I return home. A peace which doesn't last.

Our kind neighbour offers to let Sal run in his secure garden in the late evening. He suggests we come over for a cup of tea or glass of wine but advises warm sweaters as the evening chilly. Colum goes over first with the dogs and I follow later. It's all very pleasant until Colum tries to get Sally back on lead. She leads us a dance. It's after 10pm and a work day night. We all want to end the day. I start to feel embarrassed that we are keeping everybody up. We try all bundling into their kitchen to see if Sally will follow. Colum has the whacko-wheeze idea of shouting "ball coming in!" and chucking a scabby earth-laden football through the open French windows and into the pristine kitchen of our neighbours. I wish I wasn't there. Sally finally dances into the kitchen. We grab her and head out of their garden. I doubt we will get another invite very soon.

We walk the dogs around the block and back home. Sally is highly wired and hard work. Colum is totally frustrated. I want to return her. I feel we have taken on something that just isn't right.

As we get into bed around midnight Colum says "She needs us. We are her last chance."

I don't answer.

Day the Eighth

Sleep in by half an hour. Feel worn out even though it is only 7.30am. Colum takes sympathy on me and walks the dogs himself. Sal doing barking thing again. Colum brings her back to the house four times until he finally has to put on the halti. He then has to take her out again, as she still needs to do her business. Jen great. Jen a princess. Jen just lovely. Envied non-dog people going off to work. Shiny cars. Clean ironed clothes. In control. Not taking on stupid projects. I feel overwhelmed and a mess.

We talk about Sally over breakfast. Colum wonders if we can get help. I say we can't afford it. Colum checks our dog guru's website. Discovers an associate of her method resident in Edinburgh. We decide to contact her and see if we can take Sally to her. I think of how rescue dogs are supposed to be cheap. Sally is turning out to be quite expensive. Our thoughts lead on.

Colum is intrigued by the fact that Jan Fennell trains people in her own distinctive method. He says "I would love to do that."

There is a two day foundation course in England. A whole new vista of possibilities opens up. Our friends already nickname Colum as 'Dances with Dogs'. Perhaps Sally has been sent to us to teach us? Perhaps Sally is the final impetus for Colum to follow his dream?

"The problem is the way through," as my doctorate supervisor used to say.

A quiet, very tentative interior voice wonders if Sally is opening new doors for us.

Day the Ninth

Sally joins us briefly at our mediation time. Colum and I try to do this each weekday morning. For ten minutes or so we sit in silence in our designated meditation space. Jenna likes this space and, when she first came to us, quickly identified my prayer cushion as being rather comfy and now sleeps on it during the night. Sally is curious about what we are doing, or not doing, here. I dong the singing bowl as the signal for the start of our session. Sally woofs and wags her tail and tries to grab the small wooden stick. I put it out of sight. Zen-Jen is already spaced out, showing Sally how it's done. Sal thinks it looks really boring and goes off to snap at dust particles in the dining room.

I am going to track down the Jan Fennell associate in Edinburgh. Colum is off on Friday. Maybe we could go through and chat with her? If it costs an arm and leg then we'll just have to stick with reading the books.

When Colum gets home for lunch he tells me that his colleague, a great advocate of 'T Touch' training for dogs, says the halti we are using for the evening walks is barbaric. Makes me smile. After eleven years of owning dogs when we have steadily resisted using a halti, we have finally had to resort to one. Us? Cruel? Don't make me laugh. But Malcolm apparently says there is a more humane (more dogane?) harness that is much better. A halti, he says, stresses the dog even more. What fun this all is.

Day the Tenth

I have almost stopped attempting to walk the dogs on my own. Just too difficult. Problem is that Colum is very busy at work and is coming home later for lunch. Around noon, think the dogs are desperate to go out. Tell myself to be brave and fasten Sally on the waist lead, which I never use, and let Jenna run free ahead of me. All is ok for two minutes.

Approach our neighbour, Suzie, in her garden who asks "Is this your new dog?"

Sally chooses this moment to go frenetic at the sight of Suzie's cat. Suzie looks at this dog rearing up on her hind legs, at my stricken face, makes some hasty excuse and retreats inside. Colum appears cycling along the street. I swop him his bike for Sally. We go back to the house.

"Don't set yourself up for failure", Colum quotes from the dog book. I say I hadn't intended to fail, just wanted to walk the dogs.

Over a bowl of soup half an hour later I say that I am still not convinced that Sally is right for us and once again end up in tears. Colum suggests I take time out and try and get some rest in the afternoon. Feel like a gentile southern lady who has to go and lie down just to cope with life. I go to bed but don't sleep. Too busy telling myself that sleep is necessary if I am to be calm with Sally. Get up after an hour. Dogs quietly sleep the afternoon away.

Just as I am serving out a 'proper' dinner of brown rice, lemon sole and stir-fry veg – I have jettisoned the usual Wednesday night routine of joining my running group as my body needs food and sustenance – the phone rings. It is the dog guru's associate from Edinburgh. She sounds lovely. Feels as if the cavalry have phoned. I pass the phone to Colum noticing that I was about to say "As he's the Alpha male you had best speak with him," – really, where have my years of paid up feminism gone? But in dog-speak it actually makes sense. I think I could be the Alpha if I chose, but in Sally's case I'm more than happy to be second in command. I put Colum's dinner in the oven, this could be a long conversation.

Colum explains to Julie, for such is the associate's name, where we are or where we are not with Sally. She must be a good listener as he gets it all said and I haven't had to jump up and down and do stage whispers of things I think forgotten. The upshot of the conversation is that Julie has penciled in a date to come over and visit us. Hurrah! She will spend three to four hours watching what we are doing and working with us. Colum explains that one of Sally's major challenges seems to her fear of imagined and possible dangers in the dark outside. As Julie has a young family she can't be with us in the evening, but thinks that she will be able to diagnose the problem none the less.

Julie's consultation will cost a bit and I see another chunk of our very paltry savings sailing away from us. But, on the plus side, learning the tools to quieten Sally's mind will surely be worth the expense. And, as an enthusiast of this particular dog training method, Colum is already wondering where our meeting with Julie might really direct us. There are no accidents in the universe and all that. Maybe Sally is here for a reason. Maybe I'm just clutching at positive straws.

After a quick chat with Colum re our relief that there may be some help coming our way, I trot off to B&Q with my friend Frances, who needs to buy a scythe for her community garden. I filled my huge trolley with plastic coated wire fencing, a pack of clips, 5 litres of B&Q fence paint in forest green colour. Saw the same posts that we had bought at the garden centre for £3 cheaper a post. Aaagh! Phone Colum to ask if I should get them and return the already purchased posts. We decide we haven't the time nor energy. Have a cup of tea with my friend back at her house. Tell her lots of Sally stuff. Wonder if I am being really boring. Like a new parent who can't see beyond the next nappy change. But, being a good pal, she just smiles and says "I'm sure it will all come right," and gives me some lovely fresh picked wild garlic. I think of my garden and how I haven't paid it a jot of attention since Sally has come. There will be total anarchy in my potato patch.

Day the Eleventh

Lug myself out of bed at 7am. The nights seem shorter at the moment. Pull on an assortment of suitable dog walking gear. There is always a pile of such sloppy clothing on the floor of our bedroom. Avoid looking in the mirror. Aware that I feel really hungry, but there isn't time to swill down a bowl of cereal before we trog out for the first walk.

While Colum showers then irons his shirt, I make us some hot ginger and lemon – our time honoured first drink of the day – then put out the dogs' food. This is another area we need to work on. Sally eats as if we are going to snatch it away from her at any second. Jen eats in a ladylike fashion, stopping every few seconds to twist round and look curiously at Sally, who is gulping and gulping away. In an effort to ease the assault on Sally's stomach, we now spread her food out on a plastic tray. I got the idea from our friend, Siobhan, whose black Labrador, reportedly, goes mental when food appears. Siobhan told me how her vet advised her to spread Coco's food out on the back door step so she had a second or so between each mouthful. It worked for Coco so we do it with Sally but in the lack of a back door step, use a large tray.

And Jen, we now see, is a fatty. We hadn't noticed the weight creeping up on her. When she first came to us from her first family she was a shilpit wee thing. All spike and bones. She seemed to have been fed on whatever the family were eating. Money was more than tight for her first family and they just couldn't afford good quality dog food. And Jen was happy with her lot. When we first introduced her to our usual good quality dog food she walked away from her bowl and stood drooling as I chomped on a bit of bread and ham. She was also partial to milky tea and Tennant's Lager. I thought this was cute. Apparently horses like tea too, I'm not sure about the lager and I don't expect I will test the theory. Some afternoons when I was having a writing break, I would sit in the kitchen with Jen and give her a saucer of tea. I would say "Wid ye like a wee cup of tea hen? Aye, weel then, let's have a wee cuppa and wee biscuit too." And we would settle in to our tea party like two support-stocking tweed-clad ladies. Ah, it was nice. That was then, though, and this is now.

Looking at the emaciated model thin form of Sally, Jen now looks like a plump cushion, a wee French fancy, a roly-poly, still pretty, still delightful but, there's no getting around it, she's fat. So, while we focus on feeding Sally up we also focus on feeding Jen down. Sally gets a full cup of dry dog food as well as a quarter tin of wet food twice a day. Jen gets half of that. And they both finish eating at exactly the same time but Sal has also licked her tray clean. Sal then bounds over to check that Jen's bowl really is empty and only then finally understands that feeding time is, sadly, over. We then have to get Sal out of the house fairly smartish – her bowel control being what it is.

I'm quiet on the morning walk and find it hard when Sally bounds too near me. I wonder when I stopped being used to the movement of larger dogs. In times gone past I could hold onto our Lab and our Collie-cross when they were in full focused passion about a bitch in heat. I must have been another woman then. Or have I just been spoiled with Jen's self-contained off-lead behaviour? I liked being spoiled though and my tired self isn't amused with the gleeful jumps of Sal. If we could just let her off and she could tear around madly for an hour, that would be so much better. Instead we tug round the hill, down the terrace, round the block and back home. Memories of hour-long walks, chatting with other dog people as we go, are very distant; I miss them.

We have some breakfast. Me munching gloomily. Feel as if I am back in the days of being at home with a young baby when finding my hairbrush was a major feat. It's only a dog for Lord's sake! Why does it feel like we're moving through treacle? Colum goes off to work and I, after a look at my desk, see that the creative juices are just not going to flow this morning. I fill a hot water bottle, get back into my jammies, climb back into bed and fall asleep for another glorious two hours.

I wake up around 11am. Immediately feel guilty. Have a quick shower. Feel more human, more feminine, less out of control. Stack dishes. Think about putting on washing. Turn on my laptop. Let dogs into sitting room to play. Thank God they do this. Assuages my worries about their lack of real exercise. I do some basic housework and am just settling into my desk work when Sam appears.

"Mum, there's a stink in the sitting room…"

Day the Twelfth

Colum on annual leave today. Oh, the blessing of a bountiful God. In our previous pre-Sally lives, we had planned to go and visit friends in the Borders today. We weren't going to take Jen, as wonderful dog that she is, she also has a distinct fondness for the ecstasy of chasing sheep. On our last visit with these friends, she had disgraced us by slipping under a fence and tearing into the middle of a flock of said species. Colum had hurtled over the gate after her and I stood, dithering like a pathetic female, going "Oh, no! Oh, noooooo." Then my pragmatic self said "Get in there! The more people in the field the less likely the farmer is to shoot!" Belting through the field in the opposite direction to Colum in the hope that one of us could corner Jen, I thanked the universe that I was a road runner. It was true that I don't usually run with a backpack, clumpy walking boots and lots of outdoor gear on, but panickers can't be choosers and I whumped over the knobbly grass gasping "Streuth…Streuth…"

I spied Jen at the far corner of the field. She had rounded up a single sheep. Having never known her in this situation and with stories of dogs ripping out sheep's hearts in my mind, I ran faster. I was now shouting "Jen! Jen! Come here! Here!" in my most assertive I'm-not-kidding-I'm-really-not tone. Suddenly our dog guru's philosophy barged into my mind "Dogs won't come to you if they think they are about to get a severe telling off" or words to that effect. The stress of the moment no doubt making me misquote. Some inspiration made me drop to my knees, pretend to rummage in my bag and say "Oh, look! How nice! What is this?"

Jen looked at the stationary sheep and seemed to be thinking "What does one do with a stationary sheep? They're no fun," and then looked at me. Forcing myself not to make a lunge at her, I rummaged in my bag again making more noises. Jen took a few steps towards me. The sheep, bless her, stayed where she was. I flung myself at Jen, grabbing her collar. Colum had her lead but, necessity being the mother of invention, I unwound my scarf from my sweating neck and hitched it through her collar.

Colum bounded round a bush, saw that I had Jen, and said "Oh, well done!"

One of our friends, appeared at my side and said "Let's get out of here, before the farmer spots us. Quick, over that wall."

Colum vaulted over the wall, our pal picked up Jen and pushed her over into Colum's arms. I had found a place where I could get over without undignified assistance and we scrambled out into the country road.

"Well, you're the fittest pair of visitors we've had yet," said our friend. With shaky legs we walked back into the village, turned in at a bijou rustic café, ordered scones, jam and, in the absence of anything stronger, a huge pot of tea.

So, Jen wasn't too welcome where it was now lambing season but we were looking forward to some stress-free walking, good conversation and company. Now, the thought of leaving Sam, to look after not just Jen but also the madness of Sally, seemed a daft and impossible plan. And it got dafter when Sam announced that when we were away he would probably have a garden party with his mates.

"Ye know. A few beers round the chiminea, few burgers, mibbe some Pimms, and the lads can stay over."

All of that was fine with us – the lads are beyond the age of doing things like a previous amusement of a tangerine-throwing competition in our newly painted dining room – but Colum and I immediately had visions of Sally whooping over the neighbours' gardens, before being picked up hours later by the constabulary, forcing a rather tipsy Sam to go and collect her. We cancelled our visit to our friends.

Today was therefore a nice free unplanned day. A slow day. Maybe getting up around 9am. Leisurely dog walk, nice big breakfast, newspaper reading session, that sort of thing. The flaw was that no-one had thought to inform Sally.

6.30am she starts barking. We ignore her hoping she would get the message that she goes by our rules and our wishes. She keeps barking. I am conscious that the lad in the house downstairs is sitting an exam today.

I hope against hope that the exam wasn't a late start where he would no doubt bank on a good long sleep to prepare him. Sally increases her barking. By now we are all awake, including the neighbours downstairs and those through the wall.

"Do you think she wants to go out?" says Colum.

"Mmmm, sounds like it," I say, doing absolutely nothing to indicate that I intend to get up.

"I'd better take her," says Colum.

"Mmmm, good idea," says I, burying deeper into the duvet.

Nice kind man that he is, my partner gets up, and five minutes later I hear the loose concrete slab on our front path make its dunting sound as he walks over it with Sal and Jen. Sal is still barking. I can hear some kind of motorised lawn-mower giving it big licks in a garden nearby. Do they know it's only 7.00am? What's the rush? Garden police coming? Crazy people. I fall back asleep and wake up when Colum crawls back in beside me.

"Wasstime?" I say.

"Time for some more sleep," says Colum.

Sal and Jen now appear to be daring each other to run up to our bedroom door, jump on it and run back down to their baskets. Colum gets out of bed again.

"That's enough!" he shouts. "Go to your beds!"

The girls slink downstairs. Colum gets back into bed. I keep the duvet tight under my chin to stop the gusts of cold air. Two seconds later Sal starts barking again.

"Oh, I give up," says Colum and gets up. I fall drift off to sleep again secure in the knowledge that my man is on the case.

I wake at 9.45ish. Potter downstairs to the kitchen. No sign of dogs or husband. I open the blind and catch a glimpse of a figure running past the bit of the fence that we can see between the houses opposite ours which back onto the hill. Looks like Colum is playing – I presume the dogs are too. Must have met some doggy pals.

I make a hot drink, wander into the dining room and sit on my rocking chair, my thinking chair, which looks out over our back garden and over the rooftops of our town. Life feels quite good. I consider taking my drink back upstairs and reading in bed. I can do this if I want to. But the shining sun is up and the washing basket is full. A half hour later, washing chugging in the machine, last night's dinner dishes put away, breakfast table set, house plants watered, I finally take another cup of tea upstairs and sit in the spare bedroom where it is sunny and warm; I pick up the book I have been reading at night-time. Aaah, I could almost believe I am a single girl again. The front door whumps. The missing members of our household are home. I put the book down.

Colum spends the rest of the day trying to get the new fence posts painted. The weather sends down bursts of wet, wet and wetter rain and the occasional half hour of drying sun. Jen and Sal are much amused at these brilliant new sticks that their master wants to play with. They're totally up for it and appreciate his choice. Why mess around with the skinny type when you can have these huge monsters? A few hours later, a good half dozen of the posts are painted with B&Q forest green outdoor rough hewn wood paint. The teeth marks barely show.

In the afternoon I wander to the local pet store.

"How're you getting on?" asks the owner.

"Well," I say "I'm not sure if the dog is settling or it's just that we are adapting. It seems to work best if we think of her as an overgrown puppy. I've only wanted to return her twice this week, not every day."

She smiles. "Ach, you'll get there, you'll get there," she says.

I wish I could believe that. I buy another ground peg for the dog tie up. The ground pegs can take more than one dog but we don't reckon it stands too much chance against Sally's determined escape plans, coupled with Jen's agenda to rip the postman's bag off his back. Another peg seems wise. I also buy a kong – not the hollow type as the one in the shop is just too big – even though the dogs would love the fact that we would have to stuff it with a day's food ration, but the type that has rivets running round the outside. I have a stroke of inspiration with this in that I think it will suit Jen. She needs to lose weight, so a wee smear of peanut butter or fish paste in the rivets will keep her busy while Sal can fatten up trying to get out the dry food stuffed into our existing hollow kong.

"It's a complete science," I comment to the pet shop owner.

She laughs. "Aye, ither folk think us dog folk are jist aff our heids."

"And they would be right," say I as I leave.

Walk home through the park thinking how strange it is that now we have two dogs, but I seem to be doing almost no serious dog walking at all at the minute. Best not complain. It's bound to change.

And of course, it does. By 9pm I'm officially overwhelmed. Sometime mid-evening Sally takes it into her head to jump up on the on the high raised bed opposite our front door. In her efforts to find an escape route she sent a stone trough crashing to the ground which collided with another stone planter. My carefully planted poppies as well as my peppermint and lavender plants are now all strewn over the slabs. I sweep them all up as best I can then, thinking of things gardening, went down to the back garden to see how my potatoes are getting on. Far too well I think is the verdict. They have sprung up from the ground like a class of cheeky secondary kids quite aware that they have safety in numbers and their totally gullible teacher hasn't a clue how to control them. All the books nippily dictate that one should bank up the soil around the plant once it starts to show so not to develop small subsidiary tubers. Hah. Each of my potatoes has around three to four stalks now and my banking up efforts this evening with a hoe and trowel seem futile. I'm going to time the first person who walks into our back garden and says "Oh, you should have banked up your potatoes." Well, we'll just have to be the people who *don't* bank up potatoes and that's that. And my bee-and-butterfly patch needs a right good weed, and as for the "lawn" or scrubby grass that serves us as a lawn, it looks like a very bad hair day.

I cast my eyes over the side of the garden, where tomorrow Colum and my brother are valiantly going to put in fencing and ask myself just where and how they will do it. The shrubs there are all intermingled and Colum's existing woven fence is all to bits since Sally battered against it that first afternoon. I need those Ground Force folk or whatever the TV people are,

43

to come in here and start the garden for me all over again. I do some half-hearted weeding, then sit on the bench and think back to that lovely Easter Monday when I suggested that *stupid stupid* thing of us checking out the cat and dog home. Someone should have stopped me. I call it a day and come up to the front of the house.

The pots are still lying smashed; the pigeons – despite having a roofer clear out their nests from our roof – are still shitting everywhere. In Scotland we call them "clappy doos"; Colum and I have rechristened them "crappy doos". The wee courtyard bit, as I liked to call it, in front of our house used to be rather charming. Now it's all overgrown, has a bank of pots stacked up in any old style in an attempt to put Sally off attempting even higher jumps and the flimsy trellising fence that we got because of Jack and Joe annoying the downstairs neighbours with their woofing, is just a real pest. I can't deal with it tonight and go inside.

The front hall, our 'shed' as I now call it, has reached a height of mess that would have any vaguely house-proud person nearing a breakdown. I think of Jack and Morag next door who are selling their house. Their back garden is pretty, ordered and neat; their front courtyard a planned riot of colour and joy. No doubt inside the house is the same. They don't have dogs; they don't now have any children living with them. They have lots more money than us and I suspect lots more sense. How did I let my house get into this state? I come up the stairs to the living area. Colum meets me.

"What's up?" I say. There's something about his demeanour that says there is definitely something up and it ain't particularly good.

"Sally has just done an enormous pee on the turn of the stairs."

"Great," I say.

We employ the dettol again and afterwards I give Colum a litany of my moans.

He puts the kettle on. He listens then says "You should never have married me."

"Yeh, I should have married an accountant with stay-press trousers and a golf club membership."

He makes me camomile tea, puts four ginger nuts on the saucer. "C'mon, let's watch some telly.'

Walking in my socks over the carpet which has had multiple shittings on it this week I remember I still have on my gardening trousers.

A memory of my mum saying to my dad after he has hoed and raked and sorted his garden into perfection, "Oh Tom, make an effort, go and change those horrible trousers," comes into my mind. Dad would understand when changing your trousers is just too much effort. Worst thing is this is my entire fault. My entire fault. I said we should go and get the dog. I saw her. I chose her. *Stupid. Stupid. Stupid.*

Day the Thirteenth

We've had Sally a full fortnight. She's made it thus far. Had I been on the morning walk, though, I might have found myself uttering the words "That's it. She's going back!" Colum had assured me that he could cope with the morning walk and had taken *les filles* out up the hill. As he didn't have to compact the walk into the pre-work schedule he joined the 9am gang of dog people and their favourite canines up the hill. He let Sally off lead and she ran and skipped and jumped and played with Jimmy, Finn and Jenna. All good. Finn and his owner then had to go and Jen, Sal and Jimmy went to romp in Jimmy's secure back garden. Still good. A squelchy sound then emitted from Sal and she proceeded to dump nice loads of runny pooh at intervals around our neighbours' garden. Their garden stunk to high heaven and so did Sal. Colum managed to catch her and lug her out of the garden. Paul, decent, more than decent, chap that he is, said he would clear up the mess. Yukity yuk. It's ok clearing up after your own dog, but someone else's? That's triple yuk.

Across the road, cocooned in my ignorance of the embarrassing chaos happening nearby, I meanwhile had been having a busy but lovely time. Slopping around in my dressing gown, sipping tea, reading the Review section of *The Guardian*, filling the slow cooker with chopped veg and tuna pieces in prep for our evening meal, making up the spare bed in prep for our guests and doing bits of this and bits of that, all was right in my world. Conscious that my brother and his partner would be arriving in just under an hour, I have just turned on the taps to run a nice bath when I hear the front door open and bang shut.

Colum calls up the stairs "Can you run a bath for Sally please? She's got a really dirty backside."

Oh joy. Instead of adding baby oil and a pinch of lavender essential oil to the warm water, I reach instead for the medicated dog shampoo.

"Two baths in two weeks, Sally!" says Colum. "Aren't you lucky? And won't you look lovely for our visitors."

Ever the positive one, Colum soaps and soothes Sally, who doesn't look that delighted to once more find herself in the bath.

Thinking that I would now have to have a quick shower once the bathroom floor had been dried and the bath thoroughly scrubbed out, I close over the door and go to give Jen her breakfast.

Until Sal's tum settles down, food is off the agenda for her. Sod's law, really. The dog that really needed feeding up would now have to fast and the dog who could do with a week's fasting was now licking her chops at the thought of food coming her way. I give Jen her vastly reduced rations which she polishes off in two minutes and then proceeds to batter her bowl in a definite staccato rhythm of that-is-not-enough! I-want-some-more!

"Sorry, girl, that's it for now," I say.

Sally, hearing the bowl bashing verbals happening, is now whining and struggling to get out of the bathroom. I can hear her thumping against the door as Colum patiently attempts to dry her.

"You can let her out," I say. "Coast clear."

Sally tears out of the bathroom, does a skid turn into the kitchen, leaps on Jen's empty bowl, does a lap around the rest of the kitchen floor to see where we have hidden her breakfast tray and, finding not a jot of food anywhere, belts off to see if she could get Jen to regurgitate any of her breakfast.

I look in the bathroom. The mess isn't too bad. And at least we have a presentable dog again.

An hour later my brother and his partner stand in our kitchen. On the table are a bottle of organic red wine, yummy chocs and a jar of quality jam. Thoughtful gifts, but the best gift was to see these two people standing there ready to help in whatever way they can. I fling out my arms, pull them both into me and said "Thank you so much for coming". They giggle and said some muffled things like "ssshpleasuresssnobother". Although it was now after noon Colum and I are only at the mid-morning coffee stage and, as the cupboards are devoid of necessary lunch ingredients, I make coffee and open up some packets of flapjack.

Over our repast we fill our visitors in on what our fortnight has been like. It is a measure of their generosity that they let us blether about the challenges, large and small, that Sally had brought to us and listen politely, even with interest. My brother has always liked dogs. When we were children we would have an annual holiday on the Isle of Cumbrae where our parents would take a house, or rather a very small flat into which the six of us would cram and believe ourselves to be in very heaven. The glories of Kames Bay was across the road and I have a memory of seeing my brother run along the tide line with a dog, throwing sticks for him, or just walking and talking to him. I don't remember ever seeing the dog's owner. It must have lived nearby and watched for Kenneth each evening. Boy and dog. Best buds.

The scene is stuck in my mind like a postcard. Kenneth in his crew-necked sweater, trousers and wellies, the dog large like a retriever, wet, sandy and happy. Nowadays Kenneth's life doesn't allow for a dog of his own but his childhood appreciation of dogs hasn't abated. It's the old adage that dogs really don't care how much money you earn, if you have a pension plan, if your house is grand or cramped, all they want from you is some clean water, enough food, a safe and dry place to sleep, a few sticks to play with, and for you to love them. What you do for a living, how far you've made it on the ladder of life is irrelevant. Kenneth lives in a small city-centre flat in Glasgow. There isn't much room for a dog to manoeuvre but every dog we have taken to visit there, scurries up the three flights of stairs, arrives at the front door, tail wagging, bounds in, gives a few licks to my brother, does a quick sniff around the bedroom, bathroom, galley kitchen and living room, then plumps down on the mat in front of the fire and goes off to sleep. They know they are welcome and that's enough for them.

So, Kenneth and his partner, Bridget, are the perfect people to have in our kitchen this Saturday noontime. Where non-dog people might feign interest and then neatly turn the conversation to other topics, Kenneth and Bridget let us blether about "Sally this" and "Sally that" and "Jen this" and "Jen that" without yawning once. Colum and I finally came to a stop around an hour later.

"Well, will we get started on the fence?" says my brother.

"Good plan," I say.

Therapeutic as it has been off-loading our fortnight of stress, there is a task to be done and, as it looks like rain is looming, it had better be soon. The men sort themselves out with fence-building gear and stomp off, armed with an assortment of tools that they think necessary for the job and some that, to them, are just plain interesting. Bridget and I see them off the premises then sort ourselves out for a trip into town.

Two hours later we return home, lugging food for the workers and the support people. We've had a fun time. Our trip to town included the unexpected bonus of spectatorship of the 'Great Duck Race' where a hundred or so plastic yellow ducks were released into the river and then fished out by intrepid Scout Masters; a visit to the town's beautiful thirteenth-century abbey, with the added attraction of a coffee shop which does a nice cafetière of ground coffee and accompanying scone; a drop in to our local fairtrade shop, where Colum and I, in another life it now seems, are volunteers, and finally a very necessary visit to the local supermarket.

We go down to the back garden before we disrupt the dogs in the house to take orders for refreshments and consumables. The men are glad to pause and show off their work. All of one side of the garden is now enclosed in a fence high enough to stop deers in flight, elegantly fashioned in forest green mesh and occasional posts which off-set my shrubs and plants really well. I am delighted. Not only does it give shape to our garden but it looks as if it should also contain Sal. I notice I still say 'should' — this wee girl is a law to herself, and I have learned not to underestimate the power of her hind legs. She may be part deer. At least at our test session there will be four of us and that's two more pairs of hands than we had on her first afternoon. If she escapes we can always try and entice Sal back with a game of rounders up in the street.

Another hour and the garden is totally enclosed – we think. The men have ingeniously woven mesh over the existing garden gate under the honeysuckle archway which is subtle, allows the gate to open and should stop a dog leaping over it. Colum goes to get the girls. They appear puffing and straining on their leads.

"Here we go" says my brother. They shoot into the garden. I have bought the new kong on a rope, a ball and a strong plastic ring into the garden. Jen spots the toys and claims them as hers. Sally takes a momentary look at the toys then starts to circulate around the garden, ears well back, every inch of her alert and ready to spring. We watch her apprehensively while trying to look relaxed. She goes behind the wood pile.

"Are you sure that's secure round there?" I ask.

"Yes. It's fine. Relax", says Colum, but I notice he is keeping his eyes on Sal not Jen. Sal circulates a few times. Jumps up at the meshing, staring through it to the great land of freedom beyond. Jumps up, but after a few moments, jumps down. My shoulders lower a half inch.

"Seems to be working," I say, slowly, more to myself than anyone else.

We're all standing watching Sal. Jen is now chewing the kong rope delighted that she has it all to herself. Sal gives up her vigilant circuits, trots over to Jen, seizes a bright pink coloured ball that squeaks, and bounds off with it. Jen is up like a flash, tears after her. They make a figure of eight round the garden, my potato patch has had it, but I don't care. The garden is secure. It really is. A celebration is in order.

"Who's up for a glass of wine and some crisps?"

The others nod in assent.

Colum goes up to the house, leaving us three to move chairs out of the dogs' path and create a cosy sitting space on the relative safety of the raised bed of bee-and-butterfly patch. Colum returns, we open the organic red wine that Kenneth and Bridget have brought, put the crisps in a bowl – which we then have to put in an empty hanging basket out of the dogs' reach – ease ourselves down onto the bench and makeshift chairs, fill our pottery goblets and proclaim the toast 'The garden!' The dogs lose interest in us and begin a playful scuffle of grabbing and chewing each other's ears and jaw. Now that we are sitting down, it feels chilly even though we are all clad in fleeces. Colum lights the chiminea – first lighting of the year. The strong breeze lifts and fans the wood and paper into flame. We sip wine, watch the dogs; I feel the headache I have carried for a fortnight slip away.

Back in the house we prepare a leisurely meal. We are all feeling happy. The dogs are sleeping in their baskets, the wine still flows in our veins, the men have showered and changed, the CD player sings easy harmonies to us, Sam comes home from his shop job and spills free samples of soap, bath bombs, skin products and a rather strange smelling perfume called "Lust" over the coffee table. Bridget and I *oooh* and *aaah* over the products, test some out and wave our now scented wrists and hands at the men. They pretend to be interested but after a few moments start talking about the dogs again.

"Thanks so much for all your help," says Colum to Kenneth.

"It's no problem. I enjoyed it. Maybe Sally will settle down now."

"Mmmm," we say.

After dinner the men take the dogs out for the last walk. We hear Sally give her nocturnal symphony. Colum returns to the house. I look out into the street. Kenneth is standing with Jen on her lead. Jen is looking resigned. Kenneth bemused. The settled contented dog has disappeared. Jekyll is back. Colum puts the halti on Sal, goes out again. They move off down the street. We can still hear Sal. Twenty five minutes later they get home. Kenneth comes into the living room where Bridget and I are cosily ensconced around the fire with tea and the biscuit caddy.

"I see what you mean," says Kenneth. "It's like a different dog."

"Mmmm," I say.

Day the Fourteenth

Morning walk. Sal off-lead as Jimmy is there with his owner. The dogs chase around the hill and are finally corralled into his back garden. Paul, perhaps worried about a repeat of the loose pooh episode of the day before, but more likely aware that his Sunday big breakfast is about ready, drops polite hints to Colum that it would be good if Sal could go back on her lead. Colum, fixated on Sal and her behaviour, doesn't pick the hints up.

Our neighbour has to say, a few times, "Em, Colum, I actually need to go in now," before the penny drops. After a few lucky manoeuvres, Sal is grounded and brought home.

"I think I'm losing it," says Colum to me. "Paul was trying to tell me he had to go and I just didn't pick it up."

I think back to when Sam was a baby and we lived life in a haze and wonder if we have returned there. But the play session in our wonderful back garden goes well. We have a huge breakfast with all the works to celebrate and Sal gets toast and scrambled egg. She keeps it down or in. Hurrah. After brunch we drive Kenneth and Bridget home.

"It's been like a mini-break," says Bridget. Mini-break. How nice that would be. Ho hum.

Day the Fifteenth

Colum still on annual leave today, as we should have been on our long weekend in the Borders. I say to him "It would be so good if you could be off every Monday." If wishes were but fishes. Feeding Sally her breakfast she jumps up bashing her head on the underside of the plastic tray. The dry food dances off the tray and cascades all around the kitchen. Sal emits a low menacing growling at Jen if she so much as moves her eyes towards a nugget of her food. A wee piece has gone under the large swing bin. Sal digs into the skirting board around the bin.

"No Sally! No!" I cry. She persists. I pull out the bin from its usual place. Sal retrieves the tiny morsel. I put the bin back. What a circus.

After a quick run in the garden we head off out country. Erskine Beach is fairly close. Brilliant place for dogs. Bit of sand, lots of swimmable water and a long shore path which meets a forest track. We let Jen off. She runs rejoicing that we have once again come here. "It's brilliant here!" her tail says. Colum keeps Sal on the waist lead. Neither of us feels like spending an hour cajoling her back into the car later.

We do a long walk. My legs are tired when we finally get back to the car park. Jenna looks a complete waif. Wet and sandy and blissfully tired. Despite not getting to run in the water Sal seems tired too and content to lie down in the car. We retire to the Erskine Hospital garden centre. It's four o'clock. We are ravenous. The café is still open. We pile our tray with food and drink. Chink our tea cups together and say "To our holiday weekend".

A good walk and a cup of tea are age-old soothers for fraught spirits, but so are holidays, and by the time the evening comes I am back to feeling hard done by. Of late, I have been around too many friends who have secure double incomes and more freedom. One friend has just returned from the triple pleasures of a holiday in Spain, a visit to family in London and is now off to Sweden. Another friend has been for two serious pamper sessions – one in Stobo Castle and another in a posh hotel on Loch Lomond side. Since last July I have had the sum total of an overnight at my mum's, three nights courtesy of the NHS in a local hospital and one night at a friend's house. It is now May. Our Borders weekend was a bulwark against frustration but I completely stymied it by getting another dog.

And this dog, although cheap by breeder prices, was still around £100. Her first vet bill came to £43. The fencing for the garden was around £150. The tie-up and bits and pieces from the pet store have toted up to something like £40 so far and the consultancy from the dog guru's protégé will be around £150. Add that all together and Colum and I, and maybe Sam too, could have had a rather nice week's holiday somewhere. This dog that was chosen simply to be a pal to Jenna, to stop her chewing her paws, and perhaps be a bit of fun for us, is turning out expensive and exhaustive.

I give myself a shake. This is probably just low oestrogen or progesterone or lack of chocolate. My thoughts are on a no-win negative road. Since when do we measure dogs by what they cost? Since when have I ever done that? We bought our Joe as a puppy for £80, Jack was given to us by friends who just couldn't cope with the full blooded *joie-de-vivre* of a Labrador, and Jenna was also a free gift. She came to us just as our gentle Joe had died and we were bereft and dogless. Her first family had little money but they gave her free because they wanted her to be happy to be loved; they didn't see her as a money-spinning opportunity. And so we have been blessed by beings who have lived with us, loved us and whom we mourn when they go from us. And Sally, despite the path she is pulling us on, despite the nuttiness of us spending our stretched income on her and her special needs, despite the fact that we now have to think long and hard about how to arrange our days, how to plan any future getaways, feels today like she might just belong to us. And, just for the record, a pampering session at Stobo Castle isn't my style. Well...then again...

Day the Sixteenth

Back to 7am walk as Colum is back at work today. We've stopped feeding the dogs first thing. It just seemed too early and felt a bit like getting yawning white-faced kids to eat 'just something' before packing them off to school. Colum has read the chapter on feeding dogs in Jan Fennell's book and we are now adhering to the gesture-eating rule. I therefore have a scrumptious ginger nut from Sally's tray and Colum ate a gluten-free choc biscuit from both their bowls (or behind them but it worked as an optical illusion). We have to assert ourselves as the pack leaders so feeding first is a must. Can't say though that a ginger nut at 7.30am really cuts it for me.

The morning passes quietly enough. At 11am I take a basket of washing out to the garden. I think of writer Kathleen Jamie, who has written of noticing how nature seeps into her life while she is caught up with the daily needs and routines of her family. This leads me to ponder on the fragmentary life many women lead where space for creativity comes in darts and sudden shafts. Thus has it so often been for women who attempt the pen. Does that give us a more grounded text as we are rarely protected from the maintenance of day to day living? Or does it mean that our writing is rarely fully developed?

As I come back up towards the house I meet our neighbour. Morag is retired and is never done enforcing just how hard she had to work to now be able to sit in the sun. Whenever I meet her I oscillate between thinking how sad it is that she feels the need to justify her leisure years, and, simultaneously, immediately justify why it is that I am putting out washing mid-morning instead of belting off to some place of definite work, suit-clad and important looking. I remember meeting her husband, Jack, at the train station the morning I was going in to deliver my soft-bound PhD thesis to the university registry. He asked me if I was going shopping and when I demurred and told him what I was doing, he looked totally confused, as if I hadn't understood his question, then changed the subject and told me all about the profit they had made on their last house.

The moral of this tale is that one should never judge a woman putting out washing as that being the sum total of all she does with her day. She could just surprise you. Like the time a 'tree surgeon' came round to chop down a beautiful silver birch that was apparently interfering with Morag's satellite dish transmission (words escape me, but that's a rant for another day). As next door were nowhere to be seen, I took the chap a cup of tea. Even slaughterers need tea. He thanked me and then, for some reason known only to his rationale, launched into why it was that I may feel inferior to him. Seemed to be some unwritten thesis as it went on for a bit. Conscious I had teaching prep to do for the next day, I eventually excused myself and said I had things to do. Looking at my apron he said 'Hoovering and that, eh?'

'No, I've done that,' I replied. 'Just need to write up a lecture on 'Muriel Spark as anagogic novelist.'

He stared a little, decided I hadn't said what I had said, and said 'Right well, hen, I'd better get on.'

Post-feminist era? I don't think so.

Anyway, Morag is still hingin' over the fence telling me that a family with four children are really interested in it. Four children are good. They will be used to chaos. So living next door to two dogs should be ok with them. I take time to get our neighbour up to speed with the fact that our part of the back garden is now surrounded by the equivalent of deer fence. If any house viewers are unsure of dogs they now need not fear. Morag likes things to be ordered, neat and under control, so I think I score some brownie points.

Having deposited the washing basket in the back garden I go back in to get *les chiens*. They trot down fairly well. We really must get the path down to the garden sorted sometime. It's a bit of scamper even in flat wellies and a desperate handhold on the waist-high fence that divides our garden from next door. It's doable though, so I doubt any major improvement will be scheduled in the near future.

Once in the garden I let the girls off lead. Sally checks out the possibility of exit at least four times, then woofs at Jen to come and play. They romp about through my potato patch, round the whirly-gig, over the basketball court, round the back of the big fern tree, past the compost bins and back to start again. The washing now pegged out, I retreat to the bench in our bee-and-butterfly patch and watch their antics. Every now and again I call them to me, give them a wee nibble of a ginger nut biscuit before they romp off again. The idea is that they don't, or rather Sally doesn't, think that a call for a biscuit actually means a call for coming back on the lead. After a good half hour I call them to me again, give Jen a biscuit and deftly clip Sal's lead on before giving her a biccy too. Phew! Done. Success.

Out through the gate. Sal's body stance changes. She is alert, ears back, tense. This is open land. I keep a firm grip on her lead as well as Jen's and make it up the shared communal stairs, round the side of the house up to our front door. A bird, for reasons best known to itself, wings its way from our window ledge to the ash tree. Sally rears up, but I am ready for her and manage to keep a hold, get my key in the front door, lever in the girls, and shut the door with us all on the right side of it. A play and toilet session in our garden has been achieved. I need a cup of tea.

Colum comes home at lunchtime and brings out of his bag a new harness for Sal – a suggestion from his colleague at work who is the advocate of 'T Touch'. The harness is new but Malcolm says we can test it and see what we think before buying it from him. We swallow a quick lunch and take the dogs out. The harness fastens round a dog's shoulders and has various strategically placed clips which encourage the dog not to pull but to walk in a balanced manner. I am sceptical but five minutes into the walk, particularly at the usual 'red alert' spot outside Suzie's garden where her cats linger, begin to think the harness might just be working. Sal is alert but quiet, not woofing, not straining.

She is playful on the hill but even when the council recycling lorry appears and clatters past her, she is unfazed and trots along happily. Is it just that she is settling with us or is it the harness?

I wonder too if we have begun to assimilate Sally into our lives. I have stopped saying "I think we should take her back," every fifteen minutes. Although I do silently think it.

I phone a friend in the evening. A friend who has a dog. A friend who won't think we are mental getting another dog. We talk dog and dog training and dog stress. I feel better just by relating the story of Sally to her. She doesn't come out with the non-dog useless thing of "Well, you chose her," or "Well, it was your idea to get another dog," but just listens and tells me tales of the progress they are making with their family pet.

Lara is a beautiful year old golden retriever. "Fun, fun and more fun," is her logo. Maureen had once told me they had decided to get a dog as they had watched us do our lives with Joe and Jack. They were seduced by the walking, the companionship, the love our dogs showed us, the dog culture and the whole bit. Of course they were watching it from the side-lines. The times when our dogs played us up merry hell weren't in their log book and it all looked rosy and easy. So Lara was fetched from her birth home at 9 weeks old and the reality of having a dog kicked in.

My best image of how this huge bundle of fun had changed my friend's life was when they appeared on our annual caravan/camping holiday. The family have a large seven-seater people carrier. Oodles of space for two adults, a teenage son and a primary school daughter. But whereas their huge boot would once have contained their entire luggage and possibly some of ours, their car now looked like a conveyance that belonged in the developing world. Every iota of space was used up. I doubt if a midgie had a hope of a hitch-hike in it. A roof box stuffed with stuff swayed on high, three bikes hung by their fingertips at the back of the once pristine vehicle and the human occupants sat with things under their feet, things on their laps, things squashed around them. And at the back, in the boot, in gracious isolation, sat Lara in her large crate. I remember thinking as I watched them arrive how funny humans are in that we so like to complicate our lives. But that, I believe, is what makes us friends.

As our friends have embraced or rather got used to the mess and chaos a dog brings into your life, their home is one where we can visit and relax. Jen and Lara are great mates and are on a mission to see if they can achieve three times round the swing, trampoline, sand-pit, hammock and garden table in one minute flat. So far they are averaging at a minute and a half; if they can get the humans to synchronise the lifting of our wine glasses and plastic table as they whoop by mid-circuit they might just achieve their goal very soon. Maureen has devised a way of managing this by shouting "Bitch!" every time the dogs approach and, without faltering in our blethers, we all grab an end of the table and hoist it into the air as a flurry of fur passes under it. Sometimes it's just easier to go with the flow than fight it.

So Maureen was the ideal person to talk to this evening and I felt the better for it.

The late evening walk passes without major event, or rather the major event was the lack of a major event. Sal trots quite happily in her new harness, has a bit of a woof at Suzie's gate. Foxes? Cats? Who knows. We go right round the usual circuit and she is quiet and docile. Incredible. As she hadn't done her dump we thought we would go a little way along the cycle track beside the hill. The hill at night time is fox-country but in our new found confidence in the amazing harness it didn't seem such an obstacle.

It's all good until some two hundred yards or so into the track. Sally smells a fox or two, rears up, woofing, hackles up, completely tense. The old Sally reappears. But Colum holds her, talks calmly to her, doesn't change his tone. I meanwhile have turned around with Jenna and we are heading home. My neck and shoulders have stiffened again. I'm fed up with this. It's late and I'm tired and Jen and I are going home to bed. Colum catches up with us.

"Well, that wasn't too bad at all," he says.

Day the Seventeenth

I have one eye to our back garden. Sam and I took Jen and Sal out there almost an hour ago. It's a lovely windy and sunny afternoon and the girls needed some air. I drank a cup of camomile tea in the garden. Sam took photographs. When people see these photos in future they will say "Oh, how nice, there's Anne and Jenna and Sam". Sal isn't in any with people as she had switched into her dust particle manic thing. It's like there is no-one home when she does this. She twitches and skips minute skips, she stares unblinking into space, or dust particle filled space. I tried throwing sticks, a ball, tempting her with treats. No go. I just didn't exist. I picked up the lead. She backed away still looking spaced. Every time I went near her she ducked and moved out of grabbing distance. I wanted to go back inside. I had things to do. Sam had already disappeared. I put Jen on her lead, go out of the gate, pull the gate over making sure the fence wiring is looped together. Sal can't get out. Can she?

For the past hour I have dodged up and down from my desk to check if Sal is still in the garden. She seems to be engaged in the dust bits mesmerism still but every now and again does a quick round of the garden. Is it stressing her that she is left on her own? I had better get back down there. What to do? Nothing? Just sit in the sun, drink more tea? Do the thing of calling her for a treat but not putting her on the lead so she doesn't associate treats with the lead? Or try to interest her into a game? It's a real pest this. It all takes so much time. I resort to asking Sam to go down and get her. He's a skilled basketball player. Lunging for a moving object is what he does well. He harrumphs a bit when I ask him. He has a photography project to attend to, but goes anyway.

I watch him go down the communal path and into our garden. He swings a rope toy, Sal is interested. Sam bends down on his hunkers. Sal moves in to see the toy. Sam grabs her. Done.

"It's easy," he says when he brings her up to the front door. "Just grab her."

Maybe I should read the dog book again. Maybe I should take up basketball.

I go to my running group in the evening. Do a timed 5k run and a goal-setting session once back at the community centre. The organisers had provided tea and Tunnock's Tea Cakes – one of Scotland's greatest delicacies, they do them in dark chocolate now, evolution in action – and we munch on them as we sit slumped with scarlet faces and sweat-plastered hair. Perhaps it was the post-exercise endorphins, or maybe the sugar rush, but I am totally happy and so glad to be doing something non-dog connected, something that is of my pre-Sally life.

And it is good to have had that couple of hours' break. When I get home Colum reports that the dinnertime feeding session had gone to a new level of tension. Sally had snarled at Jenna when Jenna had come in the kitchen for her food and tried to bar her from the kitchen. Jenna had been uncertain and shown fear. Colum had taken action and tried to assert himself as the leader but isn't sure if it had worked. He wonders if Sal will end up the dominant dog. I'd so rather she wasn't. As I ran my bath thinking of what Colum has said, I reflect on how I don't trust Sal. In fact, I don't think I like her. I feel compassion for her. I want her to be peaceful and free from fear but I will not have our lovely Jenna made miserable.

Day the Eighteenth

This morning I take the train into Glasgow where I have arranged to meet my mum and niece for coffee. I still get up at 7, or rather 7.15 am, walk the dogs with Colum, have breakfast and hang out washing. I have factored in Sal's penchant for shitting on the carpet après breakfast and ask Sam, as he mooches sleepily by on his way to the bathroom at 9am, if he would do a 10.30 garden pee and play session – for the dogs that is. He agrees more to avoid an argument and slumps back to his room hoping to get more shut-eye. He did a midnight photo shoot as part of his college project and is still trying to get in a decent sleep. But as Jen and Sal, now filled with the vitamins of Pedigree, proceed to enjoy a wee game of coffee and dining room table tig, I doubt if Sam will actually achieve any more zeds. Hard life being a teenager really. Pity he's too old for ChildLine.

And I so enjoy my train trip to the big city. I usually read on the twenty-five minute journey but this morning I just sit and gaze out of the window. It seemed an age since I had been on a trip somewhere and it is good thinking space. Of course I end up talking at length about the dogs, particularly Sally, to my folks. I don't think they were all that interested really. My mum hasn't yet learned Jenna's name and just says "the wee dog" to cover all bases, so running Sal's exploits past her is a bit of a conversation gamble. My niece likes the account of us trying to get Sal back on the lead the first afternoon but my copious thoughts on the best training techniques fail to get much response. No matter. It is good to step away and reflect, just by boring people with my stories, how far we have already come.

On the train home though I find myself worrying away again at all the cost involved over a dog I was still struggling to like. Had we known what Sal and her issues would cost us, monetarily speaking, would we, I wonder have chosen her? Would we not have concluded that the same money could have got us a cute wee black Lab puppy? In my mind's eye I can see the hand scrawled sign on the road just out of town which read "Black Lab

Puppies For Sale. Ready Now!" And why didn't we swerve off the road and go and get one? Money. Money. Money. A pure bred is too dear, too much for our straightened purse – or so we said. Instead we chose a smooth coated confused Collie with issues. I feel sucked into a downward tunnel of regret.

I text Colum to say that I was on my way home in case he hadn't managed to get home for the lunch-time walk, aware that what I was really doing was just wanting to connect with him. Late last night, as we had finally made it into bed, I said to him "I'm still not sure of her."

And from some love and concern for animals which I don't think I have, he said "She'll come through. You'll see. She'll come through for us."

On the train I want to pick over my feelings of regret, knowing though that it would be worse if he had said "Yeh, you're right, I regret it too," I am really just asking him to assure me that it hadn't been a stupid thoughtless decision. He texts back that he was in the back garden with our downstairs' ex-partner and his two dogs. Sal was having a ball. Well, that's figuratively speaking. Literally speaking she wasn't, as Jen apparently was guarding the ball, all other toys, the bench and the water bowl. Hurrah for Jen and her bold assertion. Perhaps she would show this Sally what's what yet. Then I had a vision of Sal in the garden with the visitor dogs. Colum said she was so happy. Maybe we had done the right thing. The right thing, not the easy thing.

Day the Nineteenth

Lovely bright morning. I get up at 7am even though it is Saturday.

"You're mad," says Colum.

I go off to meet a friend and do a good hour's run. She has a dog, a lovely Springer Spaniel, we talk dog. She asks me to let her know how our day goes. Get home. Ravenous. While in shower Julie, the dog woman from Edinburgh, arrives. I let Colum deal with her. Notice a hesitance in me to get involved. Have big cup of tea. Do my hair upstairs. Get more tea and join Colum and Julie in sitting room.

A six-hour intensive training session follows. Brilliant and revelatory experience. Julie is a great woman. Knowledgeable, compassionate, but clear and assertive – with dogs and humans. We learn a huge amount in the compressed time available. When Julie first arrives Sal and Jen are in the dining room. She had requested we do this so she can watch what happens after the dogs have been separated from us. She spends time talking with us first of all about the method and seems completely unconcerned at scrabbling noises coming from the other room. Finally she says "Ok. Let's have them in." Colum releases the hounds. They run into the sitting room move swiftly past me and go up to Julie. She ignores them. Sally lifts her front legs onto the arm of Julie's chair and sniffs at her ear.

"Sally, down!" I yell.

"Don't say anything. Totally ignore them," says Julie, quite calmly.

Sally decides this isn't any fun and gets down. Jenna settles down beside Colum and lies on his feet.

"Push her off – gently." says Julie. "It might seem cute but she's actually dominating you."

Colum shifts Jen. She gets up and runs between Colum and Julie but, getting no response, sits down puzzled. Sal meanwhile has hit on the idea of chewing the coffee table leg.

"Does she usually do that?" asks Julie.

"No!" we chorus.

"Take her gently by the collar and put her out of the room for ten seconds," directs Julie.

Colum does so. She gets let back in. Does it again. Gets put back in the hall again. And so it goes on. It takes the dogs almost an hour to finally settle and lie down. What we thought "settled", i.e. when they are either sitting or in sphinx-like posture, Julie explained is not them yet relaxed. We need to wait until they flop on their sides and sigh. This apparently can take anything from ten minutes to three hours the first time the Amichien method is followed correctly, depending on the dog. So an hour is ok in Julie's book. The rule then is that we are supposed to wait for a full five minutes before calling the dogs to us and either praising them or asking them to do something. For Sally however Julie advised giving her as much as twenty minutes.

"She needs to find out how good it feels to relax," Julie explained.

Thinking of the tight-shouldered dog who stood in our kitchen on the first evening we had rehomed her, I think this is very wise. Sally hasn't been able to trust the world around her enough to relax. It is understandable that it might therefore be a new experience for her. And one that she needs to learn.

I've had two large cups of tea and almost pint of water since my run. My bladder is bursting but as it was important for us to remain stationary as Julie demonstrated the reunion technique, I didn't like to do a loo break. Colum suddenly says "Do you mind if I nip to the loo?"

"Of course not!" laughs Julie "In fact, let's break for lunch."

Colum beats me to the loo. I cross my legs as I put the kettle on and start laying out lunch. This new dog training philosophy is impacting on parts of us we hadn't envisaged.

After lunch our training session continues. I have begun to see that Julie is not so much reading the dogs as watching us. Both Colum and I had thought we knew the basics of this particular dog training method but the very fact that I call it a dog training method now tells me that I haven't quite understood it. After only a short while under Julie's tutelage I am getting the idea that it is more a dog listening or reading method.

"The dogs will tell you when they are ready for something,' said Julie 'or will tell you when they do or don't understand something. It's all just a matter of picking up their signals."

She goes on to explain that, most of all, they are looking for a leader. According to the Amichien Bonding philosophy, dogs which demonstrate 'difficult' behaviour as humans would call it, are simply operating out of the belief that they are in charge and then getting highly stressed when a situation is too complex for them to handle. The root trouble is always that the owner hasn't demonstrated strong leadership. So, at the moment Sally is the way she is because she has been hurtling around the world trying to make sense of a world which confuses her. Her stress, that goes off the Richter scale when she sees a cat or fox or bird, stems from the fact she believes no other dog or human will defend her. Strong, calm and assertive leadership from us is called for. Right. Strong. Calm. Assertive. Hmmm.

Julie works with us for over six hours. She shows us what to do when Sal jumps up at the windows. What to do when either dog insists on going through doors first. She watches us and them move around the house. Checks on the position of their beds. Asks about our daily routines. Discusses Jenna's postman problem. And a host of other detail. When she finally drives off with assurances of being at end of an email or phone line I feel both elated and exhausted. It's strangely similar to the feeling I had when I returned to university as a mature student to do a postgraduate course. After a fifteen year break from academic rigour my brain struggled to cope with the sudden and vast amount of information, new words and new concepts that queued up outside demanding admittance. My postgraduate course taught me to look at literature and language in completely different ways that I had in the past. Julie's school of thought about dogs is doing exactly the same – only with dogs as the focus not words. Before Julie came I really did wonder just what we were doing by calling her in. I really did question if we were being quite stupid by spending money on a dog consultant. But, as we discovered, we weren't so much spending money on Sally but on us. What Julie has given to us is a philosophy and strategy that we can now apply to every dog that lives with us and every dog we encounter. And that, I now know, is a total investment for life.

It is, of course, not instantaneous. An hour later and we have already done some stuff wrong. We are still staring and double checking the recipe, still pausing and asking each other "Em…what happens here?" and "What should we do if…" We already have questions which we need to ask Julie, there are scenarios that need analysis, but there is nonetheless the feeling that we now have a way forward. Pre-Julie visit, our focus was totally on Sally. Now it is on all of us as a pack. Pre-Julie visit we thought that Sally was the problem dog and Jenna was sorted. Now we see that Jenna also has issues. Pre-Julie we thought that we could read dogs rather well. Now we see that we were often reading them wrongly. So we have gone through a huge mind shift and are still reeling. But we have already changed.

One of the things Julie advocated was that we should reduce the dogs' world until they had understood that we were in charge not them. As she listened to our tales of Sally's night-walk fears and crazed behaviour, she diagnosed the problem as Sally not yet being ready to cope with all that was happening outside. We had to help her feel that we were her protectors and that she did not need to worry about anything that the evening or night might hold – that was our job, not hers. So, for the next fortnight, Julie advised that both Sal and Jen be lead-walked to the back garden and given a toilet stop only. A full scale walk, or "going on the hunt," could only happen when Sal and Jen securely knew that they were not in charge.

"What?" we said. "Toilet breaks only? For two weeks? What about exercise? They'll go stir crazy and so will we!"

But this rather negative reaction was apparently nothing new to Julie; she calmly countermanded our protests with some rational explanation.

"There's no need for walk exercise," she said. "The dogs will exercise each other in the house, they will be fed, watered, have company and be safe, that's all they need."

She then went on to talk about the commonly held view that dogs need copious exercise. "Who said that they do?" asked Julie "Has anyone asked the dog? The need for exercise is often a human need. We think that they think like us, that they need amusement, change of scene, things to do, but in actual fact what dogs like to do best is just hang out."

So, when I had sat in the garden and watched the dogs gamble about, then heaved myself up and got sticks and a ball to play with them, I was really responding to a human feeling of guilt that I should be entertaining the dogs. Whereas, by sitting quietly and watching the dogs, I would learn a lot about them. Dogs do love to run and swim and play and jump and all of that, but more than anything they want to be at peace, to chill out, to feel ease ripple down their spines and that could only happen when they felt they were 'off-duty' and someone else was in charge.

A whole other way of being around dogs has been opened up to us. For around eleven years we have walked dogs three to four times a day. Our lives are organised around dog walks. We are completely used to factoring in a major walk a day plus perhaps three smaller walks. Now, Julie asked us to just take the dogs to the garden four to five times a day. This means that in between these pit stops, we have oodles of time. This is, of course, just for a short period, just to help Sally in particular get used to the idea that there is nothing in the house or garden that will harm her and once she is relaxed we can start to work on getting her to come to us when called. Our major problem with Sally is the fact that she won't come back on the lead; consequently, we could rarely let her off unless we had a means of cornering her and getting her on the lead again. But, as Julie explained, Sal can't yet cope with all that is going on outside the home when she is still stressing about who is in charge of the pack.

And Jen. This was a complete revelation. Much of my angst about Sally coming into our home was that I was worried that she would become top dog and crush the spirit of Jenna. I had completely failed to question why it is that any dog should consider itself pack leader when we were around. Julie watched Jen's behaviour and then led us to see that Jen was convinced that she had to look after us. She identified four places where Jen was obviously guarding us – when she slept on the cushion outside our bedroom door, when she hurtled herself at the postman, when she stood on Sam's bed and watched out of his window, when she laid down on the doormat opposite the door which led down to the front door. We had seen all of this was cute and the thought that Jen had placed herself in charge of us, didn't enter our heads. And again when we let her sort out Sally. Although we thought it funny but useful when Jen would snap at Sal and tell her off, Julie pointed out to us that we were adding stress onto Jen. When she said this I remembered how

Jen had started chewing her paw again – a sure sign of stress, not boredom as I had previously thought.

"The poor lass," I thought. "She thinks we are useless and need protecting, and she's been doing it all this time."

Julie advised that we bring Jen's cushion down from upstairs and put it in a dog basket beside Sally.

"By doing this you are telling her that you don't need her to guard you," said Julie and also asked us to keep the hall door closed so that Jen couldn't charge the postman, ask Sam to keep his bedroom door closed so she couldn't guard from that angle and lead Jen to her basket to sleep in and away from the hall mat.

You may well wonder what is wrong, if anything, about a dog guarding you. Well, if you want a guard dog, then nothing, but in terms of the dog, quite a lot. The dog can't ever relax. It is like an adult in constant charge of a toddler, never off the job, and we all know how stressful that can be. Dogs can do this their whole lives and this is where the common problems associated with dogs stem from. Take that stress off them and they think "Ok, so I don't need to lead the pack, I don't need to find the food, I don't need to protect, and I can relax then."

As Julie was as interested in Jen as Sal, we asked her about Jen's penchant for chasing sheep. She explained to us that this was Jen following her natural instinct of getting food for the pack. As self-designated pack leader she believed her job was to track down and bring back food. So she belts after a herd of sheep, singles out the weakest, rounds it up, but then as she is a domestic dog who is fed regularly, and not a wild dog dependent on wild food, she then stops, confused; she knows she's not hungry enough to maul the sheep, so she just stands there. And that's when we usually catch up with her. We are angry and haul her away when all she's tried to do is bring us food. Once Jen perceives she is not the pack leader she will stop chasing sheep and leave us to find the food. Sounds sensible. Sounds simple. Somehow though I doubt it will be.

We take dogs out into the garden, try to follow what Julie had advised, Sal does a pee. Jen looks at us. We come back in, make ourselves something to eat, feed the dogs – making sure to 'gesture eat' from their bowls first – then take ourselves off to an orchestral concert in the town.

The concert is a perfect antidote to the day. Our heads are ringing from all that Julie had shown and told us, and the music and setting and people remind us that there was more to life than working with dogs. Over the tea break at the interval, some kind friends make the mistake of asking us how we had got on with 'the Dog Listener' as they seem to want to call her. And we tell them, at first in bits and pieces, but as they seemed interested we talk on right up to the end of the interval. Well, they did ask.

After the concert we invite these people back to our house. We phone ahead and asked Sam to put the dogs into the dining room and close the door. "Don't put the dogs in a situation which will stress them," Julie had advised. Our visitors trundled in and we serve tea and coffee and biscuits. The dogs make a bit of a racket next door.

These friends are mostly dog people so we decide we could let out the dogs but first ask our friends to please ignore them. It would have worked ok but for our lack of thinking through how the dogs might react to an 8 year old girl with a biscuit in her hand. So it all goes a bit wrong.

Sally comes into the room, goes up to Catriona and growls. Catriona goes to sit with her dad and Colum leads Sal out of the room. After ten seconds – the recommended exclusion time – Colum lets Sal back in. She goes up to Catriona again who was now sitting in a big armchair with her dad, and about three inches from Catriona growls again. Catriona keeps herself really still but, although her eyes go wide, she avoids looking at Sally. Colum removes Sally out of the room. Our visitors decide it is time to go. We wave them off. I feel we have got something completely wrong. Worry we put a child at risk and go to bed confused.

Day the Twentieth

Colum takes the dogs to the garden first thing. Kindly leaves me in bed. He crawls back in half an hour later. We doze off again. It is Sunday. No point rushing things, we have all week to do that. An hour later I surface and pad down to the kitchen. Get four steps down the stairs to find my slippers sinking into earth. My huge yucca plant has been tipped over and dug out. "Grrrr", I say.

Colum comes to see what is up. "Ah, a protest," he says. "They've upped the ante just as Julie warned us."

"Maybe," I reply. "Plants are one thing, but it they touch my books they're out, both of them."

I sweep up the earth strewn over the stairs and right the plant as best I can, reminding myself of times gone by when Jack, our Labrador, thought shoes and skirting boards were a tasty snack, and Joe thought a smelly sock a good swallowable chew. Perhaps I have just forgotten what dogs do before they settle down. But I am serious about my books. They can eat Colum's though. I won't fash about them.

The scene with Catriona the evening before still disturbs me. Over our muesli and coffee (or fried potatoes, egg, mushrooms and bratwurst sausage in Colum's case), we discuss what had gone wrong the previous evening. Sal had obviously identified Catriona as the weakest member of the pack and tried to pull rank on her. Thanks to Catriona's cool and her familiarity with dogs, she didn't panic and therefore escalate the scene, but we decided that in future we would have to have a much more controlled environment and safer situation for any young visitors. As Sal has an issue with food we shouldn't have let her in a room where a child was eating or if we did so, should have made sure that she couldn't get near the child, or alternatively waited until the biscuit had been eaten. We also recognised that it had been a mistake to invite people back to the house when we had just had an intensive training experience and hadn't had a chance to begin to process the new information. We phone our friends to apologise and they, being the good people they are, say not to worry about it. Every new situation is obviously going to test us and it is important for us, as much as possible, to control the situation. In Julie's words "The dogs are in a world they don't understand, we have to help them to get it right." Social gatherings at our house are temporarily suspended for now.

In the afternoon we go to B&Q. I first move the stair plants to a safer home in the sitting room. No point in tempting destruction and perhaps the plants will benefit from a move. In B&Q we buy some simple locks or catches (or 'snecks' as we call them in my locality), for the kitchen door. To alleviate the stress of feeding time, when Sally still eats like it was her last mouthful, Julie suggested we feed the dogs in separate rooms. It was necessary then that the kitchen door could be fastened so we could avoid the dogs putting pressure on each other by rushing to the other bowl once they had finished their own meal. Julie also suggested we keep the dogs out of the kitchen or wherever we are, when we eat, thus giving a clear signal that they are lower down the food chain. We haven't yet done this. There's only so much you can remember. But the door needs sorted first.

After B&Q we stay out and drive down to where there are good lochside or forest walks and a bijou café. As per instructions, we leave both Sal and Jen at home having made sure they had had ample time to 'download' in the garden. I don't know when I was last here without dogs. It seemed so strange that we decided to jettison a walk and went to comfort eat in the café.

"I miss the dogs," said Colum.

"Yes" I say. Well, I miss Joe, Jack or Jen. Not Sal.

We go to see a friend who has a huge St. Bernard dog. Rhuaridh had been rehomed five times before he came to Dierdre and, because of her huge generosity of heart, his home is now with her. When we come in the door Rhuaridh bounds up to us, joyful at there being new people. Before our intensive training with Julie, had a beautiful dog ran up to us we would have automatically patted and greeted it. Today Colum nor I make eye contact, keep our attention on his owner, sit down in chairs and when Rhuaridh pushed his fluffy face up to ours, we cross our arms, and turn our faces away. Rather hard to do this with a slobbery St. Bernard in your face. We fight the instinct to say "Well, hello there big guy? How's life with you?" But Julie had said to us "Dogs don't speak English, they only speak dog."

Rhuaridh is asserting himself as the pack leader, the one in charge, the one who welcomes you on his terms. By us refusing to give him attention we are saying "Actually you're not in charge, it's your owner". After a few minutes of persistent bumping of us and attempts to lick our faces, Rhuaridh gives up and lies down on the floor. Excellent. Stage One complete. We are supposed now to wait five minutes, but it's hard when you are in someone else's home. Ignoring the dog can be read as ignoring something precious to them. As good guests we want to show appreciation of all they have, especially if they have been kind enough to offer tea, and perhaps aware of this, Colum pats Rhuaridh while he is was only part way to being relaxed. Rhuaridh jumps up and starts licking our faces again. It matters little. His master is taking him out a walk and Rhuaridh quickly forgets we exist, he has a baby to look after. So, we didn't get it totally right, but neither did we get it totally wrong either. We are learning.

Back at home with uncooked mutton in my bag and a recipe for homemade dog treats in our heads, courtesy of Dierdre, I come up with a plan to help alleviate our dog stress. We instigate a scoreboard! – the dogs are one team and we are another. When the dogs do something which is destructive, annoying, worrying or just plain disgusting, we award ourselves a monetary point. So, a dump on the sitting room floor is £5 (the award is high as it may encourage Sam to clean it up and not shout for us); barking out of hours (pre 7am and post 10pm) is £2; destruction of an object is either to be immediately replaced should it belong to someone else, or given a financial equivalent depending on value (I never really liked the stone troughs that Sally smashed last week, so this merits no award as it didn't cause me pain), etc etc. The idea is that instead of us getting wound up by the dogs' attempts to take control back; we view it as useful and moving us towards a treat of some kind. The person with the most accumulated 'fouls', gets the monetary value and can spend it on themselves or a treat for the family – hire of a video, bottle of wine, wheat-free cake etc. Ingenious or what? But participants are not allowed to encourage any wayward behaviour and will be have their points forfeited if found doing so.

Day the Twenty-First

7am. Colum takes girls to garden. 8am. Dump on sitting room carpet. Colum awarded £5. Jen refusing to use garden for pee or pooh. Must be clenching her buttocks together. "It's a control thing," says Colum. We attempt some meditation. I think dogs should be excluded. Colum reminds me that Julie says they will learn to respect and enjoy a peaceful space. I tut and close my eyes, fold my arms when Sally comes up to face me. She gives up. Stretches out, on her side, goes to sleep.

9.30am. Walk Jen and Sal down to the back garden, both of them on leads. We process around the garden, loiter at particular areas and then return to the house. The only words I utter through the whole routine are "Good girl Sally," once. She growls and rears up at a robin who dares to land on a log in our neighbour's garden; jumps nervously as the high wind makes the lime trees sing in operatic style; snuffles frantically at a patch of earth under the hedge which smells of damp fox. I remain completely silent. Hold on to her lead tightly, pause a moment in my walk, then lead her on in the direction I want to go. She relaxes enough to do a widdle under the apple tree and is rewarded with praise. Jen mooches around, sniffs at bit at the ground, but for reasons best known to her, neither pees nor poohs.

Ten minutes later we are all back indoors. Sal sleeps in her basket in the hall; Jen stretches out across the door which leads down to the front door. I write in the dining room with the door closed. All is quiet. I do none of my usual calling of Jen, calming down of Sal, repeated instructions to "sit" or "lie down". The biscuits have remained in the tin, the dog mat in this room unfurled. I neither cajole, bribe, stroke or soothe. I simply ignore the dogs.

Despite three garden toilet breaks, Jen resolutely holds it in. I begin to worry. Just after lunch she whines. I rush her to the garden and she lets out a stream of urine which goes on for two minutes.

"There are some things, girl, which are just not worth holding onto," I say.

Still very high wind. There has been a tornado in Missouri. I am glad we live in Scotland. Sal doesn't like the way the wind ups the tempo. She seems glad to get indoors and sleeps happily in her basket. I forget to take off her harness. Find it in chewed bits in her basket. It was on loan to us. That's an immediate replacement award, but I think I merit a £1 for nuisance factor.

"When are we allowed to pat the dogs?" asks Sam.

Dogs sleep the afternoon away. Julie said they would sleep a lot more. Sometimes people read this as their dogs being depressed. Julie says they are just delving into deep relaxation. Wonder if all dogs are really teenagers at heart?

Donal, our neighbour and friend calls in with a present of fresh salad vegetables for us. I invite him in for a cuppa. Fortunately he is not a dog person so he is more than happy to follow my directions of sitting at the kitchen table with his elbows resting on it and ignoring the dogs. I had shut the dogs in the dining room when he came in; once I had made the tea and chatted a little with Donal, I let Jen and Sally out. They streamed into the kitchen and ran around the table nudging Donal. Good man that he is, he refuses to acknowledge their existence. Sally jumps up at the sink and barks at a passing bird. I pull on her collar lightly saying "Thanks Sally," and she gets down only to get up again a few seconds later. I pull her down again. She does it again. I put her out in the hall and shut the kitchen door. Ten seconds later I open it again and she trots in quietly. What Donal makes of all this is anyone's guess but he seems happy to allow me to move around while still telling me of some exciting family news. It occurs to me later that the best people we can have as visitors in the house at present are non-dog people. I never thought I would say that.

I go off to my yoga class and notice that I feel much happier with life. The past two Monday sessions I have stretched and moved to the tutor's instructions but my spirit has not been at peace. When I told people about the new dog and her shenanigans, they had smiled and said "Och, you'll get there. She'll settle down." And I wanted to reply "But it's bloody awful!" So, this evening, despite the winds battering at the old windows of the community centre, I feel that something had settled inside of me and all would be well – eventually.

We still have questions, though, so we phone Julie around 8pm. She has young children, and has warned us that there is little point contacting her before this as her energies have to be elsewhere. When we get through to her she sounds relaxed and happy to chat. It is so good to touch base with her again, like radioing to base camp when we are attempting to push up into a daunting peak. With her permission we put her on speaker phone so we can both chip in. I don't usually like speaker phone conversations, it's too public for me, but it will save me constantly waving at Colum and doing stage whispers of "remember to tell her x and y," and him getting annoyed.

We have two major questions, i.e., what happened with Catriona the evening our friends came round and also my worry about what we are doing to Jen. Julie listens really well then deals with our first question. She says that the Catriona scenario has probably nothing to do with the fact that she is a child but much more to do with the fact that we asked the dogs to cope with too much. We let them into a room full of newcomers and when they arrived there they find someone standing holding a biscuit. As Sally has food issues we should not have asked her to be calm and accepting of someone holding a biscuit when she was already coping with too much. Where we went wrong was to let the dogs into the room in the first place.

"You're trying to run before you can walk," said Julie.

She also picked up on the fact that I said both Colum and I were a bit tense as this was the first time we had introduced Sally to these people and Sal is on edge in the evenings as it is. Explained like this it made me see what twits we had been. Good intentioned twits, but twits just the same. Julie advised that in future, at least until Sal has settled down, that we keep the dogs in another room while visitors are there.

"Don't stop allowing people to come, you have to live your lives, just deal with it differently," said Julie.

Makes a lot of sense when you think about it.

We then move on to talk about Jenna. Jen is now on a much lighter diet and on top of that is getting no full scale exercise. I tell her that Jen was refusing to toilet in the garden and I am now worried that we are damaging her innards. Jen has been a favourite in our street and among our friends. Why do we want to change her existing behaviour? Won't she become aggressive if we push her too much?

"Listen to what you have said there. Think about what you are pushing her towards. You are simply trying to get her to let down her load of leadership and relax. She has had almost two years of putting herself in charge. It is going to take her a while to understand she doesn't have to do that. You are therefore persuading her to take a holiday for the rest of her life. It's like us when we first go on holiday...we rush around busy busy busy doing and seeing everything and then usually around the second week we start to slow down, to do less, to sit and read books, to chill out, and we usually feel really tired. We're letting all the stress of past months out."

I think about our annual camping holiday in Findhorn. Last year a friend asked what we had done the first week

"Not a lot," said Colum.

"And the second week?" asked the friend.

"Even less," said Colum, "and it was great."

So until Jen relinquishes her load of leadership, until she relaxes and realises how good that feels, we can't begin to work with her on the recall command. For Jen this is essential. If we really want her to stop chasing sheep and foxes and come to us on our command – particularly at times for her own safety – we need to focus on leading her to appreciate that she is not in charge. And the refusing to toilet in the garden is apparently quite normal.

"Think about it," said Julie "the pack leader wants to scent their trail and mark their territory. They therefore don't let it all out in one go but keep some back. Jen is refusing to use the garden because she thinks she will be going on a hunt (i.e. a walk), but by you continually showing her that she will only be going to the garden and back are telling her that she does not need to do this. You will lead the hunt when necessary, not her."

Apparently some dogs take much much longer to empty themselves than Jenna had done and Julie sees it as a positive sign that Jen had finally urinated in the garden in the afternoon. Julie also advises that we may have to take the dogs out more frequently, just to keep giving Jen the opportunity until such times as she performs regularly.

I also say to Julie that I feel people think we have completely lost the plot when I say we weren't as yet walking the dogs. Julie laughs and says "Yes, remember we discussed other people, particularly other dog people as being a potential obstacle to the success of the method." She says her own coping mechanism with sceptics is that she simply doesn't try to explain what she is doing unless she is asked a direct question.

"This also stops you becoming a first class bore who just wants to leap about and evangelise everyone on this amazing philosophy and also means that your own confidence is not constantly shattered," she says.

We finally put down the phone after heartfelt thanks to Julie. Colum and I are lucky that we have each other to turn to when the situation gets hard, but as we travel through the early stages of this new bonding with our dogs it is just wonderful to have a source of sense and wisdom within reach. We made ourselves some tea and watched some telly. All is calm in our camp.

Day the Twenty-Second

The high wind has lessened but it is enough to have Sally jumping up at the windows and very skittish on her garden pit stops. Colum takes the dogs out first. Sal toilets. Jen withholds. I take them out again around 9.30 am. Sal performs again. Jen finally widdles on the communal path leading back up to the house. Sal pulling and lunging on the lead as the wind whips around us. I try to keep my shoulders low and myself calm. Julie had reminded us that it was important to be calm when out with the dogs. At one point the two leads are twisted around my legs; Sal is still up on her hind legs barking at god knows what. I allow myself to sigh. Once indoors I cheer up by thinking that maybe a fraught toilet stop merits a score.

As the day goes on I find myself questioning the wisdom of not taking the dogs, or rather Jen, on a longer walk. Surely this can't be right? I am feeling low and not a little trapped. I am missing an invigorating walk round the hill. I defy the forecast of possible heavy showers and put washing out enjoying the breeze and air. The back garden is awash with large and small twigs – when we had brought out the dogs on their last pit stop, Sally had grabbed a large branch that had fallen from a lime tree and pranced around with it, thus forgetting her real purpose. I go back inside and find the rake and return to the garden and sweep up all the debris. I sit on the bench thinking how daft it all seems — I miss just opening the front door and letting Jen run out.

Colum comes home for lunch. We have a stupid argument about the arrival time of a friend who is coming for dinner tomorrow. I stomp off upstairs. Colum goes back to work and I come back down. I know I am struggling with this whole new dog thing so perhaps watching the DVD that Julie left us will help me understand more. I tell Sam I am going to watch it.

He says "Mum. Watch something fun. Forget about the dogs for a bit. Switch off."

The rain is now thumping down outside. I notice that I now don't feel like going for a major dog walk. I recklessly switch on the fire in the sitting room, make a cup of camomile tea and slip Steve Martin's remake of *Cheaper by the Dozen* into the DVD. I laugh and laugh at the slapstick antics of the family and think that perhaps our chaos isn't so bad.

The rain eases. The film finishes. We take Sal and Jen into the garden. Sal jumps at a squirrel, a passing helicopter, a loud bird, a waving tree, but still manages to pee. Is she getting more used to the outside world? A stupid cat loiters on the path up to the street as we near the house. I send it poisoned thoughts and it disappears under the connecting hedge. The dogs didn't notice it. Phew.

Ten minutes later I am back out in the street with my running gear on. I don't particularly feel like running but I think I need it both for my body and spirit. I think a lot about the dogs and our new regime as I run. My tetchiness towards Colum dissipates as the endorphins kick in. Motivational sentences begin to run through my mind. In the abbey gift shop there is a laminated card which says "It's ok to fail but not to stop just because it's hard". Am I just bucking at the first hurdle? I answer this by thinking that I actually hated having to do hurdles in school and really haven't ever seen the attraction of throwing myself over a high wooden structure which is in all possibility going to batter my knees to smithereens. So I need a better metaphor. There must be a vast store in the road running world. What's that one about it all being so much percent aptitude and so much attitude? And what about all those kick-starting jingles about striving and it all being worth it in the end? There must be something that I can apply to our new training approach with the girls. Perhaps what we need is a game plan. Something that helps us set and celebrate small targets and help us work towards bigger ones. In the running world it serves well to have a target, a goal, or half-heartedness and the whimpish "I can't be bothered" attitude gets firm hold and it's a slippy slope to apathy.

Start to dream. Colum takes redundancy. Does the Amichien Dog Listening training. We move house. Smaller house, big enclosed garden. I get a part time teaching job to support him or write a block-buster. The dream keeps me going for a good few miles.

Rain comes down hard as I near home. I quite like running in the rain. It's a peaceful experience. Some people, who normally find it amusing to shout sexist crap out of their car window, don't do so as it would mean having to roll down the window and let in nasty wet stuff. And the young lads who like to linger on the streets in packs, and get their kicks from making fun of women runners, don't like rain either as it leaves marks on their expensive white trainers and track-suits. The streets are therefore usually free of such elements and anyone I pass is scurrying along, head down, brolly or hood up and take little note of my existence. There's something too about the exhilaration that comes from doing something daft. But the best bit is getting home, drenched through but zinging, peeling off layers of sodden clothing, running a warm bath, making a big cup of tea to sip on the side, lowering my exercised body into the lovely water. Mmmmmm. Small pleasures really are the best.

Day the Twenty-Third

This morning I do a voluntary stint for our local fairtrade shop. Colum and I usually do this once a month but they have a staffing shortage at the moment. It's good to be out doing something that will take my mind off our dogs and the whole bit of it. And I notice that I refrain from talking much about Sally or Jen – my mind needs time out. It's all been a bit intensive recently and I recognise that it's me suffering from cabin fever, not the dogs. My conscience is untroubled as Sam is at home today and can cover the garden pit stops at least until I get home.

After my shift I meet Colum in a local café for lunch. Sam joins us. Sam gives us his report of the morning – "Yeh, Sal did a pee and a pooh and Jen did a whopping pooh," – just as the waitress brings us our order. I notice she turns slightly green.

The rest of the day is fairly uneventful. Martin, a friend of Colum's who is in Glasgow for one night comes for dinner. I don't see a lot of him as I have a group run which is extended this evening by a planning meeting at our trainer's house. Fortunately he is a sanguine kind of chap and Colum tells me later that he was both unfazed and interested (or at least successfully feigned interest) about our attempt to learn how to listen to our dogs. Martin is at present studying philosophy so I suppose all life experience is potential for an academic paper. We talk a little about that world – a world which I belonged to for some years and finally quit; fed up with the moans of tenured staff to people like me scratching a laughable weekly wage on hourly paid teaching. I go to bed and dream of an academic criticising the size of the last book I edited.

Day the Twenty-Fourth

I wake up at 7am and hear Colum stride down the communal path with the dogs. I should get up but the bed is comfy and I am reluctant to enter into the day. Colum leaves for London on the overnight bus this evening. And then Sam and I, but mostly I, are in full charge of the dogs and the whole bit. I finally get up and note that some of the dinner dishes are still hanging about in the kitchen. Feel taken for granted just because I am the one at home. Sal leaves a puddle on the sitting room floor. What joy. I clean it up telling myself that at least it will merit another monetary point on our scoreboard.

Sam leaves for his shop job and Colum for work. I fling on some clothes and take the girls to the garden. They both pull on the lead. Sal does a big pee, Jen does nothing. Back in the house I make a list for the supermarket. It's within walking distance so I take my trolley (and, no, it's not tartan). As I go along the street I see the flicker of Finn – a Collie-cross who is a great admirer of our Jen – running around the hill. He will be missing her. I consider going to find his owner and chat with her about our new regime but decide against it – she'll just think we are nuts. So I trundle on to Morrison's.

After shopping I reward myself with a cup of tea and a scone in the café. I notice that the people at the other tables all seem to be either pensioners or mothers with young children. I wonder, not for the first time, just where I am with my life. I think back to my dream of the night before. Academia played me some rough cards and I was the butt of some cruel shafting and nepotism, so I miss it not. And yet I do miss the status, the ease of being able to say "Oh, yes, I'm a lecturer in…" And I miss some of the teaching. I don't miss the essay marking, exam setting or exam marking, that was soul-destroying stuff, but I miss being viewed as an expert in a field. Now I float free – the desire and goal of many people – but financially it's scary and I have just gone around the aisles in the supermarket checking and cross-checking the prices of all items selected. I wonder what it must feel like to have a secure job. My thoughts run on in this negative way and by the time I get home, lugging my heavy trolley, I feel beaten and deflated.

It has also got rather muggy and I am over-dressed in my jeans, walking boots, two T shirts and waterproof. I pull the trolley into the house then clip the leads on the dogs who are standing waiting for me. They both pull like crazy. I try stopping and walking calmly but at the top of the steps down to the garden start to get annoyed and a little scared. We make it into our garden. Jen begins to pee, Sally noises into her and puts her off "Damn," I think. Sal refuses to do anything in her usual patch. A magpie flies up from a nearby tree. The game is lost. Sal bounds up and fixates on the bird, woofing wildly. Jen pulls in the other direction.

"Oh for God's sake!" I say "This is pathetic! Just pack it in you two!" I'm conscious that I am now neither calm nor in control.

I decide to take Sal back to the house and I tie Jen to the garden bench. As Sal and I trot up the path Jen howls. I shoot on and deposit Sally inside the front door. I run back down to the garden. The neighbours will have me up for cruelty. I untie Jen but keep her on the lead. She hops up into my precious bee and butterfly patch and does a huge pee on a big clump of marjoram. Perfect. That's that one off the salad menu.

We go back up the house. We go in and Jen and Sal chase off up stairs. I sit on the lower stair and sigh. The packed trolley stares back at me. I am too hot, tired, frustrated and confused about my life. Here I am the mother not of a toddler but of a strapping nineteen year old and yet am feeling as if I am having 'one of those days' at home with a fractious child. An image of me packing both Sal and Jen into our van and driving to the SSPCA and leaving them there fills my mind. I see myself telling Colum when he asks where the dogs are: "Oh, I'd had enough. I gave them away". It's tempting. It's very tempting.

I give myself a shake and get up off the step. Maybe a shower and a hair-wash will help. I must look a complete sight. It's so easy to let yourself go when working from home – who is there to dress up for and for what reason? But I feel sweaty and grotty. The chores can wait, I need some personal TLC.

The shower helps a little but I am still feeling very low. A voice starts to whirr around my head.

"Come on girl, this is time for you now. You did all those years at home, the early times when Sam woke up three times a night, the awful days when he had gastric flu, glue ear, tonsillitis, diarrhoea, a sore this or that; you watched endless *Thomas the Tank Engine* videos with him; you sang 'The Wheels on the Bus' song *ad nauseam* at numerous toddler groups; you were on the coffee and juice rota at playgroup; you thought up all the Halloween costumes; you organised and galvanised the house and hall parties; you ran in the mother's race at sports day to prove it wasn't the winning, it was the taking part that mattered (yeh, right); you sat through all the concerts where his mental head-teacher would speak to us as if we were also five; you spent near a decade around nurseries and school playgrounds; you ferried him to clubs and activities; you yelled at his swimming instructor when he tried to bully Sam into jumping into the deep end; you drove him to friends' houses, had friends over to play and to stay; you helped with school projects, listened to narrow minded teachers when they fixated on his scrawly handwriting; you helped him choose subjects that suited his talents; you cheered him on at football even when he didn't score; you watched his basketball team win the league; you helped him fill in college applications. You've done the whole package. The 'MUM' T shirt is sweaty and threadbare. So why, just why have you saddled yourself with dogs – especially a mad rescue one – just as you have a chance for some 'me' time ? Chuck it in. Take action."

And there is silence from my higher self. I text Colum.

"You had best take an earlier lunch. I have lost sight of why we have dogs."

Sparse, a little dramatic, but true. He texts back that he will leave now but needs to call into a store first to buy a travel pillow for the overnight bus. This sends me into a furious mental spin about just why it is that he is heading off for three days in London for pure pleasure and I am staying at home with the dogs. I know the answers. I do. But right at this moment I'm not sure what they are.

I go upstairs to the bedrooms – where the dogs are not allowed – and furiously begin to sort washing. It doesn't help that it has been raining for a week and there is soggy clothing everywhere. And it doesn't help that Sam has left his unwashed sheets in the machine since yesterday morning and I need the use of it. And it doesn't help when my lower self starts taunting "Just what was the point of that PhD? Just where did it get you? Sorting washing?! Looking after two crazy dogs?"

By the time Colum appears my face is blotchy again.

"We need a strategy," he says "or otherwise I can't go. I'll text Julie and ask her to phone us."

I demur at this. It will all sound so whimpish. Me in a tizzy just because I'm worried that my weekend ahead will be a total struggle. That really is pathetic. Colum hasn't been away for months – but then neither have I and, truth to tell, I am just plain envious. We go downstairs and make some lunch. I wonder if my mood is just hormonal but dismiss this. My period is a while away yet. Maybe it's just a small mid-life crisis. We eat some salmon salad left over from last night. I reflect that I only ate salad after my 50 min run last night. Maybe I am just lacking in carbs. But I pour out my moans anyway as I eat. I tell Colum of my dream last night. He knows the whole bit with me and academia, he was there and lived it with me. He is the one who encouraged me to walk away from such a stupid way of being. So I don't need to recap any of it.

The phone rings. It is Julie. Colum has to head back to work. I notice that I feel silly. Julie must think we are weaklings. This is the second time we have called for help in just under a week. Is it really only a few days since she visited us? Seems a lifetime ago. But Julie is pleasant and calm. Colum had told her I was really struggling to cope with the pit stops in the garden and the whole larger rubric, so she asks me to tell her what was up. I tell her that I found it really hard to hold both dogs and consequently was getting stressed. I ask her if it was possible to do one dog at a time, or would that upset the pack thing? To my surprise she said dealing with one dog at a time was absolutely fine. She reminded me that the *cri de coeur* of the method was an attitude of 'calm and aloof' and if toileting two dogs at once was too much for me then it defeated the whole purpose. We talked on and I told her of my worry that Colum was going away for a few days. She said this was quite understandable but in actual fact really useful.

"His going away has brought an issue into sharp focus. You've probably been stressed while toileting the dogs, and it's only the thought that you will temporarily loose the relief of literally handing over the reins to Colum that has made you say you need help."

She talked on and said that this part of the process was really hard as we were basically waiting for the dogs, particularly Jenna, to accept us as pack leaders.

"Think about it," says Julie "You're asking the dogs to trust you with their lives – that's what a pack leader does in their world, so it's no wonder that Jen is unsure especially as she senses you are stressed."

She reminds me too that there was no set time period for the handing over of leadership and we shouldn't therefore set a time limit in our heads. I had thought that she had suggested it could take around a fortnight, but Julie said that she had simply said "it might take a fortnight or much longer", it all depends on the dog and on our steady application of the method. She says that once we stop worrying about how long we will have to do garden toilet stops only, we will relax and this would show in our body language.

"When you are in the garden with a dog, just try and be conscious of the birds, the air or anything else pleasant, don't focus on whether or not they have done anything, just chill out a bit and you will be amazed how much this will help the dogs chill too."

I also ask her when we can pat and make a fuss of the dogs. It seems to me that we have barely patted them since last Saturday. They rarely do the full thing of lying stretched out on their sides, giving the big sigh etc, and if they do, it is so good to see them peaceful, that we are loathe to disturb them. I am worried that Jen will think we don't like her anymore. Julie reminds us that the dogs were making this decision themselves.

"Once they give over leadership they will lie peacefully lots of times during the day," she says, "but if they are still busy challenging you for leadership that is their decision and they forfeit the right to be petted. At the moment you will just have to get your hugs from Colum and Sam."

She said other stuff which I can't remember but the most important thing was that she said it was fine to call her whenever we felt we had come to an impasse. And I ring off feeling as if a weight had rolled off me.

I go to my laptop in the dining room and type in the words 'Calm and Aloof' and enlarge it to 72 point. Print it off and stick it on the kitchen wall. There will be some interesting conversation around it I have no doubt. Maybe I'll get a T shirt made up too.

Meanwhile, while Colum is in London, I'm scheduling in seeing some friends, drinking some wine, doing a long run (no, not immediately after the wine drinking), watching a jolly film or two, and not stressing in the least. In the least.

Day the Twenty-Fifth

Well, that was the plan. It sounds great on paper, quite decadent and luxurious. But the reality was a tad different.

The actual day was fine. Sam was at home and I had gone off to help out in the secondhand bookshop. This is an occupation I love. I don't do it very often — just when the owner needs some extra help and my payment is meeting the people I meet, being among shelves and shelves of books, pondering and answering interesting questions and enjoying the sheer delight of a real bookshop.

As I trudged home around 6pm I was aware that I really didn't want to be going home. I didn't want to be the one on duty with the dogs. I had had enough of them; I wanted to extend my dog-free hours and take myself somewhere else. I had spoken with Colum earlier in the day and he was revelling in the forgotten pleasures of London – his early morning full-scale breakfast in a posh glasshouse-kind-of-restaurant where he had met an old pal (who also paid for his sumptuous breakfast – rich guys are sometimes wonderful); mid-morning coffee with another old friend; the scents and tastes and buzz of Borough market and lunch in a serene café round the corner from the Buddhist Centre in Bethnal Green. He sounded so happy and alive. And I was deeply envious. My current woe-is-me mantra that I haven't been anywhere of significance, for what feels like a long long time, was running round and round my head. But it was good that Colum was enjoying it all. It was good for him to be there. He had had a rubbish time of it at work recently and needed a rest and some good quality input. I knew that. I wanted him to have it.

I work mostly from home. I am doing the life I want. I am lucky. But my higher self was getting some heavy pressure from my lower self and my shoulders were already slumping as I neared home. Sam had texted me at the bookshop to ask if it was ok if he went out to the cinema with a pal. He said they were going to an early showing and he would be home to help with the last garden pit stop – Sal's worst time. I said that was fine. I changed out of my nicer clothes and put on my slops. I had some dinner – homemade chips which turned out quite greasy, tunafish and watercress. A mix of health and rubbish. I really felt like a glass of wine but not a drop was in the house. I should have got some on my way home but it would have meant a wide detour and anyway, in the interests of economy, I had decided to forgo it. As it was, I ended up on peppermint tea, as my stomach didn't take too kindly to the chips.

I did a mix of exciting things, like filling the washing machine, clearing dishes, cleaning the bath. Sam phoned to say they had got the time wrong and he would now be going to the 10pm showing. So it was me and the dogs. Around 9pm I ventured forth. I decided to be brave and do the dogs both together. It would be quicker, and anyway at this time of year it is still broad daylight, so the spooks of the night shouldn't be too much for Sal. I thought wrong.

We got as far as the top of the steps leading down to our garden. Sal raised her snout in the air and let out a volley of barks and then began lunging at the lead. Jen meanwhile, possibly desperate for the loo, began to pull me down the steps. Only by sheer effort of will and the muscles my running gives me, did I not pitch headfirst down the steps. I felt as if I was sitting behind a team of frantic huskies and skidded down the path into the garden. Jen wanted to go one way, Sal the other. I was in the middle. One of the dogs did a pooh or pee, I didn't know which and I didn't know where. It was just crazy. After seven minutes of this nonsense I tugged them back up to the house. Sal still lunging. The lights were on in the bedrooms of our downstairs neighbour. I was deeply conscious of the racket Sal was making and imagined our neighbour must think we are total nutters. It is probably a matter of time before she makes her beliefs known. We got round to the front door – Sal telling the wind in the trees to fuck off. I got my key in the door, pushed the dogs in, unclipped their leads and wound it off my chapped hands, sat down on the first stair step and bubbled.

Still sniffing, I made some more peppermint tea. Carried it to my rocking chair in the dining room. Shut the door on the dogs and phoned Colum. I needed some sympathy and a huge dollop of "You're doing fine" and "Don't stress about it".

What I got instead was a slightly tipsy husband greeting me with "Yeah! You're on speaker phone! Say hi to everyone!"

A chorus of unseen voices yelled their greetings to me and wishes that I could be there with them. Tears began to trickle down my face again. Fortunately the connection was poor so I made some cursory remarks and then said "I can't really hear you guys".

Colum said "Wait, and I'll go out on the balcony." (Balcony? How nice.) A moment later Colum's own voice, now not on speaker phone said "So, how you doing?"

And I told him. It wasn't fair of me, I know. I was ruining his happy mood. I was being selfish. He was silent after I finished my catalogue of complaint. I think I ended with "I just don't relate to Sally at all. There's no point in going on."

"Well, maybe we can talk about that when I get home," Colum said. It wasn't much help but at least I had lanced a bit of my misery.

I put down the phone, fished out the video of *Pretty Woman* that had been in the 'free box' in the bookshop, went through to the sitting room, put on the gas fire (expense and extravagance be damned), slammed the vid in the machine, slumped down in an armchair. Colum had advised me to try to switch off a bit. Perhaps a bit of Richard Gere as handsome and kind rich guy and Julia Roberts as Cinderella getting her prince would help.

All was tranquil for a short while then Sal thought she would have a bit of fun by noising up Jen. Remembering that Julie had said we shouldn't rely on Jenna to correct Sally, I put her out in the hall and shut the door. After ten seconds I let her in. She pestered Jen again. I put her out again. After ten seconds I let her in. This time she ignored Jen but sprung up on the armchair near the window and woofed at the night sky. I pulled her down without saying anything. She walked around a bit and jumped up on the chair again. I took her down, led her out of the room, shut the door. Ten seconds later she got back in, went to noise up Jen. I grabbed her collar, roughly pulled her out of the room, dragged her to her basket. "Now sit! Stay there!" I yelled and went back into the room slamming the door. A few moments later she starts woofing. "Oh, for God's sake!" I said getting up again, huffing out into the hall. Sal was up at the kitchen window where some imagined fiend was trying to get in. I pulled her down and out of the room. Closed the kitchen door. Dragged her into her basket again.

"Stay! And I mean it!" I shouted. I slammed the sitting room door and turned up the volume on the film.

It took around twenty minutes for me to calm down and around ten for Sally. Jen meanwhile was curled up on the carpet, her eyebrows raised. It was the kind of feeling I used to get when Sam as a toddler drove me to distraction. I would try and work with him, suggest amusing alternatives to what he wanted to do, try to negotiate, be patient…patient…patient…then …wham! I would move into major this-is-how-it-is-happening-because-I-said-it-and-that's-just-how-it-is-end-of-story mode. I drew up a wall and was resolute against any screaming. Decision made. No space for slippage left. The way forward was simple. We were doing things my way. And a kind of weird calm always descended. Thinking about it in the light of our new dog reading philosophy I suppose what I was doing was claiming my right as leader. The originators of the method wouldn't like my shouting, wouldn't like my losing it, but they would like the final result. Sally started woofing again in the hallway. I ignored her. I didn't get up. She stopped. I finished watching the film. I felt exhausted but in control again. It was now 11.30pm and I decided to call it a night. As a girl's night in, can't say it was the best.

Day the Twenty-Sixth

Such a better day! I employed a new strategy – called 'going out'. At 7.30am I took the dogs – separately – to the garden toilet (that's probably now a fitting description. I am not thinking of my poor potato patch. I am not. There's always next year). 8.20am I set off for a run. Met my pal Rona and did a 10k circuit. Breezy day. We talked of lots of things. I avoided talking of the dogs. Running along past fields around our town I noticed I was happy. Got home. Had a big drink of water and two cups of tea and a huge bowl of muesli with Sam's homemade raspberry smoothie poured over it. Our neighbour Donal phoned to ask me along to coffee in half an hour.

I dive into the shower, dress in clothes that match, do my hair and trot along the street. He and his wife have photographs to show of their daughter's collection. Ailsa has just finished her studies at prestigious London college and her designs have been chosen for an annual press show. We sit in their dining room, sipping coffee, blethering, looking at the photos on their laptop. It's all very pleasant. They're not dog people so don't ask me about Sal. That's fine with me.

My phone buzzes. My cousin Monica wants to know if I want to meet her for coffee if I am not in London.

"No, I'm not in London," I reply. We arrange to meet later. My day is progressing well.

I jog back along the street full of coffee, toast, marmalade and good conversation. I take the dogs out to the garden. Quiet. Good. Good. I put them back in the house. Check they have water and walk down to town. There is a new café opened up in town. Monica is already there. We order and talk about her morning's tutoring work. We talk about words being magnets and stream-of-consciousness techniques and not about dogs. Our food comes – huge doorstep beef and mustard sandwiches. Turning out to be a copious food day too.

We leave the café an hour later. I walk home and take the dogs out. Still quiet. Still good. Monica comes to pick me up and we drive to the local shopping mall where Sam works. We spend a happy hour sticking our noses into curious pots and highly scented cubes of soap, body scrub, massage blocks. I buy a box of 'Cosmetic Lad' for the fifteen year old whose birthday it is tomorrow, as well as 'Curly Wurly' for my hair and a lavender bath bomb called 'French Kiss' – can't go wrong there. Monica and I stroll about till Sam finishes his shift. Monica and I need tea, Sam, as usual, is ravenous. We think 'to hang with it' and go and find a place to eat. The food is ok but I think I enjoyed the wine more – although at £3.60 a small glass my guilt factor has sprung to life and is annoying my calm mood.

I start to worry if Jen is ok. She hasn't yet fully downloaded and I really don't think she would do so in the house unless really desperate. Sal will do so without thinking so I don't fret about her. But I don't want Jen to be uncomfortable – that's just too cruel.

We finally get home around 8.30pm. Sam take the dogs to the garden. Says they are fine and both just did pees. I make tea still thinking what a waste of money the meal had been. It rankles me. I had food here. We should have come home. Reckless. Reckless. We put on a DVD of *Dad's Army* – Sam got a box set at Christmas time. We settle down. Sal jumps on the armchair. Sam pulls her off. She does it again. She gets excluded. She comes back in and goes to woof at the window. We shut the curtains.

"Let's shove her out," says Sam – he doesn't entertain guilt at his age.

I vote to give her a chance. She jumps on the armchair again. We shove her into the hall and ignore her. Two episodes later we are both yawning. Sam goes off to bed. I go and have a decadent bath with my bomb. Read a trashy novel, both enjoy it and analyse the formula and the flaws. Turn off the light at 12.30. Nice day. Expensive but nice.

Day the Twenty-Seventh

The benefits of my 'time out' spree of yesterday have lasted into this morning. I get up around 8am and take the dogs to the back garden. As I don't want to jeopardise my peaceful state, I take them separately. I manage this by leaving Jen inside and lock the top door. She isn't too happy and scrabbles at the door. The noise will wake Sam up, but that's just how it is.

I return some six minutes later, Sal poohed and peed. I take Sal upstairs, unlock the door, open it. Jen runs out and down the stairs, Sal after her. I call Sal. She comes back up followed by Jen. I walk a couple of steps into the hallway, Sal follows as does Jen. I hold Sal by the collar and push Jen back out through the top door then lever myself out too. I take Jen out and then return her to the house.

Then I go back out and pick up around four or five lovely poohs which have accumulated over the last couple of days around our back garden. I could leave them. It's our garden but it would only be a matter of time before someone or some dog steps in one. And I don't really want the garden to start to stink. So I neatly bag them all and deposit them in the bin. Hope the council refuse men have desensitised noses.

For the rest of the morning I do housework. Colum won't look for a tidy house when he gets home but I want to do it all the same. Just feels better. I had thought about going back to bed and reading our book club book – *The Long Song* by Andrea Levy which is proving both sad and compelling – but the moment has passed and I dig into tidying and cleaning. I can enjoy a good session of housework. Our old house scrubs up well if given half a chance. And I feel more in control of life. I work on for an hour or so, punctuating my endeavours with a tea and toast break. I pass my desk and think about writing up some notes. I turn on the laptop and do so.

Suddenly it's 1.45pm. Eeek! I still have to make up a chicken, apple and carrot salad, have a shower, get dressed out of my slops, pit stop the dogs and then leave the house in 45mins. I text my friend Catherine, mother of the fifteen year old birthday boy, and say "Running late. Will be with you at 3.30. Sorry." I notice there is a bit of a wind getting up outside and my insides quiver a little at the thought of driving over the Erskine Bridge. I push the thought to the back of my mind and press on. Sam has already gone off to work so he can't help. The dogs watch as I run about the house. Humans must do very curious things to their minds. They think the chicken salad is a good idea though.

At 3.15 I finally make it to the car, put the cling-film covered salad bowl on the floor along with Calum's present and head off. As I near the Erskine Bridge the overhead gantry is announcing that the bridge is "Closed to HSV" – whitsoneofthem? Oh, yes, high-sided vehicles – would it really have taken them so much more trouble to spell it out? But, more to the point, does a Berlingo constitute a HSV? Yes, I know we are probably talking about huge lorries, but at what point does a van become a HSV? I pull off into the Erskine garden centre and call Catherine's house.

Her husband answers. That's good. He's the kind of level-headed chap you need in a moment of slight stress. He assures me that the authorities will soon stop traffic if they deem it unsafe.

So, with a muttered prayer of "Be brave and bold girl! Brave and bold!" I swing back onto the bridge. I keep the car in fourth gear; fifth feels just too much on the wild side for today. The wind pushes the sides of my van but it's fine. I say out loud "I am doing it! I am doing it! Yeh!"

Twenty minutes later I arrive at their cottage. It should really only take ten minutes, but as I am on my own I have to negotiate the gate – that stops the sheep from stravaiging – and also walk the last five minutes up the track, as I think the available parking outside the cottage will by now be fully taken. I park down near the dam and get out. The sounds and scents of the Kilpatrick hills fill my senses. There are sheep, with their chubby lambs, dotted around. This was one of the main reasons I didn't bring the dogs. I try to imagine a calm and acquiescent Jen when near sheep. I can't. So I head up the track, carrying the salad and present, just enjoying the countryside air.

There are various dog owners at the party. Interestingly it is the non-dog owners who first ask me about Sally. They have heard on the grapevine about our new arrival and want to hear first-hand how it came about. I hear myself hugely abbreviating on the entry of Sally into our lives. I am aware that I am still rather raw about it all, still trying to get to grips with the whole thing and too vulnerable to hear anything that will pierce our very fragile mindset. I feel as if we have travelled a huge distance since I last met up with these friends and it's a distance that very few will want to know the details of. I am also still clinging to the benefits of doing something not dog related so swerve away from too much focused talk on Sally or Jen. Actually it's Jen that is the more difficult subject. Our friends can readily see the wisdom of keeping Sally's world small, letting her get used to feeling safe in our home and garden, before tackling the big wide world of the street and hill. But a wave of confusion comes over their faces when they ask about Jen. They presume she is just doing her usual thing and that we are walking her as normal. They think they have misheard when I say that Jen is also under this new methodology. I find myself dodging their loaded questions and dive into euphemisms in an attempt to throw them off track. Truth is that it all sounds wacky to me so I haven't a hope in hell of defending it as yet. Best thing is to steer the conversation off to safer ground, such as describing what we know of Sally's background when we had absolutely nothing to do with her, or to talk about something else completely.

I have to leave after a couple of hours. Sam needs a lift home from his shift – the buses stop early on a Sunday – and, as always, there are the dogs to consider. I go round saying goodbye to folks. Jacqui, who has a beautiful golden retriever, called Glen, hasn't yet heard anything much about Sal. She is putting out platefuls of Smarties and marshmallows and chocolate biscuits – real party food, it's just as well I am going, I doubt I could resist the Smarties for very long – and asks me the name of our method. I tell her it is Amichien. I make a mental note that I must look up the origin of this. Sounds French to me. She tells me of a spray you can buy which is said to calm down a dog. I think we would need a water canon for Sally but thank her anyway.

I text Sam when I arrive at the shopping mall car park. He texts back that he thought I said to try to get a bus so is already nearly home. The petrol light is glowing orange in the car and I huff and puff about wasting petrol. I have a vision of having to walk a mile or so to a petrol station and getting laughed at for being a stupid woman driver. This doesn't happen. There is enough petrol. I hear Colum's voice in my head "There's a quarter tank left when that light come on," but it is a twelve-year-old van, it might not obey such beliefs. I pull up into our parking bay with a huge sigh of relief. I have faced inner demons this afternoon and am tired.

Sam, in an effort to placate a possibly annoyed mother, has already taken Sal and Jen to the garden. I get in, tell him it is ok and sit down. Sam's shift was very quiet and he found it a long day. It feels like a G&T moment. I had said to Colum that I would keep my bargain three pack of ready-mixed G&Ts from M&S until he came home. But to hell with that. He's probably quaffing down the wine at his reunion lunch. There is no need for guilt. Sam and I sit at the kitchen table and drink the gin. Oh! it's good, and oh! it's strong. I feel it trickle through my veins right to my usually cold toes. My shoulders come down two inches. We talk about life and relationships. Sam is nineteen and wondering where and when his soul partner will appear – or has she already appeared? I impart what wisdom I can from my 48-year-old perspective. It maybe helped. It maybe didn't. But the gin did. Sal jumps up at the window to snarl at a pigeon. I pull her down saying "Chill, girl. Chill." We eat some bits of food. I ate at the party so a few oatcakes suffice for me. Sam wallops in to chicken and potatoes as the dogs circle. We go through the feeding sketch. It all seems rather smooth and stress-free when you're puggled. We leave the dishes, go through to the sitting room and spend the rest of the evening watching Series 6 of *Dad's Army*. Sal is given 'three strikes and you're out' rule. She spends the majority of the evening on her own in the hall.

Day the Twenty-Eighth

Colum gets home today. Strange to think that while I have been sleeping, he has been travelling. I try to imagine what the London to Glasgow overnight bus would be like. Dark, crowded, stuffy, no leg room? Or an opportunity for deep thought? As an undergrad student, many moons ago, I did the ten-hour journey, or was it twelve then? It was just what you did. Funny how things come full circle. Because of my chosen career move into writing we have little spare cash. The train fare to London was averaging at £105 against £12 on the bus. At one time in my life I could zip up and down by train to the British Library under the freedom of a research grant or departmental travel allowance. Gone are those days; it is the bus or nothing for the time being. Well, it would all be useful writing material. That's my fall-back slogan. It acts a little as a bulwark against the strictures of necessary frugalism and the challenges life throws at you. Some months ago I had to spend three nights in our local hospital owing to severe anaemia. After the hospital beings had pumped some life-giving blood into my veins and I felt like me again, Sam came in to visit and brought me a notebook.

"Thought you might need some paper to write about all of this," he said.

As the mystic Sufi poet, Kabir, sagely observed, wisdom and peace can be accessed no matter where you are.

As I lie in bed musing these thoughts. I think about Sally. Before she came, I was writing. I was in the middle of a novella. It was going ok. I was writing bits of poetry. I have no idea if they were ok. I was thinking of putting together a child's picture book and using one of my anecdotes about Jen. I was practising drawing and painting again. It was useful and entertaining. Then Sally arrived and I vented my stress on this keyboard. It has been like a fountain just gushing out. I make notes while I am sitting in the car waiting for someone. I make notes whenever I walk past my desk, I make notes on the train, in a café and other random places. The Findhorn Guidance, which is sent to our family email box every week, says something about recognising the silver lining in all situations. I must aim to remember that, when teetering on the top step with Sal, while she vents her thoughts about the foxes and all sundry life. Maybe I should buy her a diary and teach her to write.

My bedside clock clicks onto the hour. Time to get up. Colum's bus is due in at 8am and he should get home around 8.30 if he sprints to the train. And Colum will sprint. So, being the good wife I am, I batter out with the dogs, Sal lunging and plunging. Jolly good. Eat half a grapefruit, drink some water. Grab my trolley and head off to the supermarket. I get home a little later. Deposit the packed trolley outside the door where it is screened by the high hedge, and jog off over the park down to the station. Colum's train arrives. He jumps off, grinning and leaping up the steps, swings me round. What must the folks on the train be thinking? No point saying that to Colum, he would just swing me higher. We walk up the track towards home. He fills me in with anecdotes of his travels. The sun is shining. The place looks appealing. I want to say "You know, it hasn't been like this, it really has been miserable". The wee girl inside me has reared her tear-stained face. I feel jealous of all the stuff he tells me – his time with good friends, his visits to market stalls and cafés, his walks in the parks, his visits to bookshops. I've done some nice stuff too, but it was all local, all in places I know very very well. He has been somewhere different and I am envious.

He gives me a large piece of expensive ewe's cheese, a gift from one of the market stalls. I say I will taste it later. Sam appears and hugs his dad. Colum gives him some chorizo sausage. Sam tastes it immediately and pronounces it 'good stuff'. We eat a big breakfast – veg sausages, tomatoes, eggs, mushrooms, fried potatoes with two big pots of tea. I begin to thaw a little. It's good to have my man home. I can stop coping.

In the afternoon we drive out to our favourite lochside walk. As we get into the van a neighbour calls across "When are you bringing Jen over to play with Jimmy? He's missing her."

"Not for a bit yet," says Colum. The neighbour is disappointed. What a strange life we are in.

We drive to the lochside café and eat tea and flapjack. Outside the café there are dogs. Dogs in all shapes and sizes. I miss Jen. I don't miss Sal. There are three huge inflatable balls bobbing about on the loch. Children queue up to have a go at stepping inside them and tumbling and falling. I move my mind away from what could happen if Sal was here.

We walk a quarter of a mile. We usually walk right along the path and into the woods and do an invigorating hour's circuit. Today we stroll. I see a bench looking out on the loch and suggest we sit down. Tired from his eleven-hour bus journey, Colum is happy to do so. We while away an hour watching the sail boats on the loch, chatting of this and that. Two people appear with a cute-as-a-button large puppy.

"We should call them fluppies," says Colum. The pup flumps along, spies us and comes up for a pat. To hell with Amichien.

"Well, hello there. You're beautiful," I say.

The owner smiles. We talk puppy. They go off.

"I suppose I shouldn't have done that," I say.

"Doesn't matter," says Colum.

It's almost 5.30pm and the lochside is quiet. A family sits on a bench eating fish suppers. They have a golden Labrador tied up beside them. He is slabbering.

"Fancy a poke of chips?" I ask Colum. His face lights up.

We drive to the chippy in the village, carry back bags of the mouth-watering substance, park, find a nearby bench and eat our feast. More people pass by. These people have a very young black-and-white Collie. She jumps up at us. I ruffle her under her chin.

"What age is she?" I ask the owner.

"Twelve weeks," she replies.

"Well, she's lovely," I say.

The owner tugs the pup away and I sigh.

"I wonder if Sally looked like that? I wish we could have had her from a pup."

"She didn't need us then," says Colum.

Day the Twenty-Ninth

Colum still on annual leave today. It halves the load. As we come downstairs we see a curious pile of sick or pooh on the top stair.

"It's got strange green string like stuff in it," says Colum.

"My wool!" I say and leap down the rest of the stairs to check my knitting basket. Nothing has been touched. "It's not wool," I yell.

"Well, whatever it is, it's disgusting," says Colum as he reaches under the kitchen sink for the disinfectant.

Oh, it's good he is home. Sam still isn't signed up to clearing up dog mess. He hasn't had the deep life experience of dealing with squidger nappies. When that does happen I will sit back and watch with great interest. Colum clears up the carpet and takes the girls out to the garden. Men like him are so useful.

An hour later I notice that the sitting room door isn't shutting properly. Colum checks it. The lock is stuck. He gets out his toolbox and takes the lock apart. We really need this door to close for purposes of isolation. Doors that work properly are now a priority. We spend the morning driving about looking for an ironmonger who can deal with old Victorian locks.

"Oh, this is old," says each place.

"Em, yes, a hundred years or so actually. But can you fix it?" is our stock response. We finally leave it with a chap who will send it to a mate. It will probably cost something like fifty quid to mend it. Ho hum.

It is getting warm. Almost hot. We get home and begin work on the garden. Our front hedge is in bad shape, as is the side one, as are the pots, as is the raised bed opposite the front door, as is the back garden. Wonder if I will ever get a neat garden? And will I want it by then? Colum attacks the hedges. I work on the pots. I think on the countless times our dogs would be out with us in the front garden. Jack would lie out on the pavement, thumping his tail at every human who passed and either squaring up to or lying low from every dog that passed. Joe liked to sit in the open boot of our van and watch the doings of the street. I miss them.

"Shame we can't bring the dogs out," I say.

"Was just thinking that," says Colum. "Do you reckon we could try it?"

We both visualise the possible scene.

"No," we agree.

We spend two to three hours in the garden. It looks a lot better. We are pleased with ourselves. I have heard Jen scrabbling at the top door a couple of times during the session. She finally gets let out and into the back garden. Colum returns with them, jubilant.

"A pee and a pooh from both of them! I really think Jen's getting it. I really do."

Reminds me of the time I phoned Colum at work. Sam had just successfully used his potty for the first time. Apparently Colum punched the air and called out "Pee in the potty first time! That's my boy".

"That's gross," said his co-workers.

After dinner we watch the DVD that Julie left us. Jan Fennell and her son, Tony Knight, are demonstrating the rudiments of their philosophy. We find it really interesting, almost moving, as they diagnose 'problem' pets who have their owners ready for a mental breakdown. It looks as if it can actually work. And we learn a term for the stage we are at, i.e. 'foundation work'. Jan explains the obvious analogy that if your foundations aren't solid you are setting yourself up for failure. She stresses that the foundation work can all be done from home.

"Home is safe. There is no need to go out where it is scary," she says, or something like it. "You are in your safe place at home and so are relaxed. The dogs sense this."

And it makes sense put like this. As we watch the DVD Jen comes into the sitting room and stretches out on her side.

"I think she's given up leadership," says Colum.

I say I will reserve my judgment as yet.

Day the Thirtieth

Back to the usual routine. Go to the local university library to write. Amazingly quiet. Remember that term had ended. Two other students on the whole floor. They look like overseas students. Must seem crazy to them that the library is not buzzing. But I'm not complaining. A place where dishes and unmade beds and washing and grubby floors and dogs and random phone calls and chatty neighbours are not, is sheer balm to my writer's soul. And into the bargain I get a large pine desk, quiet studious atmosphere, a café which sells affordable and lovely green tea, and space to let my thoughts flow. I'm neither a student nor staff here and I am unsure if my graduation from two other Scottish universities would grant me entry. But I am a resident of the town and as this library was partly built, I believe, with public money, those residents respectful of its strictures are tolerated. While our town centre has been battered by short-sighted disastrous decisions, causing daily haemorrhage to out-of-town shopping malls, this the planners got right and I am grateful. Today, I get a good four hours writing done. Feel good. Return home.

Dumping my bag in the dining room I hear barking coming from the garden. Sam seems to be playing with Sal and Jen off lead. What the hell is going on? That's way too advanced a stage. We're not there yet! I grab a bag of dog treats from their hiding place at the top of the kitchen cabinet and go down to the garden. As I get to the gate I see Sam get hold of Sal's collar and clip on a lead. Jen appears to be tied up by the bench. Giving him the benefit of doubt before I lambast him for disregarding our careful training schedule, I call to Sam in a measured voice.

"Hi. What's happening?"

"Sally saw a cat as we were coming down the path. She went for it. Her lead broke and I was left holding the end. She pranced out onto next door's garden. I ran with Jenna down to our garden. Sal followed. I think she thought it was a game. So I decided to make it one. I left them there and got another lead. And when I got back they were having a brilliant time. They so need to run, mum!"

Having moved my judgment from teenage boy screw-up to sensible resolution of potentially bad situation, I had to agree with him. But this could put our foundation training back by quite a bit. They didn't say anything about this on the DVD last night. What happens when the training goes belly up? We seem to have shot forward to another stage and we haven't practised for 'The Hunt' stage yet. Damn it! But real life isn't a textbook.

"Ok. Well done," I say. "Now, I'm going to come into the garden and not make eye contact. We've got to reassert authority."

Hmmm. I unhook the gate and walk in like a headteacher into an unruly class. The dogs look at me or at least at the bag in my hand. I break off a bit of beef flavoured chew.

"Sam, would you like a bit of tasty snack stuff?"

He rolls his eyes but goes along with the charade. I give him an inch of the foul smelling treat. The dogs jump at me. I push them off. We 'finish' our food and then I say 'sit' to the dogs. They sit. I give them a bit of the treat.

"Right. Let's get them home!" I say, as if it is a zillion miles away.

We go back up the path. I try and do the walk guide thing of holding a treat in my hand beside my hip in the hope that Jen will trot nicely beside me. She paws my hand and I feel her claws slightly tear my skin. This doesn't happen in the books or at Crufts. Usually women with rather wide rear ends, who resemble the human form of giant Schnauzers, do a kind of pathetic flopsy lady run while their dog prances prettily beside them, keeping their snouts close to their owner's hand. They must have some better treat than I do. I decide to leave the 'heel' bit for another day and sort of run-walk with Jen back to the house. Are they now going to want a play session next time we take them out? And can I blame them?

Day the Thirty-First

Continuing in my praxis of not being around the dogs too much, I go back into the city to meet up with my mum and my niece. A half hour before the train was due I took Sal and Jen – separately – into the garden. Jen does a long pee on the communal path. Seems that she is still resisting our dictate of using our garden and our garden only. Sal also opts just for a pee but she also adds in a swear session at a robin who has the audacity to land and chirrup in our garden. I think of Julie talking about 'a happy lead', i.e. one that swings quite loosely. Pit-stops with Sally currently range from 'happy leads' to a full 'two-handed desperate hold.' I often feel as if I have a young colt rearing up beside me. Maybe Sally is part wild horse. Wish we knew her ancestry. Or maybe it's better not to know.

After the slight rigours of the garden toilet session, it's good to walk on my own down the track to the train. We are lucky that a train runs along the bottom of our garden and the station is approximately six minutes walk away. I stand on the platform and look down towards the housing estate on the other side of the track. A man and his black Labrador dog are walking toward the block of flats. The Lab looks young, maybe a year or two old at most. He/she is off-lead and is bounding along, happy happy happy. The man calls 'stay!' as a car drives out of a parking bay. The dog halts then continues on its way when his owner flicks his head to come. The dog runs ahead of its owner. In the dog training method we are this implies that the dog thinks it is leading the hunt. But in the fact that it stopped when commanded to do so, does that mean that the owner is in charge? I'm confused. And, looking at the poise and girth of its owner, leadership is definitely imprinted there. But, does it chase sheep and want to tear the postman and his 'bombs' to shreds? I will probably never know, but the sight of the happy dog makes my heart merry. We must, sometime in our next years, get another black Lab. They are just special dogs. As I wait for the train, my mind slips sideways into memories of our Jack.

Jack came to us when he was sixteen weeks. It sounds younger and smaller, put like that. Four months is more definite, more solid and Jack was certainly that. His first home was with our friends who had got him for their daughter. Their son had or rather still has, autism. Children with autism find relationships with siblings difficult and our friends had reasoned that it would perhaps be good for their daughter to have a dog, so to assuage some of the possible loneliness she felt. All very creditable. Problem was that Jack was Jack and was not going to slide smoothly into the role of quiet companion for anyone. No sirree! That wasn't Jack's style. He wanted to live life to the fullest possible percent, explore and explode every possibility, for fun. Very little made him sad, although words like 'Later' and 'All Done' caused him to sigh.

As the train moves out of the station, I think of the time Jack escaped out of the house and ran faster than the speed of time to the house of our friends, Mary and David, who then lived at the other end of our road. To get there Jack had to negotiate the fairly busy road which divides our street. My stomach lurches every time I think of it as I doubt there was much skilful negotiation going on, just sheer determination to get to his destination and answer the call of his hormones. Mary and David's wolfhound, Petal, was in heat and Jack knew it. He reckoned he was the dog for the job and never much the one for foreplay, seized his chance when it came. Realising Jack had disappeared from the front of our house where he had been happily sitting in the sun idly watching the bees, I had gone in search of him. Our dining room window affords a good viewing point over the other back gardens and as I scanned the various paths and bushes, our phone rang. I picked it up to hear Mary's voice saying 'Hi there. I've found Jack outside our front door trying to chew his way through it. Any chance you can come and get him?'

'Sure thing. Thanks. Be there in a tic,' I replied.

I belted back down to the front door, grabbed a lead and ran along the street. As I got nearer to the house I spied a 'For Sale' sign fixed on a post at the entrance to the driveway of Mary's house. Of course, they are in the middle of a major tidy-up and manicure of the house. The sight of major scratch marks on their newly painted front door wasn't, I guessed, the look of homely comfort they were trying to create. Oooops!

There was no sign of Jack but I could hear him. I rang the bell. A harassed looking Mary appeared.

'I've jammed him in the kitchen and put Petal in a bedroom. God. They've been howling at each other. Listen!'

There really was little need for her to say this. Jack and Petal were making their desire for each other's services pretty known.

'I'm really sorry,' I yelled. 'I'll take him away.'

Mary is normally very sociable and I have enjoyed many a lovely cup of coffee in her cosy kitchen but I suspected that, today, offers of coffee weren't happening. I pushed my way into the kitchen and grabbed Jack's collar as he tried to push past me to find his true love. I clipped on his lead, held it with a firm grip and hauled him out of the back door. He dug in his substantial paws and pulled backwards. I grabbed his collar and, half-throttling him, yanked him towards the gate. Once out in the road, being the affable chap he always was, he gave up struggling and let me walk in a more sedate manner back home. I didn't want to think about what Mary and David would say about their front door when they saw it.

So life with our Jack wasn't always smooth sailing. But he was so gorgeous and loveable that his many misdemeanours were forgiven, forgiven and forgiven again. His character was completely transparent. What you saw was what you got. There were no hidden agendas, no games, just pure see-through intention. Being a Labrador we could see his thinking happening. Collies are often three pages ahead of Labs when it comes to processing what is going on around them and we reckon that Sally and Jen would have run rings around Jack – and he would have loved it. Especially Sally's energy. He might, though, have shown her how to get tasty nibbles by lying quiet under the dining room table when visiting people were sitting there and stealthily making your way down to the kids' end where bits of bread, potatoes, biscuits mysteriously seemed to drop down to the carpet. He might have shown them how to lie in the kitchen with your feeding bowl over your head and sigh in a dramatic manner. He might have shown them how to Frisbee-skate in the street or sing along to the Wallace and Gromit alarm clock in our bedroom; how to find yummy chocolate angels and santas on Christmas trees; how to eat a whole bag of mini Toblerones and pooh out the silver wrappings; how to lie on the raised bed at the front door and nibble the wild strawbs growing there; how to catch a falling biscuit before it hit the ground even if two rooms away; how to biff open all doors and run in with your tail wagging so that you don't get told off; how to play dog football with Colum and any kid brave enough; how to chew the whole of the stairwell skirting board and other miscellaneous bits of wooden furniture; how to wake up sleepy schoolboys by jumping on the bed and shoving your wet nose under the covers; how to chase a full sized Highland coo and not get kicked; how to swim in the sea with Colum and scratch all his chest in appreciation; how to clap your paws and make bear noises when your favourite people came in and how to sit in the sun with your head on the arm of the bench savouring life. Yes, he would have done it all.

But Jack was part of our past lives. And when he died a part of my heart went with him. We always said his exit would be sensational. His zest for life carried him into situations where our gentle Joe cannily didn't follow. A slow deterioration and quiet slipping away were just far too boring for Jack. Instead he chose to paralyse himself while chasing a fox one moonlight night. It was the middle of August and we had been on our annual camping holiday in Findhorn where Joe and Jack had been with us almost every minute of the day. Jack loved lying outside the front of the tent watching, watching, watching all that was happening around him. He loved all the fuss and favour that dogs get in Findhorn, he loved the beach and the sea – even though the salt water seemed to act as a colonic irrigation on his bowels. He loved the crazed rabbits on the machair and the unsuspecting seagulls.

The sand was still in his fur when we drove him to the vets, Colum cradling him in his arms in the car. We knew from the vet's eyes that Jack had finally used up his allotted span of fun. As there was little the vet could do that evening but make Jack as comfortable as possible, he came home again for one last night. Colum and Sam carried him into the house on a stretcher of an old blanket. We laid him down in the hall which was still full of our assorted camping gear. Colum wanted to stay with him and so I pumped up one of our inflatable mattresses, found a pillow and a sleeping bag and placed them beside Jack's inert body. As Colum got ready for his night vigil I laid down beside Jack, tears spilling over my face, 'Jack, oh Jack, what have you done this time?' I asked him. In reply he turned his big brown eyes towards me and gently licked my cheek.

In the morning we drove him to the Glasgow Veterinary School. We are so lucky to live in the Central belt, with such an excellent facility so near to us, but it was a sad drive nonetheless. We were taken immediately by the staff there who already knew of Jack's situation – our vet having already alerted them – and they carried out a preliminary examination of him. As I watched I didn't know if I wanted him to feel pain or not. His lack of feeling meant that the paralysis was extended, but I could hardly bear to hear him moan where he had feeling. The vet in charge decided a CT scan was necessary and asked us to leave him with them for an hour or so. As he was wheeled by us on a trolley bound for the scanning room, I asked the porters to pause so I could bend and kiss Jack's cheek and whisper that I loved him. The porters must see a lot of this kind of behaviour in their job, but they went quiet as I kissed my lovely pet and remained silent as they wheeled him away.

Colum and I drove off, not really knowing where we were going; we found ourselves out near Balmore just north of Glasgow. We knew of a fair-trade coffee place there which would be quiet and allow us to think a little. We had something serious to discuss. The vet had asked us if Jack was the kind of dog who could stand not being able to run. She warned us that the paralysis could, over time, lessen and he could regain a little strength in his legs. In the meantime we would have to carry him to the back garden for his toilet needs. Even if stronger, he would need to walk in a sling for many months. We were the only customers in the coffee house – possibly their first of the day as it had only just opened, and I was glad as my tear-stained soul wasn't up for much socialising.

Once we had drunk some good coffee and eaten some cake – breakfast had been a rather scanty affair that morning and had tasted like sawdust anyway – we looked at each other.

'He will want to run,' I said. 'It would break his heart not to.'

'Yes,' said Colum 'So ... if the result of the testing shows that his spine is really damaged, we ... ,'he trailed off.

'We ask them to put him to sleep,' I whispered.

'Yes,' said Colum again.

His mobile phone buzzed, the noise seemed so loud in this quiet place. Colum answered it and said 'Right. I see. Thanks. In that case, we've decided ... we've decided to let him go.' He listened for another minute and then said to me 'Do you want them to keep Jack sedated and let him slip away like that, or do you want to say goodbye to him?'

'I want to say goodbye,' I said.

Colum spoke to the vet who said Jack should be awake in a couple of hour's time and we should come then. Colum rang off and we made our way home.

A short while later we returned to the vet school consulting room. Monica had come with us. She has somehow been around our family at notable points and had lived with us for some months and knew our Joe and Jack very well. It seemed right that she should be with us now.

The vet had told Colum that the CT scan had shown that Jack had sustained a severe stroke in his spinal column. The thought of never seeing Jack being able to run in his usual manner when his back legs went faster than his front, or even to do a moderately fast pace, was one we couldn't cope with.

We heard a shuffling in the corridor and, to our amazement Jack hopped into the room in a canvas sling held aloft by a vet. At the sound of all of us calling his name he looked up and if dogs can smile, he smiled. We were his family. We were the faces he wanted to see. The vet lowered the sling to the floor and Jack collapsed down heavily. Both Colum and I sunk down beside him. I can't remember much of what I said to him but it didn't really matter. I didn't want to watch as the vet slipped the needle into his veins. Instead I sat back up on a seat with Monica and started to sing the Taizé chant "Nada te turbe, nada te espante," a version of St. Teresa of Avila's prayer "Let nothing disturb you. Let nothing dismay you,. The senior vet had left, and the young vet designated to put Jack to sleep had told us he was from Portugal. I hadn't deliberately chosen a Romance language chant, it was just the one that came into my mind, but I saw the young vet nod in understanding.

We brought Jack's body home in the boot of our van, which I had already strewn with lavender and rosemary. Sam and his girlfriend of the time met us as we drove up. Before they carried Jack to the back garden where we had decided to bury him, Colum went to get Joe. We had read somewhere that animals need to know what has happened to their pack. I now doubt the wisdom of this – it is more essential that strong leadership must continue – but then we thought that Joe should know that Jack had died. Joe sniffed at Jack's still body curiously but then backed off and seemed not to need to see anymore. Sam and Colum lifted Jack's already cold and stiff body to the back garden. I went in front of them quietly singing as best I could, 'Remember then that day and night, remember then that dark and light are one holy circle' – a liturgical song we had learned on our holiday in Findhorn, where Jack had been so happy. Colum dug a large hole in the garden near the fence. We wrapped Jack's body in a clean cotton cloth, placed him in the ground, covered him with some of the small wild apples from his favourite tree on the hill and covered him up.

Hours later, unable to sleep, sitting in my rocking chair looking out the window down over the dark garden, I wrote a poem about losing Jack. Friends were compassionate enough to say it made them cry.

The freshly dug plot and the precious compost material it now carried was the catalyst for us to establish our existing bee and butterfly patch. I wanted to create a beautiful space in memory of our rascal boy and coupled this with my interest in helping our beleaguered bees. When a low wall had been built creating the outline of the space and infilled with top soil we asked some friends to come round and complete our goodbye process. These friends are our Taizé family. We meet in each other's home once a month for a simple liturgy, some quiet time and then a shared meal. Each person has become a close and valued friend and each person, from the youngest child to the oldest adult, knew and loved Jack. We all lit tea lights and placed it over Jack's plot. Some people said some words, some didn't. We then passed round our family Quaich.

For the uninitiated, the Quaich is an old Scottish tradition. It is a two handled or 'twa-lugged' cup of friendship made originally from wood, then silver and now most often pewter. It has been used to mark significant moments – births, marriages, deaths, new houses, a welcome to the traveller. Like the old ballads, the use of the Quaich becomes unique to the user and its purposes blend with the requirement. My belief is that you should never buy your own Quaich but it should be given to you. I don't know where I have got this from but I have stuck to it.

As I pulled out the Quaich from its box in our Welsh dresser in preparation for our Taizé family arriving, memories of my dad's funeral came flooding back with it. When my dear old Dad died, I took the decision to go and buy a large Quaich. I reckoned that as I was buying it for our family, for anyone to use whenever the occasion merited, it would therefore be a shared cup and the tradition of not buying for yourself would hold. I bought it in the gift shop of Glasgow University, as all my siblings, including myself, have some connection to the university. My dad was an east end of Glasgow man without an academic qualification to his name, it was therefore a deep joy to him that all of his four children had gained university degrees. I reckoned he would have approved of me buying it from a university shop.

The day of Dad's funeral was dreich to say the least – the wind blew open the church doors; the passkeepers had to wrestle them back together to allow the Requiem Mass to continue. By the time we got to the hillside graveyard, the sky was sending down torrents of rain. We had organised for a piper to play beside the grave. My sister had long stemmed roses to give to various people, whom she planned to ask to place gracefully into the open grave. Instead of this choreographed scene we arrived to find the drenched piper manfully trying to keep some sound in his reeds as someone else held a large billowing umbrella over him. And instead of the poignant passing around of a malt-filled Quaich and meaningful sentiments from the respectful mourners, people held on to coats, hoods, hats, scarves and small children. As soon as the priest had uttered the final blessing, all belted back to the cars. Colum was left with the full Quaich which only a few had sampled. There was nothing else for it but for him to throw the whisky out over the final resting place of my dad as the piper wailed 'Nooooooo!'

I think my sister had to hurl the roses into the grave herself. Colum swears he could hear my dad laugh. So, sometimes, no matter how well intentioned, you just can't stage a seamless ceremony.

But this afternoon, as our Taizé family passed around the large Quaich in the peaceful garden where the sun danced lightly on our shoulders and a blackbird sang its best song, our lovely rascal Jack was fittingly honoured and blessed. Back in the house, tear-stained tissues up our sleeves, tea and cake and more malt whisky or orange juice partaken, Colum presented a slide show of photographs of Jack in all his guises to a track of Bobby McFerrin singing singing Jack's signature song, 'Don't worry, Be happy.' The children particularly loved the one of Jack sitting on the bench outside with Sam's 'Animal' hat on. Jack was still making people laugh even when he was gone.

Perhaps this all seems excessive for the death of an animal. I know of some people who think a pet graveyard completely risible. But that's their outlook. For me, Jack was worth some tears and some ceremony. He brought us joy in abundance and why should we not thank him for that. I see him still in my mind's eye, busily trotting into our back garden to see what is brewing, lying flat out in front of the cooker savouring the smells around him, curled up at my feet while I type. Happy lad. I miss him.

No dog we ever have will replace Jack. They couldn't and I wouldn't want them too. He was unique. And Jenna and Sally are unique too, as was Joe. But I really don't know Sally yet. I don't know her foibles. She lunges at birds and cats and the smell of fox scent, but what makes her happy?

What makes her heart sing? Will she ever let us know? This morning as she dutifully used the pee spot in the garden she suddenly looked up at me. Her eyes were nearing softness and I smiled and said "Good girl. Good girl." She almost wagged her tail. The impulse was in her eyes it just didn't get carried to the length of her tail.

My reverie occupies my thoughts all the way into the city. I enjoy being on the train, arriving in the station, walking up to Sauchiehall Street – the street of the willow – such a lovely name. The weather is mild, everyone seems in a good mood. Tomorrow it is expected to reach 23 degrees. We have been averaging around 11 to 14 recently, so the shops are busy with people buying shorts and flip-flops in celebration of the coming weather. It will apparently then plummet to around 13 degrees in two days time. But life is fleeting and the shoppers are making the most of it.

I am early for our coffee meeting and I go into a shoe shop which promises me 50% off many ranges. I spy a trendy pair of ankle boots – everyone else is looking at espadrilles and sandals but I had such boots on my Christmas list. They never materialised and here they are reduced to half price. They will be good for the bookshop where the temp never gets much above 15 degrees. I go to pay for them. The pint-sized assistant charges me the full price. I demur and say they are half of that. Her pleasant here-to-help-you attitude suddenly stops and she looks at me defiantly and says they are the full price. I tell her their price tag is ambiguous. Perhaps she would like to go and check it? No, she's not going to check it. I say I don't then want the boots. She moves into this-is-all-too-much mode. I wait patiently. I currently help in two shops. I know how a till works and where the Cancel/Void button is. It isn't rocket science. Another assistant comes over. The situation is explained. She says to the wee one just to issue a refund. This is done with bad grace. I could kick up. I could ask to see the manager. I could call them to task for poor pricing. But my mum has already left a voice mail and a text to say they are waiting for me. I pick up the refund receipt and leave. What a palaver. I had intended going to Waterstones and looking through the pet section for a book called *How to Settle and Completely Understand a Rescue Black and White Collie Dog Called Sally in Two Short Weeks*. Now there's now no time.

I get home around 1.30pm. It was a good break and there was little conversation about the consuming topic of our dogs and their training. I didn't think there would be and that was ok. My mum has never quite got why people are interested in keeping dogs, apart from their being useful for guarding the house. Despite us having a Foxhound and two Collies over the years I grew up in the family home, I have absolutely no recollection of my mum ever walking a dog on her own. Guess it was how they divided the labour of family living – and with four children there was a lot of labour – but seems to me that she missed a lot. Maybe she was never given the chance, maybe dad saw it as a man's job, as he did gardening or maintaining the car, or maybe she just didn't want to. I'm starting to have some sympathy with that viewpoint.

I also now think back to the treatment meted out to the various family dogs when I was younger. Our dog guru would bury her head in her hands and weep. We weren't deliberately cruel at all and really thought we were doing the right thing, but nonsense like shoving their noses in pee and pooh if they defecated the house when they were puppies, hitting them on the nose with a rolled up newspaper when they were excited, tying up a dog on a chain most of the day in the garden while we were all out and believing the Foxhound had 'turned' when he apparently bit my brother and was consequently put to sleep, are memories that my adult self who has grown to love and try to understand dogs, now views in a totally different light.

If truth be told, it wasn't until Colum and I gave in to Sam's repeated requests for a pet that I engaged with what it means to build a relationship with a dog. My dad did however know some of this. When we got Joe, our Collie-cross, as a puppy and were reeling a bit, I asked my dad if he had any advice.

"Well," he said as he sipped a cup of sugary tea, "you get to know your dog and it gets to know you. And that's about it."

He was right, if you think about it.

Day the Thirty-Second

As I come down the stairs for breakfast, golden light is streaming out from under the dining room and sitting room doors. I open the doors and let the delicious stuff burst out into the hall. Colum has already had the dogs out in the garden and they are now slumped in their baskets having wisely decided it will be a slow day.

Some years ago we visited Sam's godfather, John, on his adopted Greek island. John is a Londoner by birth and formation, but some years ago had decamped to an idyllic island in search of a slower and better life. Slower he certainly got. Just before we departed our cool and drizzly land John emailed to say that there was no point in my bringing my running shoes as it was too warm. He emailed at 11 pm and said that it was 27 degrees as he typed.

I removed my running gear from my bag and we set off to catch our plane. I should have thought to remove myself.

Over the next couple of days the temp soared to over 40 degrees. Now, as a cool blooded Celt anything over 20 is hot, anything over 30 is ridiculous and I just don't do over 40. Even the Greeks were heard to mutter that it was too damn hot. Consequently swift movement, as in an easy loose walk, was way off the agenda and John advised us to adopt the Greek strategy of σιζά σιζά (pronounced "siga siga") or "slowly slowly" in English – which constituted an imitation of a stiffing geriatric who is still getting the hang of their zimmer frame.

By the time we landed back in Glasgow airport a week later I felt as if lead had replaced any life-giving blood in my veins and my head was totally fuzzy due to sleep deprivation. John's house, although lovely and authentic, didn't have the luxury of air conditioning, thus making the sweltering days stretch into sweltering nights where the escape of sleep was, at least for me, more or less impossible. The temp that morning as we stood outside Glasgow airport waiting for a taxi was 8 degrees. I shivered beneath my heavy cotton shawl which had lain neglected at the bottom of my rucksack for the whole week. But my heart was happy. My Celtic soul could breathe again and the cold air felt like a long long drink that reached to the tips of my dehydrated being.

Dumping our luggage in the hall at home some twenty minutes later, I stripped off my sweat-encrusted clothes, dived into an embalming hot bath, wrapped myself in cosy pyjamas with an extra T shirt on top, put a hot water bottle in bed, climbed in, pulled up the thick duvet around me and had the best sleep of my life. Home. It's good to know where you belong.

In Greece we had made friends with a young black Lab who spent his days sleeping on his tiled ground floor balcony, just about managing to thump his tail when we heaved ourselves by. I felt so sorry for him. Black Labradors don't belong in hot hot lands. They need cool air to jump and run and play. He did get a sea swim each evening, though, which kept him from going insane. But I didn't show him any photos of Scotland, no point in upsetting the lad. What you've never had, you don't miss.

But today was lovely. 23 degrees is just fine in my book. And the weather folk had told us it was for one day and one day only, so I was ready to enjoy it. I stroll down to our Fairtrade shop in my sleeveless tunic, cotton trousers and straw hat. How nice to feel the sun on my skin. The morning passes pleasantly. The shop isn't busy but the few customers we have are cheerful and light-hearted. Everyone comments on the warmth of the day.

In the afternoon I go out to the garden with the book group book – Aminatta Forna's engaging account of life in post-civil-war Sierra Leone, which while not exactly a 'popular summer read' is nonetheless guaranteed to take the mind travelling. This afternoon I find though that my mind is unwilling to engage with the legacy of brokenness in a far distant place. Right at the moment it is in a more somnambulant manner; much more in accord with a Wodehousian moment of guiltless ease. So I leave the Forna book unopened and sit in the shade meditating on other languid summer afternoons spent in this garden. Afternoons, when I would guiltily abandon whatever piece of academic writing, research or teaching prep I should have been concentrating on, pack a cotton bag with a small flask of tea, biscuits, bottle of water, mobile phone, sunglasses, reading glasses, sun cream, tissues, sun hat and cushion, call Jack and Joe from their baskets and trot off down to the garden. Once in the garden, I would flump in a deckchair while the dogs scattered to their favourite places. Jack would burrow under a hedge, where it was dark and cool and snooze there until called, whereas Joe liked the sun and would often lie fully stretched in it. We didn't know then he had a heart murmur and so probably rejoiced in the embalming heat. The other place both dogs favoured was under the washing loaded whirly gig, especially if there was a slight breeze as it gently fanned them as it spun slowly round. As I sit in my contemplative space this afternoon I can see their black shapes and am not completely sure if they exist solely in my imagination.

My gaze wanders up towards the house where Jen and Sal are, blinds pulled down so that Sal won't fixate on dust particles. Are they happy in there? Would they prefer to be out here? And how can we tell?

After an hour I go in to begin packing for my weekend away. A friend calls round to ask if I would write up a press release for him. We sip tea in the kitchen. He is amused by my 'Calm and Aloof' sign. We chat for a while then he goes. I suddenly only have two hours to pack, make dinner and shower. I have to get my skates on. The dogs watch me as I skid about the house. By 7pm I am ready, bags packed, dinner cooked and eaten. Can't quite believe that the weather really will change tomorrow. Hesitate about taking more than one light fleece. Is it really going to plummet to 12 degrees tomorrow?

Frances, my running buddy for the past ten years, picks me up. Irene is already in the car. The boot of Frances' car is half full already. We are off for a running weekend. Well, a weekend where we will do some running. So along with our jim-jams, ordinary clothes, walking shoes, rain jackets and food we need running gear and sleeping bags. We drive off to collect two more women. Fully loaded we finally turn towards the north and head up to Dunkeld. Beautiful evening. So good to be going away, yet aware that I will miss Colum. The Sally project has been top of our shared agenda for a month now and we are slowly beginning to see the light – I think – but it is good to work through it together.

Arrive Dunkeld. The sun has gone but the light is still with us. We swiftly unpack. Five women in a caravan. No men, no kids, no dogs. Every job to be done is simple and easily decided. It is a bit chilly but we sit out on the deck sipping tea and wine and munching biscuits and crisps. We sit until almost midnight. Frances gets her sleeping bag and curls up in it in her deck chair. I put on my second fleece, thanking my previous self that I had packed it. I feel relaxed. Note I have left my watch behind. I will just have to go with other people's timing. How nice.

Day the Thirty-Third

Wake up, to hear Frances, in the next room, say "Thought we were running at 8.30?"

I look across at Irene who is in the other single bed in my room. "Ooops," I say.

We unzip our sleeping bags and stumble out. Frances is in the living area all dressed for running. Of late she hasn't been exactly enthusiastic about the sport – maybe something to do with turning 60 and realising there are easier pursuits to be had – so we tease her about it being ironical that it is she who is getting us all up. Being women, though, we have our priorities, and insist on a cup of tea before we do anything.

Half an hour later we are out in the morning air, and make our way down through the caravan site to the banks of the Tay. It's truly lovely out here. The wide river ripples next to us as we run along the woodland track. The ground is soft underfoot and my joints are grateful. Margo and I pull ahead of the others and run up to the hermitage.

"I always think of *Lord of the Rings* when I come along here," says Margo. I say I think of Walter Scott and Dougie MacLean.

We run for an hour. We meet people with dogs. Margo is unsure of dogs off-lead and relates stories of owners taking umbrage at her taking umbrage at their dogs. I talk about why dogs are off-lead and how it should be a good sign if the owners are really in charge.

Tell her some of the rudiments of Amichien. Margo reads dogs totally different from the way I do. But then I have dogs. That automatically makes you interested and involved. And the fear Margo has, of a mad dog tearing her from her bike while sinking its chops into her leg, is a fear and experience I don't have.

After a big breakfast of muesli and toast and homemade jam, we saunter off back down the woodland track and into the cute town of Dunkeld. I already need more tea. Margo is up for a long walk. She's a supersonic kind of woman. My soul yearns for tea. I say to the others I am happy to meet up with them later. I am fixating on a vision of a big pot of tea in company with a weekend paper. Margo says I would be better off with a bottle of water.

Rosemary comes to my rescue and says "She just wants some tea. Let her have some."

Bless her Campbeltown socks. They make women generous in that part of the country. Frances and Irene say they could be tempted for tea too. Margo gives in and comes with us. Must be hard hanging out with sluggards.

We find a bijou café with a sheltered courtyard and order Suki tea, sultana scones and jam. Yum. My appetite is in full throttle. We pass a more than pleasant hour in the café then, fortified with sugar and caffeine, go on Margo's desired walk along by cathedral and up to the posh hotel. It is lovely but all the tea is making its presence known on my bladder. Margo and I go in to use the loos. I feel a right scruff and expect to be challenged. No one does. Wedding guests start arriving. I feel even more of a scruff. I remind myself of the letters after my name but still feel a scruff.

We walk back into Dunkeld and head for another coffee shop. Well, why not? I sip peppermint tea and dairy-free tiffin in an attempt to be semi-healthy. The others tuck into lattes and carrot cake. We make a shopping list for our evening meal. The local deli is delightful but expensive, so we opt to buy ham and cheese only in there. The sound Co-op supplies us with all the rest. Laden down with bags we finally return to the caravan. Footsore but happy.

Sit on the deck, munching crisps and drinking our favourite tipples. Exercise under our belts, we are ready to chill. A dog starts to bark in the next caravan.

"What does that mean, Anne?" asks one of the women.

"He/she can hear us and is a bit worried. We're too near their den." I reply.

"People shouldn't leave dogs in caravans," says someone.

I say it's fine, but silently hope that the owners are not going to make a long night of it. I feel sorry for the dog.

We move inside, as it is getting beyond chilly. We eat our shared repast. Scrumptious. Drink some more wine but, as we will run again tomorrow morning, I stop after a glass and start on the herb tea. Wild woman. Someone wants to watch *Casualty*. My heart sinks. I hate such programmes. Having lived the reality of being carted into A&E too many times for my liking with such joys as pancreatitis, a ruptured ectopic pregnancy and severe anaemia, I have no need to see a fictionalised account of it. But it sounds churlish to protest. We watch a horrendous episode – rape, trauma, death, crisis. I knit as it is on and try to block it out, but am left feeling edgy. Take myself off for a walk. Not sure if the others pick up that I didn't enjoy the programme. Phone Colum. Tell him how I feel. Return to caravan. Women are playing charades. Telly is off. Sound of laughter as I come in. It's all ok. As we settle down for the second night sleep, another dog in another caravan – a small dog by the sounds of it – begins to yap. I know I will lie and analyse what is going on. His owners are obviously having a late drink somewhere. I put in earplugs and fall asleep.

Day the Thirty-Fourth

Feels colder today. Put my running jacket on. Maybe just tired. Slept ok-ish. Caravan doors are not for the tentative hearted and need an assertive thump to open them – hence the person hoping to sneak to the toilet in the middle of the night wakes everyone up. I woke up four times and each time took a while to drop off again. But the plus side is that it's not raining and we are in a beautiful place. With smooth riverside and forest tracks at our disposal we would be fools to miss it.

Margo and I do a good hour's run. We meet more dogs. On yesterday's run I couldn't resist saying hallo to all the dogs. But today decide that this isn't in line with our new philosophy. So smile and make eye contact with the owner and thank them, for calming or holding their dogs or saying "lovely dog" to them, as we pass by. Dog owners often get abuse by frightened runners or cyclists. The frightened runners or cyclists, of course, think it is the other way round. But there's many a dog ended up in a rescue centre because an ill-informed human has misread their signals. By thanking the dog owners, I am really saying that dogs are compatible with runners. As we go along, I talk to Margo about what to do if a dog jumps at you when running. She is of the opinion that dogs shouldn't be off leads. I explain about dogs not wanting to fight – it's actually the last thing they will opt for as in the wild a fight could mean death. And nipping of heels is not biting. The language we choose to describe dog behaviour is crucial. The dog can't speak and defend itself and humans often escalate what a dog has actually done. And so the dog gets punished or sent away.

"You should write a book about this, Anne," says Margo.

"I am," I reply.

"Is there any romance in it?" asks Margo.

"Mmm, not really," I reply. Growing love between humans and dogs … would that fit the bill? I think she's thinking more of a handsome prince on a white charger kind of thing. White chargers are rather thin on the ground in my town. And I already have my handsome prince.

We pack up after a long breakfast out on the deck. Caravan emptied, cleaned, bags stored in the car within an hour. Five organised women. Easy-peasy.

Colum texts to say that he has had a breakthrough. Sally came to him after an off-lead session in the garden. He is ecstatic. I tell the women that Colum has trained the dog. This leads to a discussion about what our respective partners have done with themselves while we have been away. One husband has booked the family holiday. Two others have coped with daughters determined to do their own inadvisable things. Another has gone and played golf – but he did also supply our home-baked bread for the weekend, so we let him off. Overall we think the men have behaved rather well.

We drive down to Dunkeld again. I nip back into the deli to buy sausages for Sam. I have already bought Manchego cheese for Colum. There are sausages made from wild boar but they have wheat and milk in them so I opt instead for five slices of beef. I like watching the slicer. Reminds me of the Liptons in my childhood town. Previous to the advent of the supermarket, we would trundle down to the town with our trolley every few days and go and buy butter, cheese and meat from Liptons. The manager and his assistants wore white coats and were, in my eyes, highly skilled at cutting and measuring out wedges of cheese from huge circular wheels, at slicing into a huge butter block and patting out the amount we wanted with wooden paddles and, best of all, dumping a big rectangular block of meat onto a flat scale and rotating the slicer so that the meat fell out in neat slivers onto the waiting greased-proof paper. It's strange how nowadays that it is only the up-market delis which have reclaimed the sensory delights of the old grocery shops.

We stand about in the Dunkeld deli discussing what we will get to take back for our respective families. We eye up the enormous scones. I am tempted to buy one to munch in the car but decide to wait. The huge bowl of muesli and toast and marmalade I had only a short while ago really has no need of a top up. We assemble again. Presents bought. Make our way down country. We sing as we go. Songs from our past. 'Wee willie winkie', 'Aly baly', 'Skye boat song', 'Mairi's wedding', 'Three craws', 'Ye cannae shuv yer granny aff the bus' and 'Row row row your boat'. Who said the oral tradition was dead?

We stop after an hour to mooch around an enticing retail outlet place. There are lots of things I would like to buy, but the overdraft of last month pops up in my mind and I keep my purse in my pocket. One day, maybe one day when I write a blockbuster, then I will fill my basket with things I don't need but just like. We calculate the economies of a shared cream tea, decide it is a good idea, and sit at a white linen covered table while pots of Earl Grey and Green tea, two high cake stands filled with pancakes, wee pots of jam, ham and cheese sandwiches and cream scones are place in front of us. It's just as well we are runners. We eat to our hearts' content and wrap up the leftovers in paper napkins to take back to the menfolk.

After a long drive down country past wide open fields, leafy lanes and busier dual carriageways, we arrive home. After the lush forest greenery and silvery dance of the river that has accompanied us for the past 48 hours, our home town looks tired and forlorn. But our spirits have been aired out and our energies reset. We have no cause to moan. We don't. Well, only a bit.

Colum opens the front door and welcome me with a big hug.

"How're you?" I ask.

"Brilliant," he says. "Total breakthrough with Sal."

"Really?" I say. "Are you sure?" Colum is a born optimist. I tend to err on the other direction.

"Yip," he says "it's all happening."

I come in the house and up the stairs. The dogs rush up to me but I stick to our new guns and ignore them. There is a tangible atmosphere in the house. I sniff the air like one of the dogs.

"Happy calm," I say as if announcing the name of a new scent.

Colum makes tea. The dogs give up trying to get my attention and stretch out on the kitchen floor.

"They've been doing that all day," says Colum.

I call them to me. They come over quietly wagging their tails.

"Well, hello there! How're my girls?" I ask.

They jostle each other in the attempt to be the first to be petted. I squat down and ruffle their ears and chins.

126

"You know, I actually missed you," I say to Sally.

Colum watches me and smiles. "Ah, you're beginning to love her", he says.

That's taking it too far but I don't argue. I give Colum his present of cheese. We sit down at the kitchen table and I tell him all about my weekend and he tells me all about his. He is fair smug with himself that he had picked up on the fact that Sal was ready for a more advanced stage.

"I couldn't believe it," he says. "I had them both off lead, let them play a bit then called Jen over. She came. I gave her a reward and put on her lead. Called Sally. She ignored me. I walked through the gate with Jen and up to the house leaving Sally in the garden. I put Jen in the house and went back down to find Sal standing at the gate whining. I went through. She backed off. I called her. She came over. I gave her a reward and put on her lead. Incredible."

"Do you think it is a fluke?" I say.

"No. I did it another few times yesterday and she got quicker to come to the lead each time. I think we've cracked it. I really do."

What did I say about him being a born optimist?

We finish tea and Colum goes to pick up Sam at his work, taking Sal and Jen with him. My legs are reminding me that I have run twice in two days and done lots of walking. I pour myself a G&T, left over from our weekend, and turn on the telly. *101 Dalmatians* is on. I settle down to watch it. We are just at the bit where the puppies have been stolen – ooh, it's awful! – and my menfolk arrive home. I abandon the film, I don't like the bit where the baddies try to top the puppies anyway, and go back into the kitchen. I give Sam his present of slices of Perthshire beef and a bottle of organic cider. He gives me a big grin and tucks in. We eat salad and oatcakes and cheese and beef. Life is good.

Over dinner, the lads let me talk over each detail of my trip, then Colum asks me to come to the garden to see Sal doing her thing. I would rather go and see if the film is still on, but go anyway. Sal does her thing. Ok, so it is incredible just as he said.

"Julie said we must listen to our dogs, and they would tell us when they were ready. So I did. And *voila*!"

Back inside Sam gives me a lemon scented bath bomb from his shop. I plop it into the running water. Sink in. So good. Maybe I should go away more often. Things seem to move on apace.

Day the Thirty-Fifth

Wake to hear Colum taking dogs down to the garden. I should get up. Snooze for another fifteen minutes. My hubbie appears in our bedroom to get his work clothes on. I heave myself up. So lucky I don't have to go to a place of work today. I need a 'landing day' – to sort out washing, write up some notes, clean stuff and just chill a bit. There are huge compensations for the writing life. All the rest of the women I was with over the weekend will be up and probably out at their paid jobs by now.

Colum goes to work. We feed dogs just before he goes. Even this has changed. Colum decided he wasn't going to split up the dogs anymore. Feels that Sal isn't as frantic now when she eats as she was when she first came to us. We still go through the motions of gesture eating. That won't change.

Still in my jammies and dressing gown I do a bit of work at my laptop. Everyone thinks that writers are lazy slobs and write in their underwear so I may as well fulfill something near to expectations. After an hour or so I reluctantly change out of my jammies into semi-respectable outside gear and take the dogs to garden. Sam goes with me. I need to carry out a basket of washing too. No point in trying to be superwoman. Safely enclosed in the garden I let the dogs off lead. They jump off to leap on each other, play, pee and pooh. I watch them out of the corner of my eye as I peg out clothes. So far so good.

After ten minutes they slow down a little. I call Jen to me. She comes over. I reward her with a ginger nut – a soggy one I find in my pocket. That's another new rule that Colum remembered: Julie saying "don't bribe, but reward."

Sally looks over at us and seems to be saying "Oh, is that a ginger nut you've got there?"

I call her to me. She walks over and sits down in front of me. Incredible. She gets the remainder of the biscuit. I clip the lead on her. We three progress up the garden and back into the house. I am light-headed with the experience. The world as we knew it is opening up again.

Some hours later though the old Sally is back. It is 9.30pm and Colum and I take the dogs to the garden. Seconds into the walk down the path Sal rears up, hackles raised, woofing with all her might. Colum stops and waits. She continues her manic behaviour. Colum stoops down and holds her. She continues as she was. We struggle down to the garden where Sal dutifully pees. Stressed she may be but the routine is working in her brain somehow. A pooh though is out of the question. Jen does nothing and looks miserable. We head back up to the house feeling disappointed. Colum stops to reassure Sal again. I tell him that we shouldn't be doing that. We need to do the strong leader thingy.

"Well, what would you do?" asks Colum.

"Get back inside ASAP," I say as if wary of a possible mortar bomb attack. Colum will again be away this coming weekend and visions of shoulder-raising evening walks loom in my mind. 'Run for cover' will be my maxim.

Upstairs we discuss Sal. When do we not discuss Sal? Strangely enough two people during the course of Colum's day had suggested that Sal had perhaps been kept outside in her previous life. Thinking about it now that would make sense. She really does seem to be very scared about being outside in the evening. We wonder if she was used as a guard dog. Or was she perhaps kept in an outside shed somewhere? She would certainly be good at it but the poor lass must have been on edge the whole time. But would it really help if we knew? Julie said that dogs live in their immediate world. They don't hark back to their past all the time. Maybe not, but their behaviour seems deeply tangled up with it. I go to bed wondering what scenarios she lived through and wish I could have been there to prevent them.

Day the Thirty-Sixth

Sal is quiet this morning. The evening terrors appear to have fled from her spine and she plays happily with Jen in the hall. I suspect that Jen really wants to be left alone in peace. I call Sally to me. She comes. I ruffle her neck. She bounds back to annoy Jen again. Colum gets up from the breakfast table and excludes her for ten seconds. We are getting so used to truncated sentences just as we did when Sam was a wee tot. Good technique for life though – i.e. if you don't like what someone is doing then close a door, mental or physical, on them.

Colum goes off to work and I get the hoover out. It is Sam's job to hoover twice a week. We started this regime when he wanted to earn more pocket money. As a youngster, though, he didn't always get the timing right, often bursting through a door to begin some energetic corner-avoiding hoovering, even though a surprised and startled visitor was sitting having a cup of tea with us.

"Don't mind my maid," I would quip. "He's just a little enthusiastic."

Tuesdays and Saturdays are the contractual hoovering days but the presence of dogs in the house often means an extra session or two as well. Especially if Sam's life has been too pressured to factor in hoovering. You know the kind of thing – an important basketball league to watch studiously on the internet, or Facebook pals to chat to, and other major stresses. And his extended hours at his shop job do not possibly allow for the normal household chore quota. Despite it being a Tuesday which has followed a Saturday, our floors are showing that nary a hoover has been passed over their surfaces for a number of days.

While my laptop is warming up I get out the hoover. Sally watches warily from her basket. I open the door leading down to the front door. She will need an escape route. I plug in the hoover and switch it on. Sal leaps out from her basket, skids on the floor in her haste to get away from the terrible terrible machine, and belts downstairs. Jen looks up from her quiet doze wondering what the fuss is about, spies the open top door, thinks "Ah ha, that will get me nearer the outside world," and follows Sally, albeit in a slow leisured manner.

Our Jack would have empathised with Sal's fear. He thought the hoover an abomination on all living things. Before switching it on we had to make sure there was an open door for him somewhere nearby. His favourite safe place was, like Sal, at the bottom of the lower staircase just inside the front door or preferably the other side of it. Jack was a brave lad in lots of situations but the hoover defeated him. He would cower and run for it.

Joe on the other hand didn't mind the hoover and in fact really appreciated a freshly hoovered rug to lounge on. But, as a young dog, bring the kitchen brush out and Joe acted as if hell was truly upon us. One sweep of the brush would find him curled around the end of it, clinging with all his wee might in his furious attempt to fell this strange beast. My upper arm muscles became quite strong with the extra added weight. And don't get him started on what he thought of red post boxes, the poop scoop or dark clothed men wearing hats. Had Joe ruled the world such cataclysmic evils would have met a swift end. I suppose the answer to it all should have been our assertive claim to leadership. But then I wouldn't be able to go to the part of my mind that is marked "Memories of Joe" and find myself smiling.

After dinner, Colum and I do our 'homework.' Julie, who had lent us a demonstration DVD of Jan Fennell demonstrating her method, now needs it back for another consultation. We have only watched half of it so far, and settle down to see if we can glean any more help from the remaining material. And we do indeed glean to the extent that I feel tears just behind my eyes as I watch. In the section on 'Problems' there is a case study of a dog who fixates on light. Colum and I look at each other with wide eyes then rivet them back to the telly. Jan diagnoses this behaviour as a dog being highly stressed – and not a matter of simple boredom as the SSPCA had suggested. Her method was to go up to the dog who is staring and pawing at the particles of torch light on a living room wall and gently but firmly lead her away, ask her to sit and then give her a biscuit. She explains that a new association is needed so to break the dog's manic behaviour:

"The dog doesn't know why she is doing this. She doesn't really want to do this. You have to get her to think for herself. She will soon ask herself why she is doing this and then stop it." Or words to that effect.

I think back to this afternoon when Sal, Jen and I were in the back garden. It was a sunny hour and the dogs were off-lead. I had plumped down into a deck chair while I waited for the dogs to do their pees and poohs and play if they wished. Sal headed for the concrete slabs underneath the basketball hoop and began her strange little prancing dance while staring and staring into the sunlight. I ignored her for a while thinking that at least Jen was getting some peace then called her over. Sal came two or three steps towards me then the addiction to the shafts of sun pulled her back and she returned to her fixated state. I left her and after another ten minutes walked to the garden gate. I called Jen who came, was given a biscuit and clipped on her lead. I called Sal she came, almost sat down, thought better of it and began to walk back to the basketball hoop. I called her again, thinking that, if she didn't come this time, I would leave her in the garden. Amazingly, she came over, sat down, let me put on her lead and was given a bit of ginger nut. I wondered if the dust particle filled sunlight was fading in attraction for her.

But back in the kitchen some five minutes later here she was staring and staring into the patterns the sun was making through the window. It was just too nice to pull down the blind and block out the sun so I led Sally out to the darkened hallway and shut the kitchen door. She ran up to the tiny landing outside the door leading to the bedrooms and started her wee prancing dance in the patch of sunlight there. I walked up and drew the blind. We could put up with semi-darkness in the hall below. Sal came back to herself and trotted downstairs, got in her basket and closed her eyes. I had simply removed the tantalising light from her eyes, but even while doing so was conscious that I wouldn't be able to do this everywhere we went with her. Therefore to watch our dog guru at work with a dog demonstrating the same behaviour was a total tonic. Question is…will it work with Sal?

Day the Thirty-Seventh

On my personal agenda today is the basket which holds all our incoming mail. I try to keep tabs on this and clear it out every so often but it has now reached over-flowing stage and along with the usual pile of annoying junk mail there may be some important 'deal with me now' stuff.

I come across Sally's rehoming package that we were given by the SSPCA. The month of free insurance has run its course and ended a few days ago. Sal is now not insured. I will need to do something about this today. There are many many owners who think dog insurance a complete scam and a waste of good money, but I am not one of them. One day after the insurance package we took out for our Jack came into effect, he was in the vet's under a general anaesthetic while they removed a piece of stick which had lodged itself in his jaw. Had we not had insurance this would have cost us rather a lot of cash. Cash we didn't have. Following this Joe then had to have treatment for a recurring lameness. Jack then had to have surgery due to polyploid cystitis. And, in his final exit, had to have emergency vet consultation at our local surgery, removal to the veterinary hospital in Glasgow, consultation, exploratory surgery, a CT scan and be put to sleep. That bill would have come to something around £1,500.

Sitting in the consultation room with the senior vet on duty when we first arrived with our seriously-injured dog at the veterinary hospital, I noted she sighed in relief when I said that Jack was insured. Just along the corridor were people queuing up with the sick animals and waiting to be attended to by the PDSA charity. The treatment their animals would get would be kind but it would be basic. There would be little choice and there was a long queue.

As our dog was wheeled past them on a trolley I knew I was one of the rich whose money would pay for the best care that the animal hospital could give. But we were all animal lovers and when, some hours later, Jack's now still body was gently carried out of the room where we had said our final goodbye to him, the people in the corridor waiting for the PDSA vet all fell silent and waves of pure compassion surrounded me.

Seeing my streaming face a woman said "Och hen, it's no easy is it?"

One of the privileged owners of an insured dog I may have been, but at that moment the generous soul of this poor wee Glasgow woman recognised me as just a woman whose heart was breaking.

It occurs to me too that in the action of setting up a monthly payment for insurance for Sally I am declaring that she is staying – at least for now. It's day 37. I haven't returned her to the SSPCA despite getting very near to it. As I write this she is stretched out on the floor next to my desk. A moment ago she jumped up at the window and growled. In accordance with the Amichien method I stopped typing, got up from my desk, went over to the window, looked out, turned back to Sally, made eye contact with her, said "Thank you Sally," patted her head and returned to my desk. Sally, her job of alerting me to the threat upon the den by that cheeky pigeon now accomplished, drops down to the floor, lies on her side and sighs. I am slowly learning what works.

Day the Thirty-Eighth

Colum goes off to England this evening to spend some days with his mum. My spirit quails a little. I don't want to sink into that pathetic 'woe is me' state while he is gone, yet already note that I am feeling down. As food supplies are running rather low, I take myself and my shopping trolley off to the local supermarket. Noticed as I walk that I feel lonely. I spend quite a bit of my life discouraging people from calling or phoning me during my writing day and deliberately try not to sign up for mid-week activities. Normally a morning walk with a dog suffices to get me out and, when the walk includes a blether with another dog owner, I feel as if I have touched base with humanity. As we are not participating in communal dog walks at present that routine has changed. I now trot the dogs to the garden mid-morning and get down to work much earlier. That's all good, and the words are flowing. But today after I have whipped round the aisles and ticked off the required items on my list, I make my way to the café. I have the need to at least watch other people, to feel the buzz of them around me. There's a highly successful writer who has made her name in giving advice on how to activate the impulse of writing. One of the methods she advocates is that the writer should regularly expose their senses to some stimulating experience. Being a ranch-owning American I am sure she has something a tad more exotic in mind than a plastic-flowered supermarket café, but, in the absence of a ranch-owning income, it will have to suffice.

As I sipped my Earl Grey tea I notice an elderly man sitting a few tables away. The style of his dress is the same as my dad used to wear – a shirt and correctly knotted tie under a V necked sweater, neat silver-grey trousers, polished brown lace-up shoes, waxed jacket and flat eight-piece cap. It occurs to me that had I had the choice of who I would like to have sitting opposite me sharing tea and conversation it would be my old dad.

Dad liked supermarket cafés. He liked the cleanliness, he liked the buzz, he liked the food. Dad was a boxer in his much younger days and retained his interest in physical fitness for the whole of his life. His later passion for hillwalking and running meant that little spare fat accumulated on his body and his delight in doughnuts and sweet things were soon sweated off. I also have a sweet tooth. Along with my Earl Grey tea, I am munching a chocolate macaroon (but as it is wheat-free so maybe I still get some healthy eating points). I think of how it would be so nice if he could just materialise, sit down opposite me and ask "How're you then, hen?" I would tell him of the progress Sally was making and he would listen and be amused by our efforts to integrate her into our ways.

As an adult I have never lived in the same town as my parents; things just didn't work out like that. Being without family support in my current town I have worked hard to make friends and good friends I do have. But there are times when it would be good just to have a cuppa with your folks. Just that. A cuppa. No big arrangements to stay over. No collective family meals or occasions. Just a blether and a casual cuppa. As Dad died a few years ago there is zero chance of this happening, and, as I trudge home pulling my very heavy trolley, I think of how he would have taken it from me and lugged it up the hill.

By the time I reach home my heart is sad. I go in and carry some of the food upstairs – the laden trolley is far too heavy for me to haul up the stairs. I open the top door which leads into the hall. The black circular rug is covered in pieces of material. The lamp, which normally sits on the low chest of drawers which doubles as a telephone table, has been knocked over and its shade is in tatters. Jen eyes me cautiously. Sal is snoozing in her basket and hardly raises her head to look at me. I begin to say something like "Oh, for pity sake!" then stop myself on the first syllable, walk to the kitchen door, unsneck it and silently unload the food onto the table. Jen trots in. I ignore her and continue to ignore her as I go down and up the stairs some four or five more times, unloading the trolley and stashing the food away. Sally comes into the kitchen and stretches out on her side on the floor. She seems completely chilled and in text book relaxation mode. Jen meanwhile is still sitting upright watching me. I know that she knows that I am not pleased with either her or Sally. But not a word nor bit of eye contact escapes me. I'll show these two minxes who has the strongest female will around here.

During the afternoon I muse on how it is Jenna who is putting up the greatest fight against our adoption of the new method. Before seeing her behaviour through the eyes of Amichien I thought of Jen as an easy-going kind of dog. Easy to walk, in that she never incited a fight, but could take care of herself if another dog came too close; easy to have in the house in that she never chewed anything; easy to have around people in that she charmed them. Yes, we had her down as a good girl – until she chased sheep or foxes that is. So our recent decision to take control back into our hands is major for her. She's been on duty defending, guarding and looking after us since she first came to live with us over a year ago. Habit dies hard and my lampshade is evidence to this.

Later that day I show Colum the remnant of the shade. It really is quite a work of art. I say I think she was aiming for the 'distressed' look. Maybe I could sell it on eBay. Colum picks up the dangling wire.

"Streuth, she was lucky," he says. "She's had a go at the wiring too. One more bite and she would have hit the live wire."

My eyes sweep around the hall. "Think puppy. Think toddler," I say.

"Mmm," replies Colum. "Puts a whole new light on things."

"No, just a new lampshade," I quip.

A short half hour later Colum and I walk over the track to the train station. Feels like total *déjà vu*. Him with a backpack on looking forward to a journey. Me in my daily slops wondering how I will get through the next few days. I feel miserable and left behind. But that's just how it is. He needs to see his mum. I know that. I do. But I wish he wasn't going.

Day the Thirty-Ninth

Wake at 6.30am with Sal barking. The neighbours downstairs must be getting really pissed off with this. I lie in bed hoping Sal will settle down. She doesn't. I need to do something. I pull on my dressing gown and stagger downstairs.

Sam is already up. The new store opens today. He did a 13 hour shift yesterday and says the time between getting home yesterday evening and getting up this morning was far too short. He needs to be in the store by 8am today. I take pity on him and say I will take him in the car. Sam passed his driving test some months ago but can't drive our car as the insurance for young male drivers – even for their parents' twelve-year-old Berlingo – is completely and utterly ludicrous. Since the day he passed his test he hasn't driven on any proper roads. Stupid situation. Really is. But at 6.45 in the morning there is no point analysing it.

In return for me ironing his shirt, Sam takes Sal and Jen out to the garden. They return some eight minutes later. I suspect he hasn't given the girls long enough. He says he hasn't the time.

I think of Julie saying "When you allow an hour it will take fifteen minutes. When you allow fifteen minutes it will take an hour," and try and explain this to Sam. He isn't listening. The fortunes of the chainstore empire, to which he is a slave, prevail in his tired mind. I let it go.

At 7.30am we are in the car heading off to pick up another shop worker and friend of Sam's. The dogs are in the boot. Inspired by Colum's practice of taking them in the car with him wherever he went last weekend, I think they may enjoy a jolly in the car. Sal seems a bit excited. I hope she's not going to jump about. I don't drive enough at the moment to feel totally relaxed and need to concentrate on what I am doing. We pick up Lucia. Sal is delighted someone else has got in. She pokes her nose through the netting separating the boot from the back seat. We ask Lucia to ignore her. Lucia giggles.

"It's a bit difficult," she says. "She's licking my make-up off."

Encouraged by Lucia's giggles, Sal decides to see if she can see more of this fun passenger and sticks her full head, shoulders and front legs through the gap she has created. I see her in the rear view mirror.

"God sake!" I mutter.

I pull over and stop the car. Sam gets out, wrenches open the back door, hauls Sally out and off Lucia's shaking shoulders. I remember I had locked the boot so have to get out too. We shove Sal back into the boot and set off again.

"Who's idea was it to bring her?" I ask.

"Yours," says Sam.

Home again I put the kettle on and get the dog food out. Jen is already in the kitchen looking interested. Sal comes in. Sees the food. Sees Jenna. Sal emits a low growl, raising her hackles and doing that low shoulder thing in Jen's direction.

"That's enough," I say, then remember I shouldn't speak.

Sal growls again. Jen looks scared. I go to take hold of Sal's collar just as she lunges for Jenna. Snarls, teeth-baring and a lot of struggle happens. It's a bit frightening but I manage to retain hold of Sal's collar and bung her out in the hall and sneck the door. She batters at the door. I ignore it and continue to put out the kibble. I put Jen's bowl down for her and unsneck the door. Sal comes in like a bat out of hell. I wave her blue tray at her and in a frisbee-skimming movement manage to get it to the ground before she pounces on it. It's only 9am and I've already had enough.

The day proceeds. I leave the dogs for three hours while I go back to the shopping mall for the grand opening of the new store. It's fun and I have a happy time. My friend Joyce drives me there. I had hoped to be sitting outside waiting for her when she drove up but didn't manage it. She rang the bell and the dogs went ballistic. I ran down to the front door and mouthed to her that I will be out in two ticks. She grins but looks askance at the dogs throwing themselves at the door. I get hold of their collars and take them back upstairs.

Check there is nothing in the hall of chewable value, shut the top door on them, batter back downstairs and outside. Joyce is outside cool, calm and collected.

"Phew!" I say "Every exit is a whole logistic."

When I get back all is quiet. The carpet is not chewed nor are there any teeth marks on anything. Good. Good. The sun is shining. It has turned out a lovely day. I think I should do some writing. I had told Joyce that was what I was going home to do. It sounded virtuous. But it's sunny. My 6.30am rise is telling on me. Maybe a wee sit in the garden while the dogs gamble and frolic around me would be in order. That would be pleasant, would it not?

We go to the garden. The sun is dancing on the slabs under the basketball hoop. The dust particle switch goes 'C...lunk!' in Sal's head. She does her wee dance and all intelligent response flees from her brain. The sun goes in. Sal returns to the earth. She sees Jen who is curled up at my feet quietly enjoying the air. Sal comes over and growls at her. It's a kind of rough invite to play. Jen can't be bothered. I don't blame her. Sal persists. Jen gets annoyed and runs at Sal. She is delighted and they have a mad tussle followed by a crazed kind of figure-of-eight run round the back of a lime tree, through to the big fir tree, out onto the scrubby grass, round the whirly gig, straight past my chair and back to the lime tree again. Jen has enough and comes back over to me. Sal is fed up and takes her frustration out on the ground underneath the whirly gig. She starts to dig furiously. I get up. Go to her and stand over the emerging hole. She growls. I say "Now now," then remember the no speaking thing and look up at the sky. Sal moves to another bit of scrub grass and starts digging there. I get her lead and try to clip her on. She darts away. Peaceful this is not. My mobile buzzes. It's Colum texting to see if I want to phone him. He must be relation-free for five mins or so. It might be good to chat about Sal and her stupid behaviour. I call him.

Unfortunately this is an instance of us not being on the same page. Colum and his mum have just had a jolly family story photo session. All fired up with it, he begins to tell me something about Aunty Someone-from-Somewhere and Cousin-Something-from-Somewhere-else when Sally starts digging again. The whirly gig is in danger of collapse from the network of tunnels at its foundations. Colum chunters on about Someone-who-went-Somewhere. My patience goes. I can't do in-law family history right now. I have a manic dog to deal with. I interrupt Colum's account of Someone-who-did-Something and say I need to ring off. He goes quiet. His audience isn't as appreciative of the history of Family Doings as he had assumed. I don't care. I say quite tartly that I'll speak to him later. I need some tea. The gamble and blissful playful frolic vision isn't happening. Retreat is best.

I go to the gate and call Jen. She comes. I call Sal. She ignores me. "Right, if that's the way you want it," I say and go off up to the house with Jen. It seems unfair though to curtail Jen's enjoyment of the air so after opening the front door, I clip Jen to the long hook-up we have attached to the stairwell. Pre-Sally days Jen spent lots of afternoons, once the postman had safely been and gone, snoozing on the front door mat or just outside. I thought she might enjoy it again. She settles down. I go back down to the garden for Sally. She is standing just inside the gate and lets me clip the lead on. I take her up to the front of the house, put her on another hook-up. The sun is falling on the doormat. Sal does her wee dance. I decide to ignore her and am just going up the stairs when the dogs fling themselves out of the front door, choke on the restricting tie-ups and start barking. I sigh, go outside, grab the dogs, notice a cat slinking up the stairs, haul the dogs in, shut the front door, unhook their leads and shoo them upstairs. Why is it that every small ordinary procedure is so bloody complicated? My mind shoots to a memory of Jack and Joe snoozing outside. Off lead. Happy. Content. Not a bother to anyone. Where did those times go?

My pal Irene calls by around 5pm. As I see her parking her car I manage to get down to the front door before she rings the bell. The sun is still shining so we opt to sit outside. Actually Irene doesn't opt but I decree it the easiest thing and she falls in line. I just can't be bothered dealing with the dogs right now. They know someone is here though. I can feel their restlessness upstairs. I get a tray of tea and bics from the kitchen and go back outside.

Jen isn't pleased at all that someone is here and she can't see who it is. I hear her trying to get through the top door. Irene and I chat for a while. She tells me of a stray cat that her daughters want her to feed and adopt. It's a black cat and apparently has a broken tail and something wrong with its eye. Her girls have started calling it 'Lucky' which Irene finds rather ironic.

"I said to the girls that I'm not prepared to take in a damaged animal when we already have a cat that only I look after."

I wish Irene had been with me when I saw Sally at the SSPCA. Maybe she would have talked sense to me too.

Sam gets home from his job. The opening went really well. His whole being eminates the highly scented products that his store sells. I wonder how long it will take for him to become immune to the strong smell. Turns out it's just as well someone brings in pleasant scents to the house. Just before dinner there is an ominous stench in sitting room. Sal has left us a steaming present.

We hire a DVD for the evening. The cover description bodes well — Johnny Depp, Angelina Jolie, set in Venice, has intrigue, classy clothes and escapist fun. It promises to please the likes of a mother and son. But we only get to watch an hour of it. Sal is a perfect pest. At one point she jumps on the armchair to woof at the world, the momentum of her jump pitches her forward and her front paws land on the windowsill with her hind legs on the armchair. She is spread-eagled there. Before I get to her she falls in a heap on the floor. Jumps up and goes to dive on the chair again. Sam goes to grab her. She darts away. I try to get hold of her. She darts away. I think she may be fearful of us trying to get her. I say I will do it. She is too fast for me. Sam does it and hauls her out in the hall. I am still trying to be perfect. I give it 10 secs and she gets back in. She heads straight for the armchair again. She is back in the hall within 10 seconds and gets left there. It's now 10pm. The light is fading. The dogs need the final dump walk. We sigh and pause the film. Take dogs out.

They're quiet. We're tired. We get back in. Sam has another early shift tomorrow and no doubt so do I. I get to bed around 10.45. Colum has texted twice in the evening to say what a good time he is having. I have ignored them. He doesn't need a list of events from here.

He texts again at 11pm. He may be worrying at my silence. I call him. I moan. He listens and tries to reassure me. It doesn't work. I have visions of me returning Sal to the Rescue Centre before Colum gets home.

Day the Fortieth

6.45am and Sal is woofing. I think about going downstairs. But I am therefore responding to her instructions? I decide to wait a bit. 7pm she stops. Sam will be muttering nasty nothings into his duvet. He was hoping for a lie-in until 8am. My phone buzzes. It is Colum. Sleep, although not that long, has reset my strained nerves. I call Colum back and apologise for my defeated attitude of the night before. I say I am going to do small things today. Not try to split the atom. That can wait till I have more support.

The sun is up and today is Saturday. I have arranged a half hour run with Irene. My iron levels are not quite ready for the bigger run I sometimes do and the warm morning dictates a less rigorous route anyway. I pull on my running gear thinking of the advice of some running guide or other that says it is a good idea to get your running stuff on early in the morning as it psychologically puts you in mind for following through your plan of exercise. Truth is, if Irene wasn't coming I'm sure I would be psychologically up for a slob around the house in my dressing gown. But she is coming and the dogs need out. I manage to sort them out and clean the bathroom by 9am. Today my soul feels calm. I wonder what the difference is from yesterday. The Saturday effect?

The run is good and when Irene has gone I feed the dogs. Mindful of yesterday's chaos I keep the dogs in the hall as I prepare the food then let them in and gesture eat. Sal tries to get up on the table but after the first push off she sits and watches, whining slightly, but still sits. I put Jen's bowl down and pick up Sal's. She head butts it and the kibble bounces up and off the tray. In my post-run endorphin-filled state I just shrug my shoulders, say nothing and walk out of the kitchen, leaving Sal to scamper round the room searching for the pieces of food. Today, I don't care. Today, I am ice-cool. Today, I will walk in serenity. When I next look in the kitchen, Sal and Jen are both trying to get their paws under the upright fridge freezer where a bit of biscuit has apparently lodged itself. Oh well, they're happy. I go off to enjoy a bath-bombed bath. Life today is just fine.

The sun is still with us after I have bathed and eaten toast and jam and drunk a big glass of water. I put on shorts and stuff my pockets with house keys, phone, pooh bags and ginger nuts and take the girls to the garden. I deposit them there then go back to the house for the washing. When I get back to the garden they are both sitting mystified at the gate.

I can hear them thinking "What did we do wrong? She doesn't usually leave us here unless she is mad with us."

I go through the gate. The girls crash off through my precious bee-and-butterfly patch, felling foxgloves as they go. Sally stops to deposit a big pooh in my potato patch. Today, I don't care. Today, I am ice-cool. Today, I will walk in serenity.

I peg out the washing. My head is sore. I need tea with sugar. The warm run is impacting on me. I leave the girls.

"Again? What did we do this time?"

I get a big jug of water and a huge cup of tea and carry both to the garden. The dogs' water bowls are empty. As I pour the water into them Jen tries to lick from the spout of flowing water. I remember how last summer she loved it when we used the hose in the garden. She would dart and out of the spray squealing and jumping and highly happy. This summer we have no need of a hose. Nature is more than taking care of watering our gardens. I sit on the bench and sip my tea. The girls do their career thing around the garden. Today, I don't care. Today, I am ice-cool. Today, I will walk in serenity.

By the time we leave the garden the dogs' tongues are hanging out. Maybe Julie is right. They don't need the exercise of a 'proper' walk, they just do it themselves.

I leave them in the house for an hour to take stuff to the nearest charity shop. I had meant to do a further major clear-out of my clothes. I'm a keen charity-shopper and as a result have too many clothes. I try to follow a rule that when I buy an item, I donate an item. But at the moment my wardrobe shelves are heaped with piles of clothing waiting to be sifted. Maybe later.

I call into a newsagent to get a paper and meet the owner of a nearby *chocolaterie*. I pop into her shop after I get my paper, to catch up with her world. She tells me she is closing the shop. She says it is just too hard to carry on. She sounds both angry and sad. I think of how it was just over a year ago when I was on the point of leaving academia. I knew it was the right decision but the feeling of failure dominated any other more positive characteristic of my leaving. I was heading out into the dark, into the uncharted and it felt empty and scary. I look at the owner of the *chocolaterie* and see me. Me a long time and a mindset ago. Only a year has passed since I packed up my office and brought my crates of books home, but how far I have travelled. And how much better my life is now. I said some of this to the owner. But she's not ready to hear that kind of talk yet. But she will. She will. At my leaving lunch – organised by me, not by the department I had taught in for twelve years – a good friend gave me an envelope with pieces of jigsaw inside. I assembled these on the restaurant table. They said "The emerging picture takes a while to reveal itself. Enjoy finding the next piece."

We have to let go of what is stopping us from seizing on the next piece of life. Be it a *chocolaterie*, be it an academic lectureship, be it memories of how quiet our lives were before a rescue dog named Sally arrived.

Day the Forty-First

Sam takes the dogs to garden. Under pressure of time. Gets it all wrong. I watch him from the sitting room window and see him trying to tempt Sal with a stick so he can get her back on the lead. It doesn't work. He throws it down in disgust. I phone him. Say I will do it. He leaves Sal in garden. I go down a few mins later. She has dug a hole right beside the gate in an effort to get out. I take her up the path and put her straight in the car. A trip out might be good. We head off to drop Sam at work. Sal gets herself out of the boot and into the back seat.

"Leave her," I say to Sam. "She seems happy there. But wind up the windows. We don't need a re-enactment of that scene from *Marley and Me*.'

Driving home a half hour later, I reflect on dogs. Was in poor mood yesterday eve. Felt abandoned by Colum. Had done the garden trip some six or seven times. Last one was pathetic. Sal manic. Colum had phoned at 11pm just as I am in bed. We talked about Sal. It was the wrong time to do it. I was too tired. He had suggested I call Julie today. I had told him it is a two person job and no amount of phoning anyone will help. We had rung off, both aware there was no point talking further. But driving home today the sun is shining. The roads are a Sunday quiet. Sal happy looking out of the window. I think on how I have to get fully on board with this training thing. No point in following the woe-is-me route ...it gets nowhere.

We stop at a supermarket. I need sugar and fairy cake cases (yes, they are *fairy* cakes in this country, not cup cakes...we need to resist this global Americanisation of language ... rant ... rant ... rant). I leave dogs in the car. Come back. Look at grass verge which runs beside the river. Dare I?

I get the dogs out of the car. Jen is delighted. Freedom at last! I keep them on a tight lead. On the verge Jen does a long pee and a pooh immediately. Sal does a pee. I do a bit of 'Stop, Start, Change Direction' thing. I see people coming. Go back to car. Can't deal with interaction at the moment. The people pass by. We go back to the verge. The dogs are skittish. Too difficult. Retreat. Retreat. Go home.

I leave the dogs in car as I make up their breakfast in the kitchen, then keep them on lead as they come in to avoid hell and damnation breaking out. Get to kitchen. Gesture eat. Dogs watch. Sal jumps up twice. I push her down saying nothing. Give them their food. Walk out of the kitchen. When they finish I go back in, make myself tea and toast and sit down. There's an article in the paper, on literature set in English country houses, that I want to read. As I do so, I feel a wet nose in my hand which is dangling off the table. Sally saying hallo. I smile to myself but stop myself reacting any other way to her. Is this the first signs of her feeling affection for me? Or is she just curious about a scent from my hand?

Clean up kitchen. A pint of frozen goat's milk has split as it was defrosting and has run into the bowl containing it. I judge the mix of unwashed carton and milk unhygienic and pour the milk into the loo. Carry on with the kitchen chores. Hear slurping noises. Sal enjoying a smoothie of toilet water and goat's milk.

I reflect, as I work round the house, how you need time for dogs. I remember a friend saying of his five children that they behaved as well as he felt. Dogs are the same. When I am pressurised I don't find any of their antics remotely amusing. I read them as being tiresome and a pest. When I have time it all seems so much smoother, so much more obtainable, so much more doable.

This afternoon I am going to our family Taizé prayer meeting. The meeting today is local so no high winds over the Erskine Bridge to worry about. By the time 3 o'clock comes I have cleaned the milk- splattered loo, tidied the sitting and dining room, made a batch of fairy cakes – with sprinkles, had the dogs out in the garden twice, wrapped up a First Communion present for one of the wee girls in the group, written up some notes, showered and dressed myself in non-dog clothes. It all worked, as I set my sights low. Apart from driving Sam to his work this morning I remained at home and aimed towards getting out of the house in time for the meeting. As I drive out of the street I feel calm and in control.

Some six hours later, I return. I had no intention of being away so long but the company of good friends, good chat, good food, good ambiance was just far too tempting. I am a bad dog owner. I pull up in the parking bay, turn the engine off and listen. All quiet. I wonder what devastation may meet me. I come in the house, up the stairs and open the top door. Sally is lying in her basket. She wags her tail a bit but doesn't move. Jen rushes up to me wagging her tail much more enthusiastically. I ignore her and scan the hall. Nothing is chewed, bitten, gnawed. There are no trails of pee or steaming poohs. The dogs are pleased to see me but not frantic.

"Well done, girls," I say. "Well done!"

They leap up at me and I remember I shouldn't have spoken for another few minutes. Well, who's perfect?

I go upstairs and change my swishy skirt for my old jeans, pull on my wellies and rain jacket and head out to the back garden. Sam appears when I get back inside. I feed the dogs and we settle down to watch some telly. It is wet and miserable outside so I pull the thick curtains in the sitting room. Sal prowls around a bit then settles down at my feet. Jen is already curled up on the carpet. It is now almost 9pm. I look at the sleeping dogs, decide against a final walk. Why court disaster? Their bladders and bowels will just have to hold till morning. We turn in around 10.30pm. This was a good day.

Day the Forty-Second

A fox has been into the back garden and had some fun. A ripped pooh bag is lying in the middle of the slabs under the basketball area. Well, I hope he or she enjoyed what was in there. A small panel has been forced in the fence near the lime trees. Sal sticks her head through it. I have visions of her busting through it completely and pull her back. I look around for something to block it with. There are some slates lying nearby. I try to lever one into the gap. It keeps falling down. I find a bit of wood and prop that in. It stays put but one knock with an enthusiastic dog haunch and it will collapse. Colum gets home today. I put the broken panel on his 'To Do' list. Perhaps if I was a different kind of woman I would find some nails and wood and sort it myself. But I'm not that woman, so I don't. The bridegroom is still with me, so why stress?

Two hours later, I am on the train to Glasgow Central. Sam is at home and will do the mid-morning walk. I met him in the hall as he emerged from his room. Forty accumulated hours at his shop job over the last four days have taken their toll. He is bleary-eyed but his innate salesman instincts are awake enough to tell me what bath bomb he intends using and the life-enhancing benefits it offers. I leave him troughing a huge bowl of cereal while watching a basketball game on his computer.

It's lovely to be heading into Glasgow on the train. Trains are such thinking places. Well, our little train is. As it is now 11am, the daily work force has long done its crazed rush and the train is quiet. I feel good. I have on clean jeans, my favourite slate grey sculpted long sleeved tea shirt, my new shoes – trendy brown brogue trainer things I *did* buy for half-price – and my new jacket – a classic Italian design pin stripe which I found in a charity shop recently. I have money for my ticket, money for a cup of tea in the station and money for lunch with Colum. I have done my hair and it feels springy and feminine. I have the Arts section of a weekend paper to read, should I wish. Life is more than good.

I pull out my small hardback notebook-cum-diary – the appropriate Wildean quote fluttering through my mind — and flip through it. My eye falls on an extract I had jotted down from a book group choice – Mike Carter's *One Man and His Bike*. The main character, a chap who is cycling round the coast of Britain, is talking with a ferry man who spends his days taking people across an estuary. Initially, it drove him spare, until it dawned on him that crossing the Atlantic or a small estuary are really just the same thing. The ferryman says to our cyclist, who is experiencing a restless frame of mind, that he must enjoy it all, no matter what point in his journey he has reached, as true happiness is found in the acceptance of the here and now and not in the desire of future arrival.

I think about my own life. Do I accept where I am on the larger journey? These days I stay local and travel rarely. I spend solitary hours writing at home or in a library. I clean and sort a house. I deal with belligerent gas engineers, harassed electricity-meter-reading people, slash-and-burn tree slaughterers, worried postmen, time-consumed delivery men – all of whom tend to want to tell me how hard their jobs are. I interact with neighbours and their agendas. I run with friends. I meditate with friends. I eat, laugh and talk with friends. I help out in a fair-trade shop and second-hand bookshop. I facilitate a book group. I meet family folk every now and then. I love and care for my two men. And two dogs.

What I don't do is network at international conferences anymore or trek to the rare manuscript sections of far flung scholarly libraries. I don't discuss literary theories and traditions to university students anymore. I don't have my elbows in the academic journal circuit anymore. I don't do desperate competitive applications for funding anymore. I don't spend hours marking essays or unintelligible exam scripts, or chasing up out-of-print books for the forthcoming syllabus anymore. I don't participate in wine-soaked seminars or listen to academics trundle out their latest findings. I have retreated from all of that slightly bizarre and frantic gallimaufry.

But is my life now a small and irrelevant one? I think of Sally. The attempt to turn around the manic behaviour of a traumatised being, to encourage the buried beauty of her to come out from where it has been battened in, to help her lower her hackles and see birds and bees and foxes and pigeons and cats as all part of the unthreatening natural world, to nurture her into believing that she can be loved – is this an insignificant daily agenda? The question occupies my thoughts as the train jolts its merry way into Glasgow.

Later, over lunch in an enlightened café which offers wheat- and dairy-free options, Colum and I discuss how to manage our annual camping trip. Should we board Sally or take her with us?

Topped up with his mum's excellent food, refreshing long sleeps and the reflective quiet of an inter-city train journey, Colum says "I've decided to manifest a miracle".

I pitch in with my more earthbound suggestion that we need to do some intensive training with Sal. I ask if Colum can take off time from work to work with Sal? He likes the idea but his annual leave quota isn't up to it. I sigh and put the problem into my 'Deal with Later' mental box.

At home I show him the hole Sal has dug beside the gate.

"I can fix that," he says.

I show the broken fence panel.

"I can fix that too," he says.

Everything minimises. Good to have a helpmate. Think of women I know who do life on their own. Not elderly ones who have had the benefit of long marriages and few remaining responsibilities, but younger women still bringing up children, still coping with mortgages, rents, school agendas, busy households. Must be so enormous a task. But maybe they would be sensible enough not to try to rehome a crazy dog.

Feel flat. All very well discussing the way forward over lunch. Seems simple then. But the reality is that we still have a rescue dog that is spooked by the just about everything. Can we possibly take her camping? I wonder if we should just abandon the idea of having a holiday this year. The thought makes me feel even flatter. Colum detects my change in mood. I say it has been a long haul over the last few days. Was hoping he might bring me back some nice present. Not expensive. We can't do that. Just small and nice. He gives me a jar of chutney. It is nice. But.

He disappears. I go over to a neighbour's garden to water the plants in their conservatory. They are on holiday in Cornwall where, according to their postcard, it is apparently raining. The sight of their beautiful garden doesn't help. Go back home. Where is Colum? I phone him. He is down in the local supermarket. With the dogs.

"I thought we weren't at 'The Hunt' yet?"

"Sometimes you have to break the rules," he says.

"But I would have come with you. I felt like a walk and thought it was a no-go as usual."

I meet him on the road coming back. He is carrying a bouquet of white roses. For me. They are beautiful.

Day the Forty-Third

Write at home in the morning. Have to close the windows shutting out the sound of birdsong as it upsets Sally. It is mid June and our winter was long. I don't want to shut out summer. But needs must.

I do a stint in the fair-trade shop in the afternoon. A friend comes into the shop. She is just home from a cycling trip along the Danube. Molly is an energetic, caring woman of great integrity with a sharp wit and caustic tongue for those who exploit others. I like her grit. We share a cup of tea and blether about this and that. I am envious of her holiday. Apart from having no money to fund such an adventure, Colum and I now have a Sally who needs to be in our care if we are to follow through the Amichien method. We are effectively grounded.

I am envious of people who were not stupid enough to try to rehome a rescue dog.

I am envious of people who have a rescue dog but who is at least attractive to look at.

I am envious of people without dogs.

I am just an envious woman.

In the garden, later in the day, I watch Sally as she does her dust particle thing. Her whole being looks as if an electric current is flowing through it. Her face takes on a 'Gone to Lunch' look. I sit on the bench and wonder why we have her. Would I feel this if she was a cuddly chubby black Lab? A floppy-eared, glossy-coated Spaniel? I find myself wondering how long she will live. Collies are expected to have a life span of anything around twelve to sixteen years. As I watch her do her daft prance this seems a long, long, time. I think of parents whose child is challenging them in some serious way. Do they have days when they find it hard to love their child? Those parents would think me way beyond the ludicrous should they read this. To compare a child with a dog? But my mind persists. I am also one of those dog people who take pride in what their dog looks like. Is my love for dogs only then skin deep?

Words from the wise grandmother in Alistair Macleod's novel, *No Great Mischief*, who perceives that all of us need love if we are to flourish, circulate in my mind as I watch Sally. If we manage to reach in and massage her frenzied soul will a buried beauty emerge?

Colum comes home from work and joins me on the bench. I tell him my thoughts.

"But look at her," he says. "She's happy here."

"Do you still want to keep her?" I ask.

"Yes, I've committed to her," he says.

Day the Forty-Fourth

I go down to write at the university library in the morning. I have books to return to the local town library, which is also having a book sale, and there is a nice café just opposite which sells quality loose tea in ceramic pots. Small pleasures but delightful ones. As I cross the park I see a young Beagle skip out of a car and gamble up the hill. Jimmy, our neighbour's Weimaraner, stands at the top. The Beagle runs up to Jimmy who woofs in pleasure. Jimmy is a great mate of Jenna's. Has her place been usurped by this new dog? Has the local dog community reshaped itself since we have retreated from it?

In the library I return my books and potter amongst the rows of books for sale. For the humungous price of a pound, I purchase an Anne Tyler novel and another one about a woman who gives up on her dead-end life in England and goes to live in Paris. The second one is not high literature, but who cares. It will take my mind on holiday when I can't go in reality. And I like Anne Tyler's writing. I like the sound of her as a person. She said in interview that she writes four days a week and and uses the others for keeping up with necessary household chores. She sounds like the kind of woman who understands about the necessity of keeping the domestic and intellectual plates spinning as she writes with the doors and windows open to the sounds of the neighbourhood. No ivory tower for her. As a Pulitzer Prize winner the method appears to pay off. I wonder if she has dogs.

In the café, with a pot of exquisite green tea in front of me, I get out my phone. Two window cleaners are battering about and I think it a matter of seconds before they engage me in banter. I can't be bothered, so use the shield of my phone. Nan, our former dog walker, texted me a week ago and I didn't reply. My phone is a basic one, and texting demands patience, but this feels like a good moment to wrestle with it. I tell Nan that Sally has come into our lives and that it has all been a bit of challenge. Nan is a Cesar Millan devotee, so she will probably have reservations when she reads that we are following the Jan Fennell Amichien method. Doesn't matter. She's still a dog person. But I have visions of her dropping by and making a fuss of the dogs. Will be hard to ask her to ignore them. It will go against her principles. But as she now lives way up north any future visits will be very rare.

I think about how it is now difficult to ask anyone to walk our dogs. At least at the stage they are. Sal definitely couldn't be let off lead up the braes as yet and Jen could easily take off too. What we need is another Amichien follower. Julie, away over in the east, is a geographical world away. Maybe Colum could initiate the philosophy over here. He could be 'Colum of the West'. Has a ring to it, does it not? We might need to get a dry-ice machine though if he needs a photo for his webpage and maybe a voice-over from Annie Lennox.

Day the Forty-Fifth

Saturday. Glorious day of the week. Colum was supposed to be helping my brother with some major maintenance job, in return for Kenneth's help Sally-proofing our garden, and I wasn't looking forward to being in charge of the dogs for the fourth Saturday in a row (not that I'm counting), but the arrangement has been cancelled. This means our Saturday can take a different shape. It is a wet day and we opt to do something different like taking the train into Glasgow and going to see a film. *Potiche* is being screened at the Glasgow Film Theatre and I have had my eye on it. The film stars Catherine Deneuve – who plays a seventies housewife, Suzanne Pejoul, married to a factory-owning bourgeois and chauvinist man. The factory is mid-strife and strike as the workers campaign for better working conditions. It all gets too much for the retrenched owner and his health breaks down. Suzanne steps into the breach. Her husband sees her as purely a figurehead who will smile prettily and do nothing until he can return. Of course that isn't what happens; Suzanne discovers she is rather good at the business of running a factory. Her now-recovered husband returns; she refuses to hand over the reins. There are machinations. She loses her position of power. She decides to divorce her husband and become a politician. Which she does. The film is quirky, humorous and yet strangely thought-provoking.

Colum notices that I seem quiet after the film and suggests a cup of tea. We chat about the film as we walk to a café. I tell him that such films always make me assess where I am in life. What I am doing with my life. Am I living up to my potential? And all that kind of stuff.

The fact that I earn very very little these days bugs me. I feel guilty about it as if there is some tight-lipped authority watching over my every move and tut-tutting. On reflection, though, the film was placing paid work over unpaid, recognisable occupation over the unrecognised. Catherine Deneuve's character takes over the factory, not so much because she wants to run a factory, but because her family disregard who she is a person. She is a kind of non-being in their eyes who has a blank life. She sets out to change this and does change it. My family don't view me as a non-being but I question if what I do has validity.

And I question if by taking on a rescue dog that I have subconsciously put a block in the way of me taking up full-time paid employment. Colum says that he only wants me to be happy and it's really up to me how to achieve that. All this from a Saturday afternoon film.

When we get home Colum goes off, taking the dogs with him, to collect Sam from work. They've been in the house all afternoon and we think a car trip will amuse them. We have been invited to my cousin's house for dinner this evening. We're hoping Sam will leave work sharpish so we can get to Monica's on time. I remember we said we would take some ice-cream with us, so text Colum to ask him to pick up some. My mobile phone rings. It is Sam.

"Hi mum," he says. "We're in the supermarket car park. Sally got out the van and she's running around the place and won't come and there are cars and we can't get her back and it's horrible and I can't take this. I'm tired, I'm hungry and…and…oh…oh…brilliant…a guy has just grabbed her…oh thank God."

In my place of calm I say "Right. Ok. See you in a bit then." I close my phone with a sunken heart. What happened there? Did Colum over-reach himself and think Sal was chilled enough to do a walk with her? Are we now right back to Stage One?

The menfolk get home. Sam looks totally fed up. I know that look. It needs food and then talk. And in that order. I feed the dogs and then leave the guys to get themselves ready and go and wait in the van. I sit in the driver's seat judging that Colum may be a tad too stressed to do more driving. As we make our way to my cousin's house, I tentatively ask what happened.

"When I got back in the van after getting the ice-cream we smelt this ominous smell. I thought maybe Sal had done a dump in the car and quickly opened up the boot. She slipped past me as I was trying to get hold of her and started skipping round the car park. I called and called. I tried to keep calm but it was as if she had no notion of who I was. We tried retreating to the car and leaving her outside but it was too dangerous. I was at my wits' end when a youngish chap loading up the boot of his Audi called over "Having trouble mate?" I told him what had happened and that Sal was a rescue dog whom we hadn't had very long.

He then put down his shopping bags, hunkered down and said in a soft voice "C'mon sweetie," and Sal trotted right over to him. It was amazing. Really nice chap."

"Couldn't you have got a lead on him, too, and brought him home?" I ask. "Sounds like the sort of chap we need here," I say.

"Yeh, and he had a really nice car too," says Sam.

"Well, we could find a space for that too," I say.

Day the Forty-Sixth

It's Father's day. Sam has already gone to work but has left a card for his dad on the kitchen table. Colum takes the dogs to the garden while I set out breakfast, adding napkins, a lit candle, bowl of chocolate bits as well as the usual muesli and tea cups. Colum wants to spend a little bit of his Father's Day remembering his own dad and mine. Both of our dads died some years ago and both dads were almost daily communicants in their respective parishes, so it seems a small yet significant gesture for us to go to Mass and remember them. Neither Colum nor Sam nor I go to Mass regularly. Sam goes not at all since he left his Catholic secondary school and it matters not. Colum and I both go when the mood takes us. Established church structures don't serve our souls anymore but sometimes we dip into our local parish just to see what's happening, and enjoy a coffee and a blether with people in the hall afterwards.

As we walk over the park towards the church we talk about Sal. Our routine for years was for Colum to walk to the paper shop first thing on a Sunday and take whatever dog or dogs were with us. Very often on his way there or back he would meet another dog owner with their dog and the dogs would have a good run and play. This morning we meet Ella, with her dog Sylvie. We haven't seen Ella since Sal came to live with us.

"I heard you had got another dog," said Ella. "How's that going?"

"It's slow progress," I say, "but I have to keep reminding myself that she is a rescue dog and we're her last hope."

A wave of compassion sweeps over Ella's face. "The poor soul," she says. "She'll be needing a lot of love."

Time is pressing, so we say goodbye.

"The dog community really is amazing," comments Colum. "Word about us has got around even though we think we are out of the loop."

After Mass we loiter a little and chat with people we know. I notice that neither Colum nor myself mention the arrival of Sally in our lives since we last saw them. Feels like too big an effort. We get home, come up the stairs and find the underlay of the hall rug in bits. We collect up the bits without speaking. There doesn't seem much point.

A Sunday afternoon is designed for a walk. At least it is in our calendar. But the list of reasons why we aren't ready to do that circulate around our minds. After Sal's debacle yesterday it would seem stupid to try to force the pace of her training. I wish we had some enclosed space we could take her too. Enclosed space. Dog exercise area. Mmmm. Possibilities. I float my idea to Colum. He's up for it.

We get the girls into the car and drive up to a local park. This is a quiet park. There is no children's play area. No zoo corner. No café. Nothing really but open space and what I think I remember as a dog exercise area. Jen is ecstatic that we are out out. She pulls me on her lead. I debate about stopping her but think that she may be desperate for a dump. I'm right. In fact she does two dumps within a space of two minutes. Her bowel control is incredible. We explore the designated dog exercise area and discover it's not such a space. The gate doesn't shut properly and the fence is a bit too low for our high-legged Sal. Also it is really big and we can't see if it is fenced in over on the other side.

We keep Sal on the lead but let Jen off. I am a bit nervous about this. Jen *was* good off lead, but will she have changed in behaviour now that we are attempting to take the leadership role from her? She trots around quite happy. Happy not excited. We definitely can't let Sal off. We opt instead to do a bit of lead training.

The area is quiet. There are only ourselves here. Perfect opportunity. Both Colum and I do a bit of 'Stop. Start. Change Direction' each time Sal pulls ahead. We have forgotten to bring treats so have to use lots of praise instead. Jen has gone ahead so I go after her leaving Colum to work with Sal. I call Jen to me. She comes. I make a fuss of her then clip on her lead and start to do a bit of lead work with her. It works okayish. I'm not sure if I am doing it correctly but basically follow the rule that every time she goes ahead or pulls me, I take calm control. I wonder if the people in the flats overlooking the area can see us. Will we look like professional dog trainers or just a couple of nuts who can't make up their mind what direction they are going in.

After twenty minutes or so I rejoin Colum. Both of us think it went quite well. Maybe we are just so pleased to be in a park with dogs again. We take the girls back to the van. I nip into Monica's house which is very near to get water for them. Monica invites us in for tea and cake. We settle the girls in the van and go off for a very welcome cup of tea. I feel we have turned a corner.

Day the Forty-Seventh

Monday morning. It's 9.30 and I'm on the cusp of settling down for a writing session. Colum has gone to work and Sam is still in bed. It's a lovely day; I really wanted to walk down to the university library and get a few hours writing done in the focused peace and quiet there. However, our annual gas check is happening at noon, and I need to clear the area around the boiler in the kitchen, make our bedroom look respectable (as the gas chap will need access to the radiator there), encourage Sam – when he eventually gets up – to clear the debris around the radiator in *his* room, go and buy a pint of milk in case the gas chap wants a cuppa and have lunch ready on a tray in case the gas chap comes when we all need lunch. So there isn't enough time for me to go to the library if I also have to factor in the walk there and back. It's one of those days when the catch phrase is "Keep it Simple". I really must get a T-shirt made up with that.

Jen is ensconced in the landing leading down to the front door. This is a house-guarding position. I should really lead her away from it but she's curled up in a tight ball and is sleeping. Why wake a sleeping babe? The postman isn't due for a couple of hours yet. And Sal is lying upstairs. I can see her in the mirror. She seems relaxed too. I sit at my desk. Deliberate about leaving the door open so the dogs can wander in if they want. But there is a lovely shaft of sunlight falling just beside my seat. Dust particle land. I keep the door shut. I calculate I have around an hour of quiet providing the door doesn't go or the pigeons rampage on the roof.

This is what isn't shown in the dog training DVD, i.e. the constant negotiation and path-finding through the minutiae of the ordinary day. Colum and I watched some of the 'The Walk' DVD on Friday evening. We were both feeling that we need to move the dogs on to the next stage but recognise that we need to get it right. Sal's frantic refusal to come back to Colum on Saturday evening has reminded us that we are a long way yet from walking with her on a loose 'happy lead'. On the demonstration DVD it all looks very simple and the dogs featured there seem to get what is asked pretty quickly. And the dogs on the DVD are not fairly newly rescued dogs nor dogs that are new to Amichien. There's a major difference then. I would find it much more useful to see a demonstration of 'The Walk' with dogs who have issues. It could also be a bit of a giggle – the professional dog trainer getting in a fankle. Slapstick always makes me laugh. Seems to me that the DVD shows the perfection to be aimed at and not the messy reality that goes with the journey.

Colum comes home for lunch just before the gas chap phones to say he is on his way. It's all working out. Colum takes Sal and Jen to the garden and I follow with a tray of tea and a tupperware box of chicken salad. I think of Julie saying "Help them to get it right" and "Don't set yourself up for failure". Keeping the dogs out of the house while the gas man is here feels like the perfect thing to do. There will be days when it is pouring rain and the dogs can't be out while we attend to visitors, but that is all in the future. Today the sun is shining. Colum is home and peace reigns.

As we wait for the gas chap to do his list of checks we do some lead training with the girls. Today I have some chocolate substitute drops in my pocket. The girls love them. Colum entices Sal away from the dust particles playing around the compost heap and she weaves around the paved area following his hand with the choc drop in it. Jen sits on the bench with me. I have invited her to do so, so she is there on my terms not hers. We're doing it all by the book today. We're not stressed. We're at home. Colum has taken a longer lunch and I'm sitting in the sun with one calm dog watching another at work. At the moment all is very good.

Come dinnertime, some hours later, Sal decides she has had enough of being the good dog. I have been out to my yoga class and we are eating a late supper of hardboiled eggs, potato salad and tuna fish. On reflection it was the tuna fish that tipped the balance. Jen loves fish of any sort. It is a total myth that it is only cats who appreciate this food. Every dog we have ever owned has drooled at the smell of fish, especially the oily type. As I opened up the can Jen materialised in the kitchen. I put the tuna into a small dish and placed it on the table. There was a low growling. I turned round to see Sal doing that low shoulder stalking thing. Jen was her prey. Colum came into the kitchen. I told him what was going on. Hoping to stymie a potentially ugly scene between the dogs, he takes hold of Sal's collar; she lets out some rather threatening-sounding snarls. Colum hauls her out of the kitchen and into the dining room.

"Thought she was going to go for my hand there," he said.

"I really don't like that," I say.

We wait for a minute then let Sal out. She comes back in the kitchen where Jen and the tuna still are and repeats her behaviour. She ends up in the dining room again. This time she isn't quiet but lets out a series of barks. I worry about my books, the contents of my desk. She goes quiet. She gets let out. She does it all again. This time we ignore her noise and sit down to eat our supper. I should have learned by now that just when Sal seems to be settling and getting the rules she does something that resets my opinion of her. I'm glad Colum was there. I'm not too keen on putting my hand on the collar of a snarling dog. And I really don't like it when Sal seems to intimidate Jen.

"Seems to have been a tidal shift," says Colum. "Wonder if Sal's taken the position of top dog?"

I really don't like the sound of that at all.

Day the Forty-Eighth

It's the summer solstice today. The rain is pouring down. Real wet rain. Big brolly stuff. The sky last night was rosy velvety pink. Shouldn't that mean a good day today? Apparently not. I had entertained visions of us taking the short walk to the top of our hill this evening. I saw us sitting looking out over the Clyde valley as the longest day wound to a close. It was light yesterday evening until almost eleven o'clock. As I emptied stuff into the recycle bin outside around ten last night, I paused before going back in, drinking in the light and the stillness. The only natural thing our senses will drink in this evening is rain or maybe the dregs of the bottle of Cairn O'Mhor elderberry wine that I bought back from the recent jaunt to Dunkeld. Beautiful stuff. Just right to toast an equinox with.

My peaceful state of mind fragments however later in the afternoon as I cost out the necessary expenses for our annual camping holiday What?! What!? We can't afford that! I try to think of options. How about we go for one week only and maybe take Sal with us but don't camp and book a house instead? A house has sound proofing and has doors that can be closed. I spend the next two hours searching the net for a suitable house that has a secure garden, is in or very near Findhorn, is available the dates we want and is within our budget. The list I end up with is very short. And I am now totally depressed. Owners of houses seem to want hundreds of pounds for one week. It seems avaricious and I am left wondering if we should just cancel our holiday. The dogs are restless and, checking the clock, I note they haven't been out for hours. I text Colum to see when he will be home. Not for a while yet. Ok. Time to bite the bullet. I have been let off lightly the past couple of days and have done almost no garden pit stops. It is still battering down rain but the dogs need out, so out we go.

I have of course set myself up for failure. I'm feeling miserable at the thought of staying home this summer and having to listen to lots of folk expounding about their holiday travels. I'm also hungry as I only had a small salad at lunchtime and its now 6.30pm. As we start to go down the path Jen pulls the opposite way. I tug her lead and get her to follow. We get to the top of the steps. Sally pulls to the right, Jen loiters. I stop and breathe a bit. I don't feel steady on my feet and the steps suddenly seem rather steep. We go down slowly. I pause on each step so to get my balance. We make it into the garden. I let Jen off. She just stands there in the rain. I keep Sal on the lead. She wants to play with Jen, I want her to do her business. I drag her about the garden to all her favourite pee places. Nothing doing. She just wants to play. I don't want that to happen as the garden is now just a big mud patch. I am wondering what to do when Colum appears. I tell him I can't get anything out of the dogs.

He puts Jen's lead back on and says "Right, just leave it then."

We trog back up to the house. That was a complete waste of time.

In the kitchen with our coats dripping over chairs. Colum says we must phone Beth, the dog boarder, this evening. I tell him the staggering amount of money our two-week camping holiday is going to cost. He starts to say that we should maybe just take Sal with us. The pent up misery inside of me comes flooding out. I say there's no way we can have Sal with us in the tent, the other campers would think we were mental and things will be said. And we can't afford to board her for the planned 14 nights. And. And. And.

"I didn't sign up for this. Everything is just miserable and life is so complicated since Sal came to us," I wail.

Colum kneels down beside me and wraps his arms around me.

"I think we really need a holiday this year," he says, "and we'll find the money somehow. We'll just have to go for a shorter time that's all. But we need to contact Beth first and take Sal for a visit before we make any decisions."

The catharsis of a 'good greet' has worked. I blow my nose and nod. Colum fishes out the last of the elderberry wine, pours two small glasses, dumps a box of oatcakes down on the table and we sip and munch and I feel better. I forget about toasting the equinox.

Day the Forty-Ninth

I am writing in the quiet of the university library when my mobile buzzes. There is a message from Sam saying "I'm locked in!"

Oooops. I did that. I was so focused on getting out of the house and securing everything against escaping dogs, that I had forgotten Sam was still at home. I pack up my books and head home.

Winning the Booker Prize will never be achieved at this rate. I think of E M Delafield's frustrated diarist who carries a hundredweight of pens, notebooks, refreshments and furniture to her sunny garden in the hope of a decent writing session, only to be called back in immediately to deal with the pantry sink, garden fête arrangements, the butcher order, the laundry list and the vicar's wife. And having dealt with all, the sky then clouds over and the diarist carries the whole accoutrement back in from the garden. Despite the difference in our generation and class, she and I have a lot in common.

This morning as I packed my briefcase for my library stint I put in Jan Fennell's *The Practical Dog Listener*. This book has lain around our house over the last few weeks. Both Colum and I have dipped into it but, if truth be told, I have not actually sat down and read it seriously. As a former academic I know that an informative book is essential to decent research. If you don't know the discourse then there's little point trying to write about it. So, in the spirit of putting in effort, I read the opening pages. What this book reminds me is that taking on a dog is a major commitment. As a precursor to getting a dog, Jan advises that owners ask themselves some searching questions — such as are the new owners prepared to commit to the sacrifices entailed in understanding the dog's language? Well, no, quite frankly. My idea of getting a second dog was that she would be a playmate for Jen and a bit of fun for us. I had presumed she would shake down within a few days and become part of our family. We would love and care for her. We would all be happy. What I didn't mentally sign up for is was a damaged dog who was totally befuddled by everything that had happened to her. And the perfect image I had of her assimilating into our ways has been at total war with the reality of her living with us. Until I let go of that perfect image and also let go of my regret that we didn't wait until we could afford a pedigree puppy or until a more balanced rescue dog came our way, then I can't move on. Trouble is that I am a Libran and we swing around backwards and forwards. I commit to something one day then loosen my commitment the next. Depends what it is of course. But committing to Sally and her special needs is what is necessary if I am to begin to understand her. And all thoughts of returning her to the SSPCA need to be eradicated from my mind.

Later, I read the dog book in the quiet of our kitchen. It is mid-afternoon. Sally and Jen are quietly sleeping in their baskets. I have closed all windows so the noise of the men working on the roof next door doesn't worry them. It's peaceful. Right at the moment I can commit to our girls.

Day the Fiftieth

Our friendly dog neighbour has asked if we could possibly walk his dog, Jimmy, today. He actually asked Sam, but Sam couldn't see how he could walk Jimmy without Jen. He explained to our neighbour that we weren't yet walking the dogs. Must have sounded nutty to him. I tell Colum about the situation. Colum says he will do it and do it with both Jen and Sal. I say I thought we still weren't doing proper walks yet. Colum says the combination of Jimmy, his enclosed garden which is accessible from the wide expanse of the hill, and the French window doors opening into a kitchen are the perfect set of factors to test if Sal will respond to the "Consequence of Action" rule. It should be easy enough to get her back into the garden as Jimmy and Jen will be playing there, then Colum plans to use the principle of exclusion to get Sal back on the lead. Well, we'll see. I might or I might not go and witness what happens.

I do go as the day has turned lovely and my soul wants to be outside. Jen can't believe her luck when we turn up the steps towards the street and, joy of joys, towards Jimmy's house. She pulls like crazy on the lead. I'm conscious of time so don't do the 'stop start' thing with her. She greets Jimmy like a long lost friend and all three dogs start frisking about the garden. Jen finds an old deflated football and waves it at the other two. Colum opens the back gate which leads directly onto the hill. Jen runs through it with her new toy and Sal and Jimmy belt after her. They have a fantastic run about and we get them all back into the garden after twenty minutes or so. Stage One accomplished. Colum needs to get some lunch so I suggest I run back to our house, make up some sandwiches and bring them back over. It seems such a pity to lock the dogs up again. Colum is more than happy to sit down on our neighbour's patio chair and watch the dogs play.

I return ten minutes later with sandwiches and tea bags. I guess that our neighbours won't mind if we pinch some hot water from them. Colum already has the kettle boiled and we sit in the sun and munch our lunch. We then try to get Sal back on lead. Ah. She has remembered the dust particles and is deaf to all commands, and doesn't care a wit about being excluded from the pack. Why should she when there is vast entertainment to be had with her dust particle friends. Colum puts Plan B into operation, i.e. a game of football where he will try to grab hold of Sal's collar. After some deft dribbling, with all three dogs involved, Sal is caught and tethered. Phew. Colum has ten minutes to get back to work and cycles off once Sal and Jen are back home. They are highly content and sleep all afternoon.

I do a bit of emailing and then take Jan's book to the garden. I'm still hoping that by digesting this book the rudiments of her method will become second nature to me. Or, at least I can say hand-on-heart that I have tried. I'm ruminating on an example of two dogs who challenge each other for leadership and take lumps out of each other when they do, when our friend Donal appears. He has come to tell me the good news that his daughter has been awarded an excellent mark for her honours degree dissertation. Our talk moves on to other subjects and I see him looking around our garden. Donal, being an excellent gardener, must be aware of just how unkempt our garden currently is. He politely comments on how well the new fence has been constructed and is also interested in a huge plant in my bee-and-butterfly patch which has withstood the rampages of Sal and Jen. His fingers must have been itching though to sort the whole place out.

"We've had to give up on the garden for the time being," I say. "The dogs, you know..."

It won't make any sense to Donal. Not being a dog owner he won't get why we are sacrificing our garden for the training of dogs. I'm not sure I get it either. But that's where we are with things.

It's still sunny when Colum gets home in the early evening. I have washed the pigeon shit off the table and chairs near the front door and we sit in the warmth and share a bowl of crisps with a G & T. I tell him of Donal's visit and my shame about the garden.

"The garden will recover," he says. "We'll just have to be patient."

He's right of course, and, although I really want to plunge into a moan, I try to be positive and say that I suppose we need to focus on the progress Sal has made. We make up a list between us which amounts to:

A. She seems to be more or less house-trained now.

B. She knows her new name.

C. She will come to us in the house when called.

D. She is much better around food.

E. She stays near us when off lead in the garden.

F. She isn't barking so much at birds landing on our windowsills.

What we need to get her to is the major landmark of:

G. Coming to us on command when outside the garden and off lead. That's such an easy sentence to write and so so hard to deliver in practice.

We have some dinner. I would like to go for a walk. But a walk with Sal and Jen means either an arm-pulling session or a heart-stopping session of wondering if we will get Sal back on the lead. We're just not there yet. I could go on my own but it seems pointless. As the saying warns us though, I should have been careful for what I wished for.

We take the dogs to the garden for their last pit stop. Sal does her thing of darting away when we ask her to come to us. We leave her in the garden and start to go up the path with Jen. Sal is whining.

Colum says "I'll get out of sight then go back for her. She has to learn to come when we say," just as a black and white shape dashes past us, up the steps and up into the street.

"Oh, God!" I say.

God slinks away back to what he/she was doing and leaves us to cope.

"She'll aim for the top of the hill. I'll get a football and see if I can tempt her to come to us," says Colum.

I hear some cars in the street and worry that our mental dog is skipping around up there and causing chaos. People will think us really negligent if we don't appear soon. Colum goes in the house and starts to pump up a football – why it needs pumped up is beyond me. I hear another car arrive in the street. Good. One of Jimmy's owners is home. I run over to her.

"Annabelle, our mad dog has got out. Can we use your garden to get her back please?"

"Sure thing," she says. "I'm just about to get Jimmy out anyway for his last walk so I'll meet you up the hill."

Thank the lord for easy-going people.

Colum has already gone up the hill and just as I am jogging along the street my mobile buzzes. It's a text from Colum saying "Sal is here with me. Off-lead".

Well, that's something. At least she is safe and nearby. I get up to the top of the hill.

To the casual observer's eye all must look quite harmonious. Colum is playing football with Sal and Jen and Jimmy is louping casually between the dogs and his owner. Jimmy doesn't believe in too much high energy exercise. My heart rate slows down a little. Annabelle asks me how it has been going with Sal. I say that some days it is ok and others I just want to give up, but what stops me from doing that is the thought that the SSPCA would probably just put her to sleep.

"If we can't cope with her," I say, "I doubt if anyone can."

"Well, there's no point beating yourself up about it," says Annabelle. "You have really tried. No one can ask more than that."

Her words make a huge amount of sense and 75% of me wants to quit and take Sal back to the rescue centre tomorrow. But I look at her playing with Colum and Jen in the evening sun. She is so happy with a man, another dog and a ball. I suspect just the man and ball would do but Jen is an added bonus as she makes the game more interesting. Just a few words and some decisive action from me would take her away from all of this and probably end her life. They are huge and immensely weighted words. If I was doing this on my own I would say them. But I am not doing this on my own. There is a man playing football with Sal who wants to save her, wants to give her a happy life. The 25% of me that wants to save Sally too might be enough if added to the 150% that Colum offers. It just might.

And we do get her back on the lead in Annabelle's garden. Sal is knackered by then and she doesn't have the energy to dart away from me when I grab her by the scruff of her neck. We give her a big drink then she flumps out on the kitchen floor of Annabelle's kitchen. Jimmy snuffles in my pocket. He can smell the wee bits of cheese I have in a bag there.

"Do you want to come home with me Jimmy?" I say. "How about a swop, Annabelle?" She looks at me with a smile.

"Em. No thanks," she replies.

We thank her for letting us use her garden. She thanks us for looking after Jimmy earlier in the day. Oh, it's so good to have neighbours who are dog people.

Back at home Colum says to me that he has been noticing how people appear to help us just when we most need it.

"Angels. That's what they are," he says. "Angels. And I'm learning to trust that they will appear in the right place at the right time."

My mind flicks back to today's daily guidance written up by Eileen Caddy, one of the founders of the Findhorn Community, which says that we are surrounded by divine laws, not human. I have been forgetting that.

Day the Fifty-First

I spent the night dreaming of the dogs – of Sal and Jen and Jimmy. It's as if I can't switch off. I so want Sal and Jen to arrive at the point where we can go for long walks together and be secure in the knowledge that at the end of the walk we will all come home together.

Colum is already up and dressed by the time I surface at 7.15am. I had forgotten he has an 8am meeting at work. Crazy time. Or maybe not. It's another lovely day. A few grey clouds about but by and large a promising start.

In the library that morning, as I reach for a journal or newspaper to secure my seat while I take a break, I notice an advert for an article on the writer Elif Shafak. Actually what I notice first is her lovely face on the cover of the journal. It's a publication called *The Third Way*. It has apparently been ordered by the Scottish Baptist College. I have no need to be coverted to the Baptist church, good singers though they are, but the mix of a beautiful face of an older woman who has the kind of eye make-up I need to learn, the fact that she is a novelist, and the cover quotation – which asserts that true learning comes from understanding people who view life differently from us — is enough for me to pick it up. I'm glad I did so. I like what she is saying in the interview, such as the capacity of women to re-invent themselves. I think of my life now. My final serious bit of academic work, while still involved in the university world, was to produce a new annotated edition of a Victorian novel. It was a lot of work and the result was worth it. But my spirit is loath to engage in anything of the sort again. Many would say this is a waste of my skills but it feels as if that kind of writing is so remote now. Instead I am writing about the life I am living here and now. I have, as Elif Shafak argues, recreated myself. That feels good. It gives credence to the direction I am now going.

And it also gives credence to the change that has happened with the arrival of Sally in our family life. The days when I despair of her and question why we have her, are the days I am looking back on the pattern of our lives as they were.

Last night Colum said to me "We're in it for the long haul." He is a man who doesn't look back. Who doesn't do regrets. Indeed he wants Edith Piaf's 'Non, Je Ne Regrette Rien' played to accompany his coffin – preferably with exotic sultry weeping women shimmying behind – and it would indeed be a fitting song for him. I do think about the past and I do worry I have taken an inadvisable road in being a freelance writer, but to cease to change is, as some mystic said somewhere, to cease to live.

Day the Fifty-Second

My dear friend, Catherine, stayed overnight last night. This morning as we sat around the breakfast table – it being Saturday today there was no rush to be out and achieving – Sally came in the kitchen, stretched herself out on the floor and sighed.

"That's the full relaxation mode," said Colum to Catherine. "You can call her to you now if you want to. With Sally we usually either leave her or wait for a good ten minutes, but you've been waiting to chat to her since yesterday evening, so we can bend the usual rule."

Catherine quietly called "Sally!" and Sal came up into a sitting position. "Can I have a paw?" Catherine asked her.

Sally obediently gave her a paw. Why humans like this is a mystery to her and any dog, but it seems to please, so she gives it.

"Aw, you're a lovely dog," said Catherine.

Colum looked at me. He didn't say it but I see written in his face the words "See? Other people can see Sal's lovely nature." I wondered to myself if this works as some kind of inverse of the general rule that you can see what is wrong with other people's children. Maybe it works the other way for dogs.

Earlier this morning for example, as Colum was coming back from the paper shop where he had taken Sal and Jen for an unscheduled outing, he met Gerry, an owner of Finn. Gerry had asked Colum how we were getting on with Sal. Colum gave a potted history. Gerry said "She's a lovely dog".

"Anne doesn't see it," said Colum.

"Has she been to Specsavers?" asks Gerry.

Colum chortles all the way home.

Day the Fifty-Third

It's almost one o'clock in the afternoon and I am sitting writing in the kitchen with one ear listening out for sounds from the hill. Paul, our dog-friendly neighbour, texted a half hour ago to say that he was taking Jimmy round the hill and did Colum want to join him with our girls? We don't tell the dogs they have an invite, we can predict their answer. And if the girls get to tear about the hill and can be captured in Jimmy's garden, then they will sleep for the rest of the afternoon. And that means we can leave them with an easy conscience. We need a cooking station for our camping holiday and there is a discount outdoor store some miles away which we need to check out. So, hopefully if Colum doesn't have to spend two hours trying to get Sal back on the lead, we should be on our way soon.

The interlude is also useful in that I'm hoping our friend and previous dog-walker, Nan, will phone me. Our camping holiday is looming ever closer and we need to make a decision about Sally. Beth, the Amichien woman in Edinburgh, says she will contact us on Tuesday and arrange for us to visit. We may still do this. But Nan lives roughly half-way up the road to Findhorn. That would cut out the trip to and from Edinburgh each side of the holiday and also cut out the expense of it. Nan isn't Amichien trained but she is kind, conscientious and loves dogs. Do we really need any more? I was thinking last night about what a friend said to us when we told her I was expecting Sam. "You'll not be perfect parents, but you'll be good enough." And nineteen years on we don't see this as faint praise, just recognition of reality.

It's the same with our care of dogs. We try our best and sometimes it will work out and lots of times it won't. But it will, I hope, be good enough.

Colum returns from the romp around the hill.

"Success!" he shouts up the stairs. "Sal came into their kitchen quite happily. I didn't have to cajole her at all."

Sal and Jen appear. They look exhausted.

"They had a great run," says Colum.

This is brilliant. This is exactly how dogs should look after an exercise session. We have now bought ourselves some downtime of roughly four hours. Colum has a quick shower – his football game up the hill has left him with more than a manly sweat – and we head out to the outdoor store.

We find the exact table/cooking unit we need and pay for it. I wander around looking at lots of things I want but can't buy. No matter. I am trying to follow the 'Less-is-more principle' anyway, and recently donated four bags of clothing to a charity shop. My shelves are now ordered and neat and I can see exactly what clothes I have. I intend to try to keep it this way at least for a while. We leave the temptations of the store and drive a short distance to Pádraig and Maureen's house. They have said we are welcome to pop by for a cuppa and catch up chat.

Our friends are the owners of Lara – the lively golden retriever. As we approach, I wonder how I should behave with Lara. Our house rules and dog training is personal to us. Just because we ignore our dogs after a separation doesn't mean we have to do this with all dogs, does it? But if it actually helps dogs to relax maybe we should apply the rules at all times. But it's hard to ignore the lovely bundle of joy that Lara is. She bounds up to me, wagging her fluffy tail, as I come in. I hug Pádraig and his daughter Catriona.

"I'll pay Lara attention in a minute," I say. At least I am acknowledging her existence. Catriona and her dad have just started a game of table-tennis.

"Good timing, Anne," says Pádraig.

I pick up the paddle which Pádraig has just put down.

"You put the kettle on and I'll try and remember how this is done," I say.

Lara meanders around as we bash the tiny ball around. I am amazed she isn't going for it. What a chilled dog. She must have read my thoughts because she then scrambles after the ball which has just landed on the floor, again, and puts her chops around it.

"Leave, Lara, Leave!" says Catriona and tries to prize open Lara's mouth. Lara is having none of it but thinks this a exciting game judging by how hard her tail is now thumping. As I watch Catriona wrestle with Lara I reflect how just how far Catriona has come in her relationship with dogs.

As a very young girl of three or four she used to physically climb up her dad if any of our dogs went too near her. But there is a great determination of spirit in this wee lass and, as she saw more of Joe and Jack, her curiosity about how dogs worked got the better of her fear. She stopped climbing up her dad and opted for clinging to his legs instead or sitting on his lap. Then, one day, as our dogs were crashed out on the carpet having had a good long walk, she got off her dad's lap and edged centimetre by centimetre over the couch towards the collapsed dogs. Jack opened his eyes when he sensed her coming but kept still. Jack liked wee children. He thought they were good value as they seemed to come with a trail of biscuit crumbs and the potential for fun. Catriona stretched out her arm and touched Jack. He grunted in appreciation and wriggled a bit. As he moved Catriona scrambled back towards the safety of her dad, but instead of climbing right back into his lap, she stayed on the couch. She looked back at Jack who was now deep in the land of good slumbers. She got off the couch and walked as quietly as she could back to Jack, bent down, patted his furry side then jumped back to the safety of the couch. Breakthrough.

From there she progressed to being quite happy to be in the same room as our dogs, to throwing a ball for them, and one day to climb right into the boot of our van to sit down beside Joe and Jack and give them both cuddles. She has her own dog now and Lara will take first place in her heart. But the dogs who helped her overcome her fear were our boys. When Jack died she gave me a small ceramic statue of a black Labrador which now sits beside the photo of Jack in our hall. And when we passed the silver Quaich around at the first New Year bells after Jack's passing and gave our individual toasts, Catriona said "I want to remember Jack. I'm never going to forget him." And I doubt if she ever will.

Maureen comes home while we are there. She has been out for a road run, so we talk running for a bit while Colum takes over my place at the table-tennis. Being Colum, the game extends boundaries immediately as he seizes two paddles, one in each hand, and starts playing with two balls. Catriona giggles and gets another paddle for herself. Lara is equally delighted at the double chance of getting a ball into her mouth. She zooms around under the table highly delighted until Pádraig decides he's had enough and she gets put out into the back garden. Maureen now has a cup of tea in her hand and flops down onto the couch beside me. Lara gets let back in and promptly starts to climb up onto the settee where Maureen is. Maureen is interested in what we would do in this situation. I say that we would do exactly what she is already doing i.e. turning her face away, refusing to make eye contact with Lara and gently pushing her off the couch. Lara tries her luck again.

"Oh, she's so persistent!" says Maureen.

I tell her of the Amichien method thing that if a dog does something a hundred times, you simultaneously insist on the behaviour you want a hundred and one. After eight tries to get on the couch, Lara gives up and lies out under the table despite the zooming balls.

"Look," I say to Maureen, "she's in perfect relaxation posture and now she will sigh ... there she goes ... perfect."

What a great dog.

Day the Fifty-Fourth

Spend some time this morning fixing up boarding arrangements for Sally. As we now think that taking her all the way to Edinburgh to Beth isn't practical, I investigate the possibility of Nan taking her. I call her mobile and hear her cheery tones. It's months since we have spoken and I'm relieved she isn't distant with me. I tell her of Sally and her issues and ask if it would be possible for Nan to board her. Nan doesn't see why not. She also says she has a garden surrounded by a six foot fence and most of her walking is on lead anyway. Sounds good. I initially book Sal in for a week, then wonder if we could stretch to two.

I chat with Colum when he comes home for lunch. He says he will find the money for Sal's boarding somehow if it means we can get to Findhorn for a full two weeks. Must admit I am now working on the Trust philosophy. Maybe the tax gods will decide they owe me a fortune and a cheque will miraculously appear, or, more likely, I will just stop worrying about our cash flow and start to trust. I text Nan again and book Sal in for the full fortnight. Done.

In celebration I decide to test how far we have come with Sal and put both Sal and Jen on the tie-ups at the front door which have lain dormant for the last few weeks. Last time I tried this it was disastrous as Sal flinched and lunged at any sniff of a cat, any flicker of a bird. This time I take the precaution of smearing butter into two hollow bones and taking them down with me. The girls are delighted. Getting to sit outside and with a yummy bone. It works quite well. Sally more or less gets that she is restrained and doesn't try to do crazy jumps up to the flowerbed. I go down and sit with them for a few minutes. This is an improvement too. Maybe because my expectations are less even being able to sit with them calmly for a minute feels like progress. We do around ten minutes then Jen and Sal start their crazy woofing. Colum appears at the top of the steps which lead into the street.

"Postie coming," he says.

That's my cue. I get up rapidly, grab both girls and pull them inside. I need no second warning.

"Postie" is a high alert word round here. He's actually quite a nice guy. He has dogs himself – two Collies as it happens. But Jen can't cope with him. It's all to do with her defending the den which is under attack from the 'missiles' this man insists on firing it. I get her reasoning but trying to explain this to a justifiably irate man who is concerned for his ankles, is a touch difficult. Nowadays we just circumvent the issue by getting hold of Jen and putting her in the dining room when she scents the possibility of the daily attack. Julie had advised us to "help them get it right" and Jenna's one time record of nipping the postman in the leg was her getting it very wrong certainly in his eyes. He threatened then to stop delivering to our address – again, quite understandable – but there was a background to the incident. I was in hospital getting blood transfusions to sort out severe anaemia and Colum, being very worried about me, wasn't functioning on his usual rational cylinders and had opened the door when he saw the postman approach. He acted out of a mistaken belief that it might be a good idea for Jen to meet the postman and so lessen her fear of him. His good intention backfired however, as, being a sensitive animal, Jen had picked up Colum's anxiety about me, had seen that the pack was less one member and the tension in her promptly cranked up. She saw it as her job to at least rid us of one menace and went for the unfortunate postman.

When I got home some days later, now more or less recovered, I wrote him a note of apology and explanation and sellotaped it to the front door. A day or so later I saw him approach the house and ran downstairs making sure Jen remained upstairs. I stood by our makeshift gate as the postman turned towards our house.

"I'm so sorry about the other day," I said.

"It's ok. Forget about it," he muttered without meeting my eyes. He shoved our letters into my hand and strode up the path.

It wasn't the best of reconciliations but it would do.

Day the Fifty-Fifth

As I walk up through the architecturally graceful streets of Glasgow's city centre towards the where I am meeting my mum for morning coffee, I think back to my Dru yoga class of the evening before. Steph, our teacher, had led us through a movement that helped accept change in our lives. I swung my arms in rhythm to my breath and thought of how Sally is slowly becoming part of the family. Just before I had left for the yoga class I had heard a snuffling sound in the kitchen and found Sally enjoying a refreshing taste of some past-its-best tomato and lettuce salad which I had been about to throw into the kitchen compost caddy. As I pulled her down from the worktop I said "Sally Scriven, what a girl you are!"

It's the first time I have used our family name for her. I smile to myself as I stride up the street in the morning sunshine. It is good to feel we were slowly getting used to her.

The sun is warm and my thoughts move to the enormous pile of washing accumulated on the floor of Sam's room. I pull out my phone and dial Sam's mobile. A rather annoyed sounding teenager greets me.

"Did I wake you up?" I say. It is ten o'clock in the morning but, in the teenage world, this could be considered early.

"No," says Sam. "The dogs woke me up a while ago, and they've eaten the landline."

"The landline?" I say. "The whole thing?"

"No, they've just knocked that out the cradle but chewed right through the wires. They could have electrocuted themselves."

I notice that Sam is speaking in the plural. Without witnesses it's hard to pin the crime of a single dog. My heart plummets anyway. This seems to be the pattern. Just when we feel small victories are gained a rather considerable landslide occurs. At least no-one was hurt. Just means our answer machine is now out of action. We will have to revert to the old-fashioned low-tech method of waiting for people to phone back. I wonder what will be the next target. The skirting board? The low chest of drawers the phone normally sits on? There isn't really anything else left in the hall. I'm glad I am not at home.

The day continues to be pleasant weatherwise. Down in the south of England the temp is soaring to over 30 but here in central Scotland, we have a mild 18 degrees going on. That's fine with me. I like my green and temperate land. It is perfect walking weather and after a morning of breathing in city scents it would be good to do just that. But. But. But. Usual scenario. I think about rebelling against the Amichien praxis and taking Jenna up the hill. Yes, this would set up a hierarchy. Yes, this would say to her that she is still in charge. Yes, Sally would not be chuffed. But I so miss being able to come in, change into my dog gear, put on trainers or wellies and get out to clear my senses.

I busy myself with other things when I get home to avoid temptation but the temptation doesn't go away. At 5.30pm I phone Colum and say what I am thinking of doing. He says he will come home and help me take both dogs out. He does so and twenty minutes later we head up the hill. As I feel guilty at disrupting the routine and insisting on 'The Hunt' instead of a garden pit stop so try to do a bit of heel work as we go along the street. Nothing doing. Jenna, whom I have on lead, has sensed waving grass, wide space, fresh air and freedom and pulls like mad. She does sit when I ask her but ignores my command to "heel!" We stagger along to the park – at least Sally isn't going mental at the possibility of cats – and I let Jen off lead. She skips and jumps and snuffles happily around and promptly lets out a pee and a pooh. Colum takes Sal up to the top of the hill. Jen and I join him there and we all sit down for a good gaze over the valley. Sally gets jumpy as two swifts begin to dart around.

Colum says he will do some "Stop Start" stuff with her. I put Jen on the lead and walk her a slight distance away to do the same. I don't know if she really gets it at all. And it must vastly amuse the neighbours should they happen to look out their upstairs windows that overlook the hill. I look back at Colum and Sally, they seem to be working quite well. I continue on for another ten minutes or so then let Jen off and tell her to "Go see Colum".

She does so very happily.

We are just thinking of going home when a voice calls "Hallo, there, strangers!"

It's Jenny with her wee Cairn Terrier, Iona.

Jenny is one of those people you never mind spending time talking with. She's a bright and bubbly kind of woman who listens well and asks good questions. The dogs though are not too sure about the extension of the pack. As Iona comes in closer Sally, barking, lunges at her and Jen follows up with a run-in. The humans spring back, pulling our pets with us. The retreat calms the dogs a little.

From a distance of some twenty feet I call "Hi Jenny, good to see you!"

We all laugh. Iona decides to have another go at leadership. Pint-sized though she is her spirit is huge and she darts towards Jen. Jen snarls and shows her sharp teeth.

"Iona!" yells Jenny "No!" She tries to get her on the lead but Iona is too quick for her and jumps away.

"S'alright,Jenny," I say. "Just ignore her. She'll calm down in a bit."

Colum holds on to our two and the calm slowly descends. Jenny comes in closer and we begin to chat. She wants to know how it is going for us. We tell her some of it. There is so much to tell but how much do people really want to know? Iona begins to jump at Jenny trying to get her attention. Jenny yells at her again.

"Don't look at her," I say. "Ignore her."

As her owner isn't giving her attention, Iona comes over to try her luck with me. I mentally assess the fact that I have on old jeans and ignore her as she starts to jump at my legs. She gives up when I don't move. She moves off back to Jenny and slumps at her feet.

Both Colum and I notice that she is lying on Jenny's feet – a sure sign of dominance – but she's quiet and it isn't time to start saying anything. Iona isn't our dog. We don't need to do anything. Our two stretch out on the grass. They're in sphinx position but that's good enough for now. And it's lovely standing there in the early evening sun, catching up with Jenny and talking dog. She asks about our training programme. Programme? That sounds way too structured. We're more involved in a slow trudge. But we run through the rudiments of Amichien. Jenny is interested as she is experiencing various problems with Iona and Colum offers to lend her the DVD. She's unsure of the ignoring thing though.

"Trouble is," she says "I live on my own. Iona is who I talk to when I get home."

I can see her point.

"It all depends on what you can cope with," says Colum. "If you're ok with how Iona is then why change it?"

Looking at Iona sleeping on Jenny's feet it seems to me that a few tweaks are all that is required. Compared to Sally's messed up mind it would be a skoosh.

Day the Fifty-Sixth

It is 4.15 am but it is already light. I am too hot. Levering myself up onto my elbows, I see that Colum has thrown all the duvet onto me and wrapped himself up in a light blanket. I'm also thirsty and my half-cup of water on my bedside cabinet doesn't satisfy my dry throat. Some action is required, even though my mind is still fuggy with sleep. I drag the duvet into the spare room and pick up the single light duvet lying on the guest bed and throw this onto my half of our bed, pull on my lighter dressing gown and make my way downstairs. There is a curious kind of light emanating from the dining room and sitting room doors. I go into the dining room, closing the door behind me. It's too early for Sal to be moving around.

Moving over to the large windows overlooking the back gardens I pull open one of them fully and lean out. The bird community are waking up and throwing salutations to each other. A fox sits grooming itself on a neighbour's lawn. The texture of night-time still lingers amid the early day. I take long breaths in and out. Such a blessed moment, overlooked and unseen by most of us. I think of George Eliot's thing … what is it? … something about hearing the squirrel's heartbeat and the clamour that lies on the other side of silence. I look behind me to check that the dining room door really is shut … Sally and Jenna might not quite appreciate the poetical metaphysics of a squirrel's heartbeat. I consider staying up and writing or looking for the exact wording of the quote but a wave of drowsiness wafts over me from nowhere. I close the window and return to my now cool side of the bed.

A few moments later it is 7.45am and I hear the crunch of the chuckie stones way below our bedroom window as Colum takes the girls to the garden. I get out of bed and open up the curtains. The silky air of a few hours ago has gone and a dull grey overcast sky has taken its place. It's the kind of morning, though, when I would enjoy a quiet meditative walk with Jen. I know she would too. But then, but then, all the issue of 'The Hunt', etc, would kick in and the agenda becomes laden and heavy. I let go of my desire and go downstairs. I hear woofing coming from the back garden and wonder what's going on. Sally doesn't tend to do this anymore at this time of day. Five minutes later Colum appears.

"Bloomin' fox," he says. "Just standing there looking in at us in our garden. Sally clocked it and went nuts. She almost tipped over the bench in her effort to find a way out of the garden. You'd think the thing would have more sense than to infuriate dogs right near it."

I wonder if it is Brother Fox of the 4.15am sighting. Just as well I didn't let Sal peer out the window with me. The whole neighbourhood would have involuntarily joined us in our morning reverie.

The advantage though of no proper dog walking means that I gain an hour each morning. The girls are still a bit edgy post-fox and keep trying to look out the kitchen window.

I take my laptop into the kitchen table and sit there sending out decided "I'm in charge" signals. The girls take themselves off duty and go and lie down in their baskets. I write for an hour or so. Make some tea, draw up a shopping list and then take myself and my trolley down to the supermarket. Sam has got up and has taken Sal and Jen to the garden. A good time for me to exit.

I walk down the street thinking of all the times I would take a rucksack and a dog or dogs with me. Joe and Jack liked supermarket runs. They would sit outside the entrance and revel in all the attention they got. I would speed around the shelves at the speed of sound trying to put aside thoughts of someone stealing my lads, only to rush back outside to find some kind person squatting down beside the boys quietly stroking and talking to them. Quite often people would tell of me their own loved dog who had passed away and who they still grieve for. I was always glad that Joe and Jack did something to help them name their grief and do a little towards their healing. I know that my heart lurches when I see a silky black Lab and my hand comes out to touch it. There are times when the ignoring rule of Amichien Bonding is difficult for humans.

I walk home from the supermarket musing on the radar of my life at the moment. It is, in many ways, a small life. But smallness has its place. Like

Virginia Woolf, I am a great defender of the small, apparently insignificant, people who appear to do insignificant things but who, viewed with a perceptive eye, are indeed remarkable. In *Mrs Dalloway*, and other novels of Woolf's, we are told there are no insignificant lives, only inadequate ways of looking at them.

As I trudge up the sloping street which meets ours, I have no idea of just how fate is about to demonstrate the value of a middle-aged woman pulling a shopping trolley at noon on an ordinary Tuesday.

Smasssssssh! The sound breaks though the air like a wraith. It's a sound I have never heard before and I pause mid step trying to locate the source. I look up to towards a house diagonally across from ours. Our neighbour, Johnny, is standing at the top of the steep flight of steps leading to his front door. He sees me and waves frantically at me to come.

"Oh, dear God, not Cameron," I think as I run over bumping my heavy trolley behind me. "but it can't be wee Cammy, Johnny wouldn't still be standing on the step."

Johnny shouts "An intruder! Surprised him. Jumped out through the window.

"Unconscious." I hear him say to his mobile "Police. Yes. Police and Ambulance."

Now, 'tis strange what the mind does in these situations. I may be rubbish at Maths but the mum bit of my mind, which far outweighs any paper qualification demonstrating ability with number, calculates that I have around a minute or so max to do something practical and effective.

I shout "Be back in a moment!" and run to our house. Drag in my trolley. No sense leaving it in the street. Belt upstairs. Find Sam in his room busy playing his X box.

"Sam! Need your help over the road! Maybe your first aid knowledge too." Something in my tone tells him that this is no time to debate if what he is wearing is fashionably suitable for public scrutiny and, good lad that he is, he pauses only to pull on some shoes and run with me back over the road. I tell him what Johnny shouted to me as we go.

"Heavy stuff, Ma," is his comment.

I wonder if I should take over some medical gear but have no idea what, so just keep running. We sprint up our neighbour's steps.

A young man lies spread out on his back, his head propped up on a small raised flowerbed. Johnny has put a soft brown jacket under his head. There are huge shards of glass all around. The young man has blood on his hands. I bend down beside him. He stirs. The mother part of me kicks in. Yes, he is a criminal, but he's also just a lad and is bleeding. I talk to him quietly, thinking of all the times I have been seriously ill, and the way medical staff seemed to think it important to keep me *compos mentis*. So I do the same. I ask him his name. He tells me. He wants to know where he is and why he is there. I keep it brief and say "You've had a wee accident. Just lie back. The ambulance is on its way." And other such stuff. I call him "Honey" and keep my tone soft and soothing. I don't know what I'll do if he tries to get up.

His sweatshirt has the Celtic football club logo on it. I ask him if that is his team.

"Aye, bloody right," says the lad.

As this isn't the time to tell him I have zero interest in eleven overpaid men punting a ball around a park, I say "Oh, right, it's good to have a sport. Good for you. Do you play football yourself?"

"A wee bit," he says, then tries to shift his position a bit. "Christ, ma neck's sair."

"Yes, it will be, but you'll be ok," I say.

I worry that he will try to move too much. Sam and Johnny are there, but it could be horrible if they have to try and restrain him. He wants a taxi to go home in. I say a taxi won't take him in his condition. He tries to get up. Sam comes closer and says "Just lie back. You're hurt. You need to take the pressure off your ribs."

It's maybe the sight of Sam's strong body that makes him give in and sink back down again. I ask him if there is anyone I can phone for him.

"My gran," he says and begins to say the number. Not too much wrong with his long term memory then.

I dial the number and speak to a croaky out-of-it voice telling her, without complete detail, that her grandson is seriously injured.

The woman says "Ah cannae handle this. And ah cannae go up tae the hospital. I'm no well. I'll tell his mum tae dae it. Thanks for phoning, hen."

Poor lad. Not important enough for rapid action or intensive questioning of what's happened to him.

I shift my body stance a little and my head swims. This is no time to faint. I sit next to the lad on the low wall and take few deep breaths. We hear the sound of sirens.

"That's the ambulance. They're going to take care of you," I say to the lad.

A paramedic estate car pulls up and out jump two green-clad men. I have a long-held theory that the best jobs in the world must be being a paramedic and a florist delivery person. I mean, really, are there any other jobs when your arrival brings random people sheer relief or pleasure?

As the men take the steps two at a time – actually that's not that impressive, I did that and I'm at least ten years older – I register the fact that their uniforms really do add a certain frisson to the human body. I'm obviously not too stressed then.

They hunker down over the lad and, feeling like a nurse on duty, I say "He's conscious, but maybe concussed. Has no short term memory but could tell me his name and his gran's phone number." The medics nod and swing into action doing paramedic things.

I continue to stay where I am and send soothing sounds to the lad. They have a slightly rougher approach that I do and I suspect it won't wash well with this customer. One of them opens up the lad's sweatshirt to reveal a large screwdriver stuck into the belt of his jeans. The paramedic sighs and lifts it out and puts it aside. He pulls the lad's T-shirt up and reveals a crumpled hospital gown.

"Have you been in hospital recently?" he asks the lad.

"Aye, this mornin," he replies.

"Right," says the paramedic.

The plot has definitely just thickened.

There's still a bit of blood leaking from somewhere but the green-clad men are struggling to locate it, as they are trying to dodge the glass strewn everywhere. We haven't moved anything – I'd like to think this is perhaps because I have read almost every one of Miss Marple's cases and I know you should never disturb the scene of a crime, but it's really that the glass was useful in deterring the lad from trying to get up. One medic – the chap with the interesting Aussie accent, or is it New Zealand? Is there a difference? – asks if they could have a broom. Johnny goes inside to get one. I call to him and ask him for rubber gloves – another pair of hands may be useful.

I help clear some of the large half-inch thick triangular shards of glass nearest to the lad. This allows both paramedics to kneel down and examine him better. As a paramedic loosens the boy's waistband some money, around £20, falls out onto the ground. The boy stirs.

"Don't worry, sweetheart," I say. "I'll put your money in the pocket of your sweatshirt."

The paramedics lever the lad up a little and one of them tries to reach a big piece of glass which seems to be lodged into the waistband of the lad's jeans. He can't do it as they are both holding him.

"Do you want me to do it? I don't mind." I say.

They go silent. That means 'Yes' but they're not allowed to say it. Health and Safety and all that. Well, sod it, how hard can it be? I pull the huge shard of glass gently and it comes away quite neatly. Well, it's not any yuckier than changing a squidger nappy or picking up stinking dog pooh. You just have to get on with it. I'm quite proud of myself.

"What else do you want me to do?" I ask.

"Nothing," they chorus.

Well, cheers, chaps. Did your mammies never teach you that politeness costs nothing? But ok, that's my cue. I'm out of here.

As I stand up, Mhairi, Johnny's wife appears. She must have arrived some minutes ago. She starts to ask me what's happening then looks tearful. She tells me Johnny's father died a few days ago and they are in the middle of arranging his funeral.

"And now this," she says. Her voice breaks. I hug her.

"The good thing is that Cameron isn't here and Johnny isn't hurt," I say. Cameron is their beautiful little boy who is safely at his nursery. At

Cameron's name Mhairi's eyes fill up again but she wipes her eyes.

"Do you want a cup of tea?" she asks.

"That would be great."

She also asks Sam to come in but he's not a tea man and opts instead to go home.

Just as I turn to follow Mhairi I feel another pull on my arm. I look round to see Natasha from-next-door having a major stress moment.

"Oh My God!" she wails "My kids were in the garden! My kids!"

Dredging deep into my hugely depleted store of calm I say 'Oh, they weren't anywhere on his radar. He was after other things.' I make it up. I have no idea what he was after but Natasha can't cope with that and, right at the moment, I can't cope with her not coping.

She turns and dashes back down the steps towards her own house. I hope she does at least three laps around her garden to defuse some of that nervous static she is giving off otherwise her kids will think there's a maniac loose – and it's not the chap currently lying on the ground.

As I go up the steps to their hallway I see that my newly washed pseudo-Converse shoes have blood stains on them. The stain is evidence to my brain that it all really happened. The steps suddenly feel really steep. I need some tea.

"And I didn't even wash the breakfast dishes," says Mhairi as I enter the kitchen.

"In the scheme of things…" I say.

We laugh and she puts on the kettle. I have never been in their kitchen, or indeed in their house since they have moved in, and normally I would hover politely until asked to sit down. Today I say "Mhairi, I'm sitting down."

Extraordinary situations sometimes deflate stupid niceties. I then look at my hands. They are sticky and dirty. I hadn't thought to ask for gloves earlier. My head swims a bit again.

"Can I wash my hands … the blood, you know …"

The sink seems a long way away, but I want to get my hands clean. Mhairi shows me where the soap is – nice scented bottled squeezy stuff, not like our Aldi economy large bar stuff – and I scrub my hands.

When I get back to the table, still doing some deep breathing without making it obvious – Mhairi has had enough without me going to bits – there is a cup of tea waiting. It's too strong for me. I swither whether I could ask her to weaken it but I don't think she would have the energy. And they say that strong tea is good in a crisis. But I wish it was weaker. No matter. It'll do the job. I put in a teaspoon of sugar … sugar … good thing for shock is it not? The hot sweet liquid helps bring back some equilibrium.

We talk a little of what has just happened. We keep our tones light. Neither of us wants to think about what could have been the outcome. We finish our tea and I get up to go. I don't want to be in the way. I'm superfluous now. We move through to the living room and hear movement outside the window. The young lad is being carried away on a stretcher his head in a neckbrace, his body strapped down. The police are now here as well as plain clothes people – must be CID. So, they think this is an important one then. Mhairi and I stand at the window and watch as the lad is carried down the steps.

"He's someone's son," I say. "What a shitty life he's having."

She murmurs agreement. Had my house been broken into, and had my husband been threatened, I might not have reached for compassionate interpretation of the facts. But Mhairi did and I admired her for it.

Johnny comes into the room. For some reason I hadn't been thinking of what the lad might have had time to steal from their house but apparently he swiped their old laptop, a huge defunct cast iron key, some £20 in cash (ahem), and what is rather more sinister, a large kitchen knife. On his person has also been found a nurse's fob watch and a credit card belonging to someone else. The CID have also told Johnny that the lad was a psychiatric patient in the local hospital and had busted out that morning. Apparently he is very very well known to the authorities. Looking at the faces of Johnny and Mhairi I think that in this instance less information might have been better. They need a moment or so together. I make my excuses and leave the room.

There are a number of police people around outside. One of them asks me if I was a witness and I relate my side of things to them. He decides that he had better take a statement from me and pulls out his notebook. And he starts carefully filling it in. My head switches back from 'mother' and 'concerned neighbour' mode to 'English teacher' and I find myself wanting to correct his misuse of the collective and the apostrophe as he writes "witnesses' report". I want to say 'Now, think about that. How many witnesses were there? Only one? Right. So perhaps that should be "witness' report"? But I don't. And does a formal police report need always open with 'I was proceeding along the street...'? I never proceed. I was walking. I was trundling my trolley. "Use the wide vocabulary available, young man!" I want to say. But I don't. I just tell my piece slowly and steadily. Waiting for the young officer to get it all down. He finally does so. I'm done.

I walk back down the steps which I had hurtled up an hour or so ago. This day had begun in such an ordinary way. A short while ago I was but a woman returning home from the supermarket thinking about the current shape of my life and wondering if the dogs had behaved themselves while I was out. The dogs. I look over at our house. Our messy lovely house with its dog trounced garden. I can see Sally's form at Sam's window. She is staring out into the street. She's not normally allowed in his room – but, right at this moment, it's lovely to see her there. An intruder would need to be totally out of their box to attempt to wander unannounced into our place and if they did she would quickly persuade them to wander out again. Maybe Colum is right. Maybe she is our Silver Lining Sally. Bless her highly wired socks.

Day the Fifty-Seventh

I've been thinking about morality. Why is it that that young man yesterday thought it ok to walk into someone's house and lift things that didn't belong to him? Why is it that Johnny, who owned the burgled house, put a soft jacket under the young man's head as he lay unconscious? Why was it I went to help a neighbour and show compassion to the injured young man? Why was it that the paramedics came and tended to him despite his abusive attitude to them? Maybe we all had different reasons. But what strikes me is that we were all trying to do what we thought the right thing and therefore not to add any more wrong to the situation.

I am writing in the university library. I have just read an interview with the doyenne of Canadian literature, Margaret Atwood. The interviewer asks Atwood about morality; she replies to the effect that morality is something we do that we know if we didn't do, it would result in suffering. I think of this concept of extension where inertia causes harm. My thoughts shift from yesterday's incident to Sally. It's not yet plain sailing with her. We still can't get her out for proper walks. She still has the occasional accident in the house – Sam texted me five minutes ago to say he found a pooh on the stairs. She is costing us significantly more money that we envisaged. My bee-and-butterfly patch is knocked to smithereens, mud has replaced the grass and there are stone-filled holes dotted around the garden. I miss the air and exercise of long walks and feel divorced from the dog community. So, why is she still with us? Because the alternative is a concrete cage in the rescue centre, perhaps another rehoming which would no doubt result in failure and lord knows what after that. I know nobody would blame us. Indeed many would think we had just come to our senses. It would be a justifiable decision. But such an action would add suffering to a life that has already known too much. Do we have the right to do that? Perhaps if I spend long enough asking this the need for an answer will become negligible.

Day the Fifty-Eighth

Sally is sick. Yesterday eve she spewed up her dinner and left it in a huge pile on the sitting room carpet. It had barely been digested. And through the night she did the same. We initially think it is just a minor stomach upset but the second lot of spew had blood in it, so Colum takes her off to the vet despite the fact that he should really be heading to work.

The vet says it is just a stomach upset and the blood was probably just a blood vessel popping. She gives Sal an injection to calm her stomach, advises no food until the evening, water little and often and also prescribes special dietary tinned food. As Sal is calm getting back into our van, Colum decides to take the conference call, for which he had sent his apologies.

All goes well for a few minutes then a seagull takes a moment to do a fly-past the boot of the van. Sal goes into a spin. Colum perseveres with the phone call even though he can only hear every fourth word. It isn't working. He makes his apologies and drives home.

I could have taken Sal – my voluntary stint in the Fairtrade shop isn't until 10am and it would make logical sense for me to do it. I did hesitatingly suggest this but Colum had replied, "I care about her more. I've taken her on. So I'll do it."

I didn't haggle.

And now my lower self is at war with my higher self. The lower self is thinking "Maybe she'll get really ill and die and then problem solved. And at least we will have made her last few weeks happy." While my higher self weighs in with "That's shocking! Shame on you! The poor dog is sick and all you can do is think maybe you'll soon be shot of her." At least I am honest. And her being ill reminds me that there is no guarantee that dogs live out their expected life span. Jack died age 8, Joe age 9. Way too young for their breeds. The lesson I learned from Joe and Jack's death was to enjoy a dog while they were still with you. But that's the thing. I'm not enjoying Sally.

Day the Fifty-Ninth

Glorious morning. Out of sheer compassion, I let my partner snooze in bed while I take the girls to the garden. It isn't much of an act of goodness as the morning is wonderfully warm and sunny. My spirits want more though. I put Sal back in the house and take Jen up the hill. Oh happy happy girl! Jen runs ahead of me, delighting in her freedom. I am aware I am putting the hunt training back. But so, life is short. I want a walk.

We skirt the top of the hill. Last night's revellers have left the place in a fine mess. Bottles and cans and blue plastic bags everywhere. I collect up the plastic bags and stuff them full of debris. Jen watches me as I trudge up and down the hill to the litter bin. My hands now feel filthy and I'm also hungry so we head home. Sal is quite content in her basket. She probably has little energy at the moment. The vet said to allow her food from 6pm yesterday eve but only a teaspoon per hour. A teaspoon! Poor lass. No sooner on the tongue than gone. But she hasn't been sick again so that's good.

Today is Sma' Shot Day. This is a festival peculiar to our town. The history of it stems from a nineteenth-century protest. The Sma' Shot was an invisible but vital thread that held together the intricate and colourful cloth woven in Paisley and, as it couldn't be seen, the mill owners, in their wisdom, said the workers were to buy it themselves. The workers protested and went on strike. They won their case and, in 1856, the first Saturday of July, traditionally a holiday for the weavers, was renamed "Sma' Shot Day". Since then there has been an annual festival on this date to celebrate the rights of workers. A procession forms in a local park and members of issue groups, unions, dancers, drummers, pipers, as well as a local drama group dressed in mill workers' costumes, process down into the town led by a burly chap battering on the huge Charleston Drum – which was originally used to call weavers to a public meeting. If the weather is fine, it's a great joyful event. If the weather is rubbish, it's still a good event. Paisley people turn out in force to Sma' Shot.

We go down to the Abbey Close just before the procession gets there. The place is already busy. There are craftspeople selling their wares, there are bookstalls and tombolas and a children's games area. The RSPB is here, and Scottish CND, and green groups and political parties. A tea dance is getting ready to kick off at 1pm in the town hall and around 181 white-haired shampooed-and-set pensioners appear to be having their tea and homemade cake in the abbey cloister café, in preparation for tripping the light fantastic. I buy two 'carry out' teas and go back out to the sunshine.

Colum and I sit on a low wall watching the crowd. A young man walks past leading a chubby black Labrador puppy on a lead. I feel a lurch of envy. I think of what we have instead.

I say to Colum, "You know, if someone wanted Sally and we knew they would care for her, I would give her away today."

He sighs. "I've given her my heart," he says.

"Why?" I ask. I know there really isn't an answer to this but I persist anyway just to be thrawn.

"I think she's beautiful," Colum says.

"Hmph," I say.

"And she'll repay us a thousand-fold," Colum goes on, "and I also don't see why we should go through all this hard work then give her away."

All I can see is the uncharted work we still have to go through. We do a round of the stalls, buy some books and CDs for a bargain price. It's now really noisy. A boy/girl band is singing – or sliding around some notes on stage; since when did singing involve so much off-key shouting? My head starts to bang. Colum goes off to see a stunt cyclist and I go home.

The quiet walk up to the house is good. I really am quite an introvert. I only do so much noise and people and bustle. The dogs are quiet when I get in. I do the ignoring thing for a while then call them to me. Jen wriggles over on her tummy to be tickled. Sal gives me a paw.

"Ok, let's try, Sally, let's try," I say.

I stand up to put the kettle on. While waiting for it to boil I put on one of the bargain CDs – Enya's *A Day Without Rain*. A verse of one of the tracks, which says that only time will provide understanding, seems incredibly apt.

I find myself humming it as I take Sal and Jen to the back garden.

Day the Sixtieth

"How would you feel if the dogs chewed up one of your wood carvings? That's how I feel when they rampage through my bee-and-butterfly patch," I say to Colum.

"Difference is that your patch will grow back," he replies.

But I could see it had struck home.

Later he says "When we get back from our holiday we'll sort out the back garden."

I want to reply that we won't have any money left by then but I have been negative all day. There are words best left unsaid.

A lovely food fight occurs in the evening. I find myself pinned into a corner as two dogs snarl and snap at each other. The kitchen windows are open and the ugly noise floats outside. There are neighbours sitting outside enjoying a barbeque. I call Colum as calmly as I can. He comes in and takes hold of Sal. She squirms out of his grasp. He grabs her again and she ends up upside down in his arms as Jen jumps up and snaps at Sal.

"Pack it in, Jen!" yells Colum.

He drags the armful of dog and appendage to the dining room. I get hold of Jen's collar and pull her back into the hall. Colum emerges from the dining room where Sal is now deposited. We shut Jen in the sitting room. Go back into the kitchen. I notice that the neighbours outside are silent.

"Want a cup of tea?" I ask Colum. "Or a dram?"

Day the Sixty-First

The heat of the day is lingering into the night. At 2am I come downstairs to get some water. A tell-tale smell hits me. Sally has emptied her bowels on the stairs. I actually think of leaving it for the morning. My head and body are befuddled with sleep and I can't be bothered with this. But it is horrible and unhygienic and we have a friend of Sam's staying over. I go and get the rubber gloves and all the paraphernalia that goes with cleaning up dog shit. As I put the pooh bags outside the front door I linger a moment to register how still and beautiful the night is. Dawn is only an hour or so away and everything is at rest. I watch the sky for some minutes then close the door and pad back upstairs to bed.

I wake some hours later as Colum comes in the room. He has already showered and as he changes into his work clothes, I sleepily mumble "Sal left a nice present for me at 2am this morning."

"Another one?" says Colum. "I've just cleared one up too."

Oh, joy. I get up and wash my sticky body. I am towelling off when I hear Colum come back in from the garden and feed the dogs. There is an escalation of growls. I'm glad I'm in the bathroom. The kitchen door opens and shuts. I hear scuffling in the hall then silence.

"What's going on?" I ask when I emerge.

"No idea," says Colum, "but tension was rising so I bunged them out."

We talk about Sal. Is this behaviour just because of the combination of an upset tum and hunger? Has something else happened?

"I think I'll phone Julie this evening," Colum says.

I go in the dining room to pack my briefcase. My eye falls on one of Jan Fennell's books. I flick it open and come to a passage about an owner who is at her wits end with the aggressive behaviour of her dog. She sobs down the phone to Jan that the only thing stopping her giving the dog away is that she doesn't know anyone who will take her dog and keep her alive. Sounds familiar. I keep reading and discover that it takes this woman almost four

203

months to assert leadership and for the dog to accept it. I wonder how long we have been at it. It seems around three months anyway. The hardest thing for the woman was the fact that her family refused to have anything to do with the dog. Yesterday I was nearing that decision. I keep thinking of how much easier life would be without Sally. Over breakfast I ask Colum if he feels alone in it all.

"Sometimes," he says, "but my worst fear is that you will say you don't want her here. I'm trying to prevent that happening."

I tell him the four months story. "Makes me feel a little better," I say. "But I think we need to protect our relationship. This is stressful and it's so easy to pull in opposite ways."

"Well, the new Julia Roberts and Tom Hanks film is out this week I think," says Colum, "we could go and see that together."

I think of the looming MOT, Road Tax and the camping holiday.

"Yeh, perhaps, but I am thinking more of making sure we communicate better. I suppose what I am really saying is that I'm back on board – today at least."

Colum hugs me and goes off to work.

I take the girls into the garden before I go to the library. It is another stunning day. Apparently it is to reach 24 degrees – that's really hot for us. At the moment the back garden is cool and shady. I wonder if I should abandon the library and write long-hand, down here. Then a neighbour starts up his strimmer. No, the library is the better choice. The sun brings out too many people.

I collect the leads from where they are hanging on the gate. Jen is already waiting there. I look for Sal and see her deep in the foliage of a large plant which grows underneath the Rose of Sharon. She is lying in sphinx position and pokes her head out when I call her name. Her long thin face is surrounded and softened by crushed greenery and flowers. I smile and stretch out my hand to pat her head.

"Is that a nice place for a hot day?" I ask her. Her eyes seem to smile at me. My mind flicks to a photograph my sister has of a family dog, Ruillean, taken when he was a very young pup. Ruillean was also a black and white Collie but had a much nicer start in life than Sal has had. He was born on a croft in Morar in the West Highlands which is owned by some friends of my sister. His parents were working Collies (you know, dogs which did actual work as in herding sheep and things, not dogs which only carried the name of a 'working' dog – I really don't get why some people say that their dogs are 'working' when they are quite clearly spending their lives chewing stuff, playing, going for walks, eating and lolling about. On the other hand, as the majority of dogs are actually trying to look after humans, perhaps they can all be counted as 'working' and not just the posh pedigree types. The paradigm of the term obviously needs to be expanded. Rant over.) Anyway, we were only allowed a pup because Mairead and Catriona knew that we were an active family, who liked walking and would look after a dog properly, or so they thought. My sister and my dad travelled up to the croft by train and brought the wee pup home in an open shopping bag. He was a gorgeous bundle of fluff and we all loved him, but the transition to our home from his must have been really traumatic; he spent lots of time burying himself deep into my dad's flowerbeds and hiding there. As I look at Sally I can also see Ruillean. Sal may be older and leaner but as she peeks out of the foliage at me, I see a little frightened pup who isn't yet sure of the world or how it works.

"It's all right, wee girl," I say to her. "It's all right."

True to his word, Colum contacts Julie in the evening. There are a growing number of questions we need to ask her, the most major being: Just how much longer will we have to do this full-on training?

When Julie phones Colum on his mobile our landline also rings. I go and answer it, as I suspect it will be my mum asking about our meeting tomorrow. I hope to make it the briefest of calls, but my mum has been at a funeral that day and is a little upset.

By the time I get back to the kitchen Colum has moved on from the first question of how the holiday boarding could effect Sal, to the recent behaviour Sally has been treating us to. I also suspect that he may have told Julie that I was finding the whole thing really difficult and have been teetering on the point of giving up. Colum puts Julie on speakerphone and I say hallo to her. Speaking to Julie is like plugging into a power source when your battery is almost dead. It's such a relief to talk dog with all brakes off. Reminds me a little of a comment my doctorate supervisor said when I was preparing for my viva and feeling rather nervous.

"Look at it this way," she said. "No-one will ever be as interested again in your research. So enjoy it."

And she was right, no-one ever has been.

The upshot of our long conversation is that Julie thinks that Sal's recent slip back into challenging Jenna over food and defecating in the house is her making a bid for leadership as, in her eyes, we don't seem to be making a good enough job of it. Great stuff. Here we are busting our guts to make a good home for this mut and she apparently thinks we are inadequate. Julie locates the problem in our recent practice of taking Sal up the hill. The weather has been so nice that we have felt the need to get out and in doing so, have forced the pace of Sal's training when the outside world is still a scary place for her.

"Think about it," says Julie. "Are you happy and in control when you have her out with you?"

Colum and I look at each other.

"Em, no, not really," Colum answers.

"So, Sally senses that and thinks that she had better take charge. But remember, she's in a world she doesn't understand and is confused."

It's all making horrible sense to us. Yes, we have been trying to move her on to be a 'normal' dog and of course she isn't ready. I leap in to ask my main question: "But Julie, just how long are we looking at here? I notice that in the DVD and books by Jan Fennell that she seems to sort out a problem dog in an afternoon. Although today I did read of a case that took four months for the owner to manage. We are now over three months. Do we just have a particularly difficult dog?"

"What you have to remember is that that owner took four months to begin to work with her dog. You guys are already working with Sally. You are already seeing progress. And it's not helpful to think in terms of time-scale as it just puts pressure on you and Sally. You said you were at a yoga class this evening, Anne. Well, would you say that even after years of learning yoga that you know it all?"

"Absolutely not," I reply.

"Well, it's the same for Amichien. It is a lifelong learning process. You just move deeper and deeper into it."

Again, this makes huge sense. I have been desperate to know just when we can expect Sal to settle down, to learn our ways, to stop woofing and lunging at birds, foxes, helicopters and cyclists, to stop straining on the lead and dodging coming back on the lead and stop fixating on sunlight and dust particles and fighting over food. Ok. So there isn't a scheduled time. I have to pull back my thinking and accept Sally as Sally just where she is. Right.

Meanwhile Julie advises that we narrow in Sal's world again. Stick totally to garden pit stops, don't try to venture anywhere else with her, do lots of assertive calm leadership around her. As to the holiday Julie thinks that will be ok as Sal with accept it as different place, different rules. The important thing will be for us to re-unite with her in the Amichien way and so reinforce how our pack works.

"And you'll both be much stronger and calmer for the break from her."

"So we see it as respite for us," says Colum.

"Exactly," says Julie.

We ring off. Colum has taken notes during our talk. I suspect they might be very useful over the next few days.

Day the Sixty-Second

A sultry oppressive moody headachy kind of day. Waiting for a storm to break. Food fight in evening. I speak with Colum's sister, Anna, on the phone. Anna is a cat person. She tells me that she had to spend £80 at the vets today.

"But when you decide to take on an animal you have to live with that choice," she says.

"Yes, but I didn't know I was choosing a nutty dog," I want to reply.

Day the Sixty-Third

There is an exercise we do at yoga which encourages us to view life from another perspective. It involves raising an arm – left or right it matters none – up over your head, continuing to bend it in a (hopefully) graceful curve, ballerina style, while you turn your neck and head to look under and beyond your raised arm. Sally appears to be interested in mastering the philosophy behind this stretch as she once again ends up upside down this morning as Colum carts her off into the dining room, with Jenna snapping at her dangling ears.

I watch them go, think about following and saying to Sally "You know girl, life could be so much easier if you wanted it to be," but instead I just grab hold of Jen's collar as she makes yet another attempt to get the upper paw of Sally and push her into the sitting room.

Colum comes back into the kitchen. We look at each other, shrug our shoulders and get on with our breakfast. I begin to laugh. Colum raises an eyebrow in my direction.

"I'm just thinking what future visitors might think if they witness the break-up of a food fight. You walking calmly past them with a mental dog the wrong way up and me rugby-diving Jen – and all without breaking our flow of conversation. They'll think we've totally lost it."

"I'm glad you can laugh," says Colum. "Streuth. It's only 8.20 am and I'm already exhausted."

We munch our muesli ignoring the barking from respective rooms. Time the neighbours were up anyway.

Sal continues to escalate her push for leadership. Through the day she stalks Jen glaring at her and daring her to move right or left without her permission. I push through the dogs on my way upstairs, downstairs, in and out of rooms. I know I should take hold of Sal's collar and put her on her own in another room, but my spirits quail at the cacophony of barking and complete stramash which I know will happen should I do so. The best I can do is close a door on the dogs and take the audience factor away. I feel for Jen. This isn't nice.

Got a court citation in today. They are calling me in as a witness to the incident over the road. Start to replay in my head what happened. Keep seeing the huge bits of glass and the blood on the paving stones. Don't sleep too well.

Day the Sixty-Fourth

I have a meeting with the secondhand bookshop staff today. Come August and I will be a proper member of the team...hurrah! When ask what days I can work I say "Any but Tuesday." Those who have dogs give empathetic nods when I explain that Tuesdays are problematic as Colum can't get home for lunch and someone needs to sort out the dogs.

Those who don't have dogs just say "Ok, so what days are good?" I reflect how much easier my life would be without dogs. But the fact is that they exist and I have a contract to them. For the moment at least.

Later in the day, another example of when owning a dog gets a little difficult illustrates itself. Our neighbour's married daughter recently acquired a beautiful golden springer spaniel. The whole family have been invited to a wedding and all was jim dandy until someone said "What will we do with Rosie?"

Ah, Rosie. Every member of the family is going to said wedding. But Rosie, beautiful though she is, hasn't been invited. What to do?

The answer apparently presented itself one morning as I trogged past my neighbour intent on a garden pit stop. The neighbours. The dog-owning neighbours. Useful. Initially the daughter hit on the idea of asking Sam, which she duly did. He agreed to go into our neighbour's house, let the wee dug out, walk her twice round the garden, give her some dinner, freshen up her water bowl and pop it and her back in her crate. Voila! Done. And the payment would be a couple of bottles of his favourite cider. All was again fine until yesterday evening, the evening before the wedding, when Sam realised he was working this evening. The neighbours' problem suddenly became our problem. And of course good old mum bailed out her son. Truth to tell I didn't mind agreeing to take Sam's place. I thought it might make a very pleasant change to be in charge of a cute pup. I had plans to bring her into our garden and let her play with Jen. Sal, I assessed would be too much for her. But a good romp around our secure garden with Jen should fit the bill. I reckoned however without the thunderstorm.

Around 5pm the sky darkened and that peculiar eerie light, that tells you something is about to happen, filled the street. As if at the flick of a switch, rain began to batter at the windows; rumbles of troubled thunder shifted above us. Jenna shifted and buried deeper into her basket, Sal whines a little from her position on the top stair. Thoughts of romping in the garden exit my mind. We're down to basic needs now. My dogs are fairly settled, it seems daft to stress them by taking them outside. But what of the wee dug next door? Maybe the weather is freaking her. I decide to investigate. I turn the radio up a little so to drown out any more worrying thunder noises, put Jen in the living room, leave Sal in the hall and go down to the front door to where our wellies are stashed.

Outside it is really gloomy. It's hard to believe it's only just after 5pm. I sprint up our steps, turn into our neighbour's path, down their steps, skip over to the front door, pull their key out of my pocket and let myself through the storm doors into the tiled porch. All is quiet. I open up the inside door. All is still quiet. Then I hear a quiet whimper. In the middle of the huge hall is a smallish dog crate with a duvet cover over it. There are more whimpers and some movement. I squat down, pull up the duvet cover to reveal a wee golden face and two big brown eyes staring up at me. My instinct is to say "Well, hallo there! How are you?" but I don't. I need to assert leadership. If Rosie is concerned about the storm she needs to believe that I'm in charge and will protect her if necessary. I let her out of the cage without looking directly at her and walk into the kitchen. She pads in after me jumping at my legs. I ignore her. Outside the sky is still quite black but the rain has lessened. Maybe we could make a dash for the garden. Rosie will probably have a full bladder. The family went off to the wedding early afternoon and I don't really fancy clearing up any unforeseen mess. I pick up her pink lead and clip it onto her pink collar. Her fur is soft and kitten like. She jumps up at my bent face. I straighten up without saying anything. I'm in charge. I'm in charge.

We go through the two doors. Rosie is overjoyed to be outside and begins pulling up towards the street. Perhaps that's not such a bad idea. We hop up the steps and turn towards the cycle track. Rosie strains like crazy on her lead. Every few seconds I stop and wait for her to calm down. She pauses for a milli-second each time. We get into the park. She does a long pee. Good. A bird flutters up from a bush. Rosie jumps up on the hind legs and wants to tear after it. I hold onto her lead silently. This is all very, very, familiar. And I have to say that she's doing a lot of stuff that Sal does. Maybe Sal really is just an overgrown pup.

Difference is though that Rosie is what we would call a kenspeckle dog i.e. eye-catching. She's cute. She will be forgiven just because she's beautiful. Whereas our Sal hasn't a huge amount going for her in the looks department. Challenging behaviour and non-cute body shape aren't a useful combination. I know it's not fair to compare them but I can't resist. And Rosie is a blank page. She hasn't been messed up. Yes, she's excitable, but she's a pup, all she needs are some firm boundaries put in place now and they will keep her right. Whereas Sal ... well, you know.

Rain comes back on and I tug Rosie's lead. She leaves the long blades of grass that she was challenging and we make a quick dash for home. Inside I dry her off. She wriggles and squirms under the towel. Our neighbours are in the process of moving and there are boxes all over the place. I also notice that there are lots of open doors. This is also not a good combination. I pop a protesting Rosie back in her crate for a few minutes, then go round the house, shutting any door I can find. I also notice the new cream stair carpet bought, no doubt, to enhance the allure of the house for prospective buyers. New carpet and a puppy. Again not a good combination. But hey, it's not my problem.

I go back to the crate and let Rosie out. I don't need to do this. I could just leave her in the crate with her food and go away. But she's a young pup, the house is empty, it's miserable outside and I'm not in any hurry. I go in to the kitchen to locate her food. There is a tin and some dry dog biscuits on the counter. It looks far too much to me. I measure out half of the amount into her dish and put it on the floor. Rosie bounds over to it and starts eating enthusiastically. I search around for the kettle. I don't think the neighbours will grudge me a cup of tea. I find the kettle and then spend some minutes finding the cups. The kitchen is half-packed in boxes, but there are still a few cups in one of the cupboards.

Now tea bags. Tea bags. Surely they've got tea bags? I find the caddy. There are three bags in it. When they get home tonight from the wedding will they want tea? Will they notice that there are now only two tea bags? Well, they can share. I put one in my cup, pour boiling water over it, add a wee touch of sugar and sit down on one of the high bar stools around the unit sipping my brew. A feel a tug on the hem of my jeans. Rosie has finished her dinner and wants to play. I smile but ignore her. This has to be on my terms. Yeh, you're cute, but I'm still in charge. I finish my tea, wash up the cup so no evidence is left and replace it where I found it.

I suddenly wonder what our back garden looks like from their sitting room. Does it look the total mess it really is or do the neighbours' bushes screen the worst of it? I go towards the sitting room door and open it. A cat leaps out. A memory of my neighbour saying "We'll put the cat in the sitting room and keep the door shut," comes floating into my mind. Why did I have to be nosy? Serves me right. But what to do with the cat? Rosie, fortunately, doesn't seem to bothered with the cat. Would be a whole different scene if Sally was here. The cat seems to have gone upstairs. I think I shut all the bedroom doors. I go upstairs. Rosie follows. The cat is propped up on a pile of boxes. She isn't too enamoured by Rosie and starts spitting. I turn tail and go back downstairs. Cats are not my specialist subject. I don't know what to do with them. And I really don't fancy stretching out my unprotected arm and trying to grab her collar. I check my watch. Colum should be home about now. I text him and ask if he can come over and help me with the cat situation. Two minutes later he appears. Like me, I see him deliberately ignore Rosie.

"She's lovely, isn't she?" he says to me.

"Yeh, lucky people," I say.

I consider putting Sal into Rosie's crate and taking Rosie home with us. I decide however that although the drink may be flowing at the wedding reception, the neighbours still wouldn't addled enough not to spot the difference.

Colum goes up the stairs to track down the cat. I hold onto Rosie. Colum appears two minutes later with a furry bundle in his arms talking quietly to it. I open the sitting room door and he lets the furry bundle down. I quickly shut the door.

"Phew, disaster averted," I say. "Want some tea?"

We sit in the kitchen as Rosie charges around our feet. She hasn't let up since I came in over an hour ago. Not once has she sat still or flopped over. She's taken us on as her responsibility. That's too much weight for such a wee scrap of a thing. We watch her running about in circles for another ten minutes. Our dinner is calling. Time to put her back in her crate. I hesitate though. The family said they will be home around 10pm, that's still a bit of a stretch. I think a tour round the garden is necessary.

Colum goes off back home to start cooking and I take Rosie out on a big adventure to our neighbour's back garden. Our own garden will be a quagmire after all the rain, and I don't fancy clearing up a very muddy pup. We circle the garden twice. Rosie sniffs at every plant and bush but does absolutely nothing. So be it. I take her back up the path, in the double doors and straight into her crate. I want to say "Well, Rosie, it's been real," but I don't. I'm in charge. I decide when I come and go – so says the text book. A hear a tiny whimper as I close the first door. I stand and listen. Some scuffling sounds, a flump and a sigh. She's settled.

Much later, as I lie in bed reading, I hear the family come home. It's after 11pm. The drink must have been flowing. I reckon I could have swopped Sal for Rosie.

Day the Sixty-Fifth

I'm working on the 'good enough' philosophy. Take Jen up hill without Sal. I reckon that, if I do this occasionally, it won't upset our leadership stance. Lovely day. Sunny and breezy. So easy to walk Jen. Meet a chap with his wee cairn Terrier – Archie – whom I haven't seen for over a year. Jenna jumps and skips around with him – Archie that is.

"Last time we met," says the owner, "you recommended a dog training book by someone whose name is a plant."

"Fennell," I say, waving my hands to imitate teasing the delicate lacy herb through my fingers. "Jan Fennell."

"That's it, knew it was something horticultural. Are you still following her method?"

I am in mid sentence about how the Amichien training is really helping us assert leadership when a wee black and white beagle appears. Jen snarls, runs it off. Both dogs disappear.

"...and, as you can see, we now have a totally obedient dog," I conclude.

I start to go to find Jen, spy the beagle's owner in the distance, think better of it. "Actually, Jen will come back if I don't look for her," I say, hoping Jen won't chose this moment to disprove the method.

Archie's owner runs off to track down his dog. He reappears a minute later running back towards me, with Archie.

"Puff...puff...best...to...run...in...opposite...direction...when...I... need...him...to...come," he sputters as he rushes past. Seems like he doesn't need Jan's book. He's already worked the method out for himself. Jen appears over the crest of the hill looking scampish.

"C'mon you, you're just embarrassing me,' I say to Jen when she appears

Tired out from her run, Jen snoozes happily on her bed pad all morning – the dog baskets are now in the loft and will remain there until Sally Scissorhands has stopped her new pastime of ripping up stuff. Sal is quiet too. She isn't jumping, barking or stalking. She actually seems quite peaceful.

At noon we have a visitor. Andrew is the partner of Nan who is going to board Sal while we are in Findhorn. He's come to take a look at Sal. I have sent various emails stressing her particular penchants and Andrew and Nan are envisaging a raging beast. What greets Andrew is a placid black and white Collie, who gently gives him a paw and listens to him with rapt attention as he asks her if she would like to come to his house. I interject with a thesis-worth of Sal's history and her recent regressive behaviour. But that dog appears to have gone. The dog in front of Andrew is another one. I could lay money on the fact that Andrew will report to Nan: "Don't know what the fuss is about. There's nothing wrong with that dog."

Well, a fortnight of being with Sal might slightly change his first impression.

Watching Andrew pet Sal and watch her lap it up, and hearing myself tell him of what she likes and doesn't like, it dawns on me just how far we have come. Just how much we know her now. We know what will make her edgy. What will help her feel secure. What to do when she does this. What not to do when she does that. For the first time I start to believe we will get there.

Day the Sixty-Eighth

Three days have gone by and I haven't felt the need to lance my stress on the keyboard. A seismic shift indeed. Nothing miraculous has happened. Sally isn't lead-trained, she hasn't stopped worrying about foxes, birds, cats and other things that go bump in the night. We didn't take her out for a walk off or on-lead. But a shift has happened nonetheless. Sal spent the weekend slumped out on her bed-mat in the hall and she idly watched us out of one eye as we went about our curious human business. She trotted out to the garden four to five times a day, was kept on-lead so that she wouldn't fixate on the colonies of sun particles in the garden, and brought back inside. She listened to Classic FM, Radio Scotland Outdoors Show, Five Live Extra test match special, to CDs of Gregorian Plain Chant, Chett Baker, James Taylor, audio tapes of Billy Connolly's tour of Australia, and an assortment of beats and voices emanating from Sam's room. She had her dinner from a new bowl that Nan sent us – a wonderful invention that "slows down the chow" by being split into sections so that the dog has to take time to tease the food out instead of assaulting their stomachs with huge mouthfuls. She wrestle-played a bit with Jen but mostly she just chilled out, did nothing and was happy. We minimised her world and she liked it.

In Sally's case, less is definitely more. In drawing in her world, giving in to her own particular needs, I stopped trying to move her on, stopped trying to 'normalise' her but instead accept her just as she is. Andrew's visit allowed me to sit back and view from the sidelines the advances we have made since that fateful Easter Monday afternoon. Since Sal has come to us we have changed the way our garden, our house and our thinking works. In the garden the six-foot wire meshing keeps Sally in and other threats out. My bee-and-butterfly patch is a mess and the grassed area has disappeared and been replaced by mud. But this morning I found myself looking at these areas with different eyes.

After our holiday I plan to move the roots and remnants of the ground-cover plants up to the raised bed in front of the house leaving only the wall climbers and small sturdy shrubs where they are – they should be able to sustain the mad romps of the dogs. The grass/mud area will be paved over – we already have an offer of free slabs – and thus eradicate the minefield of potholes that the dogs have created. The back garden needs to become functional rather than aesthetic. I've let go of how it has been and am now thinking of how it could be.

As the Buddhists say, 'resistance to change only brings suffering' or something like that. And I have been highly resistant. In the house, doors that had locks which didn't work now have fully functioning ones. Ironically there have been a couple of incidents of burglaries in the street but, thanks to the needs of Sal and Jen, our house is now more fortified. We also think that any intruder would have to be really mental to want to break into our house – the postman still thrusts letters in as if they are ticking bombs and random delivery people or those coming to read gas or electricity meters, still need assurance that I won't let the dogs out for the three minutes they are on our doorstep or in the hall.

During Andrew's visit I also understood how much we now know about Sal. She came to us with huge blanks. No-one knew her name, no-one knew exactly how old she was, where she had come from, why she ended up as a stray, how long she had been a stray, what happened to her when she was out there on her own and what exactly went on in her other rehoming episodes. And Sally couldn't tell us, couldn't give us words.

Instead we had to learn to read her through her behaviour – her wee prancing dance at sunlight and shadows, her desperate frenzy when food appeared, her raised hackles and stiff shoulders at unseen evening dangers, her phobia about the lead, her sheer joy when a ball is produced, the gradual softening of her eyes, her courteous play-bow when another dog appears and her contended sigh as she stretches out on her side at our feet.

As we move day by day with her, as I write about her and our life with her, we thus construct a history which all beings have the right to have. She will not end her days as an unknown and perhaps that is the greatest gift we can give her. Jeannette Winterson, says says in her memoir *Why Be Happy*

When You Could be Normal that adopted children often experience a sense of severance from one's own story, one's own narrative. So it is with rescue dogs, there is no previous owner to tell you what they did or didn't do and why the dog now behaves the way it does. And perhaps we wouldn't really want to know. But the hiatus is still there and is powerful.

Vets tell us that dogs live in the Now. Maybe that is true but their bones remember past experiences and when Sally fixates on dancing light or shadows she is operating out of a time previous to us. Our job then is to bring her into the Now. To help her believe that her now is safe, that there will be food enough, sleep enough, play enough, and hopefully, if my patience holds out, love enough.

Respite and Ruction

And with those wise philosophical words I packed away my laptop and went on holiday. We dropped Sally off in Fife with Nan and Andrew, having given them written detail of Sally's likes and dislikes, then, feeling that we had done our best for Sal, drove off up to the Moray coast and Findhorn.

Jen had had to sit at my feet on the journey to Nan and Andrew's, now she stretched out in glorious isolation in the space we had put Sally. I noticed she didn't seem remotely curious where Sally was.

And we had a great holiday. It wasn't just the soul-enhancing beach which I ran along, it wasn't just the walks around Cluny Hill and round the Findhorn village, it wasn't just the dip into the excellent second-hand bookshop in Logie Steading or the swim in the Findhorn river, it wasn't just the time we had to to sit and read, read and read, it wasn't just the calm of the free meditation sessions, the evening of sacred dance or the daily Taizé prayer in the Foundation, it wasn't just the tasty scones and soya cappuchinos in the Blue Angel café or the freshly baked spelt bread, the ewe's cheese or the mellow Scottish red wine that made their way into our daily repast, it wasn't just the meals with friends and the making of new connections with other souls on the road, for me it was simply that I didn't have to think about Sally, write about her, attempt to walk her, work with her or do anything at all with her.

Colum, not being me, kept in touch with Nan and was concerned about how Sally was doing. He asked me if I would also phone Nan.

"Why?" I asked.

He was disappointed in my response but I couldn't do anything about that. My mind refused point blank to mull over Sally and her needs and when I did drag it to think of Sally, usually when Colum wanted to share his report of her with me, I just thought of a black fog. My unspoken wish was that we would end the holiday, get to Nan's and she would say that they had grown so attached to Sal that they wanted to keep her.

Meanwhile we had Jen with us who was lapping up the adoration of the campsite. The wardens timetabled a daily stop at our tent to chat and pet her and a brilliant wee six-year-old chap called Alan – a real boy boy – lost his scampish heart to her and was gloriously happy when we asked him to help feed, groom or play with Jen. Watching her stretch out on her back to receive yet another tickle, I wondered for the umpteenth time just what we were thinking of by getting another dog. And with 24/7 attention, three or four walks a day on the beach or machair or wood, Jen seemed blissfully happy. I did mention Sally to some people if we were doing dog talk, but all the while felt as if she was just a complexity that belonged to our home life and had no bearing on our present state. Oh, it was veritable rapture.

I also stopped worrying about money. Just before travelled north our dear old van went in for an MOT; it failed, failed, failed and finally passed to the tune of £400 the day before we were due to go on holiday. Any extra money we had had now gone. My sensible head said we shouldn't be going on holiday, shouldn't be boarding Sally, but staying at home and just tholing it. There is however such a thing as "The Findhorn Effect" and it swung into action, just as I was sitting at our kitchen table, sniffling into my dinner saying that we should just give up on the idea of a holiday this year.

The phone rang. Colum answered it. I was feeling too miserable to chat with anyone and continued gloomily munching my oatcakes, salad and humous. Pádraig was ringing to say that he wouldn't be joining us this year in Findhorn as his elderly father was very ill. Pádraig's wife and children were already in the caravan park in Findhorn and had been there for almost a week.

"Maureen has decided she wants to come home and is bringing Catriona with her, so our caravan is all paid for and free for the next six nights if you guys could use it. The only slight thing is that our lad would like to stay on, if you wouldn't mind looking after a teenager?"

A broad smile appeared on Colum's face.

"Well, I think the answer is 'Yes please!' but will check with the missus and phone you back. Thanks! That's really thoughtful of you, and the timing couldn't have been better."

They talked a little of Pádraig's dad and what was happening there then rung off. Colum turned to me "Findhorn is On" he said and then told me what Pádraig had offered.

"So that means we don't have to pay for six nights ground fee," I said "that will really help and we get to stay in a snug caravan. Bless him."

"I take it, that's a yes, then," said Colum and, without waiting for my reply, rang our good angel back and said it was a deal.

Things like this happen around our Findhorn holiday, actually things like this happen quite a lot around our lives. Just when we are wondering how we will find the cash to do stuff someone says "You can stay with me," or "I've got slabs you can have," or "I've just done a clear out of my clothes and wondered if you could use any?"

I so often forget this powerful network woven around us. A network that doesn't run on financial profit or gain but on sheer giving to the other when the other least expects it, but when the other could really use it.

Another example of the 'Trust effect' came to us at the end of the holiday. We had had fifteen days of freedom from Sal and her issues and my spirit was really struggling with the thought of having to factor her into our daily lives again. As we approached Nan and Andrew's house my spirits were sinking. I really didn't want to pick up Sally. I would so have liked to just drive on and go back to being a family with one easy dog – well, one that chases sheep and doesn't like the postman, but one that we can cope with.

Colum, of course, being the more compassionate half of our partnership, said "I'm really looking forward to seeing Sal. Wonder if she will recognise us?"

I don't remember answering.

When we pulled up at their house Andrew was just coming home with two of their own dogs. He gave us a big smile and shouted "Just give me a minute to settle these two and I'll let you in."

We busied ourselves re-arranging the dog spaces in the van while we waited. Jen would have to go back at my feet again while Sal took the larger space behind. It felt like she was encroaching on our new-found freedom immediately. Andrew appeared at the front door.

"C'mon in," he called. "Sal's waiting for you."

"Would it be possible for us to re-unite the dogs in your garden?" asked Colum.

"Sure thing," said Andrew.

From my position on the front door mat I could see in to where Sal was standing up on her hind legs at the dining room door dog gate. She was wagging her tail and barking. Did she actually recognise us? Or was it Jen she recognised? Or was she just happy to see people? At least she wasn't unhappy to see us. I closed the front door and went with Colum and Jen round the path at the side of the house which leads to the garden. By the time I had closed the latch, and checked with Andrew that it was secure, the dogs were chasing each other around the garden. No issues of re-uniting there then. Andrew offered us a cup of tea and as it was brewing we sat in the evening sun on the back door step watching the careering dogs.

"How'd it go then?" asked Colum.

This seemed to be the question Andrew was waiting for and he launched into an account of the last fortnight – how they had given Sal some long walks every day, how they had used a halti as they quickly saw that she would pull them off their feet if they didn't, how they had got her to slow down her eating, how they thought she had dominant issues, how she loved the play sessions with some of their own dogs, and how they used a covered crate in the dining room as Sally's own private space. It had obviously been a long haul.

Listening to him I felt both justified and disheartened. A fortnight of Sally had indeed opened their eyes as to her issues. But no magic wand waving had gone on, and Sally was still Sally, and she was definitely coming home with us. Nan came home as we sipped our tea and she reiterated some of what Andrew had told us.

"She's a good dog," she said, "but you've got a lot of hard work ahead."

I wondered, as both of them filled us in with more detail of the doings of Sally, just what they had said to each other in the privacy of their own space. What did come across is that they thought the only way forward was for us to walk, walk and walk Sally. We nodded and smiled but didn't comment. They also told us how they had used the crate and offered to loan it to us. I demurred – it seemed too much to take it from them, surely they would need it for other dogs?

"That would be brilliant, thanks," said Colum, ever a man not to operate with false politeness, and promptly went off to our already loaded van to see if he could find space for it.

And, thank the lucky stars, Colum did find space for the crate. Over the next few weeks we were to bless Nan and Andrew over and over again for gifting it to us. During one of the meditation sessions in Findhorn I had thought about Sally and asked that we would find a way through with her, or find a new owner who would be prepared to continue to work compassionately with her. The way through has proved to be the crate. When we arrived at our own home a whole new challenge presented itself as Sal decided to make a bid for the upper hand.

The dogs had been running around the sitting and dining room while we brought in the whole paraphernalia of our camping gear. Sam, who had been at home for the previous week, had the kettle on, the floors hoovered, rooms tidy and an atmosphere of calm floated through our home – it remained like this for roughly ten minutes. Then a growling emitted from the hall. Sal had Jen backed into a corner and was giving out low growls if she attempted to move. As Colum took hold of Sal's collar she bared her teeth, reared up and lunged at Jen. Jen, in turn, showed her teeth and ran at Sal. I was in the kitchen unpacking a food box and as the ugly noise rose and decided to stay there – why keep two strong men if you can't depend on them to sort out a dog fight? With the help of Sam, Colum pulled Sal away from Jen and tossed her into the living room and shut the door.

"What's that about?" asked a stricken looking Sam.

"Just resettling stuff," said Colum calmly.

The "resettling stuff" continued over the next day. Whenever the dogs were together Sal would attempt to subdue and dominate Jen.

"We have to assert leadership," said Colum "Sal obviously thinks we are not doing a good enough job."

"Oh, what fun," I replied. It seemed to me that we were back at square one, in fact at negative one. Before our holiday, Sal had more or less got along with Jen, now we had two dogs who weren't at peace with each other. Great.

Had we not had the crate I think Sal would have been rehomed that week. As it was we did have it and it gave us a path through the craziness. If we had had to isolate Sal in a room on her own she would, no doubt, have taken her frustration out on anything chewable. Instead of this, we set up her crate in the dining room and partially covered it with a dark travelling rug. This became her home within our home. Colum called it 'Sally's Sacred Space'. Sam and I named it 'The Slammer'.

Resetting

We contacted Julie, who said separating the dogs was the right thing to do and not to rush re-integration. She was sure Sal's behaviour was rooted in her fortnight of having to face the world and take on a responsibility she wasn't ready for. We had to go back to minimising her world again, making it safe for her. And the crate was an excellent idea in Julie's eyes.

I thought of how much we had changed in our own perspective. When Jen first came to us, her first owner also gave us the crate they had kept her in. Neither Colum nor myself were advocates of crates as we viewed them as nothing more than a euphemism for a cage. Now, with our new philosophy of making the world small and safe for a stressed animal, and the highly practical issue of stopping our house being ripped apart, we thanked the bountifulness of Nan and Andrew for loaning it to us.

It wasn't plain sailing though. For the next week we had to pause at each door, open it a fraction and shout "Jen alert!" or "Sally coming through!" Getting the dogs toileted and fed became a finely tuned manoeuvre. If visitors called in during one of the 'Change over times', they found themselves locked into the kitchen sometimes with a dog while we corralled the other dog into a room, or out through the front door. The hall became the equivalent of a decompression chamber.

"So, remind me why we have a second dog?" I asked Colum after three days of this. "She spends a lot of her time in her crate, she wants to eat Jen, she has gone back to defecating on the carpet and howling at the moon."

"I agree with mum," said Sam coming into the kitchen behind me. "I can't stand this and I'm surviving it by saying to myself that I'm only doing one more year at home then getting out."

"Well, that's it," I said. "I'm not having Sam moving out just because of a dog. If he wants to move out because it's a natural progression, being almost twenty and all that, that's fine, but I will not allow him to leave home because of Sal."

Colum sighed. The game was up. The deck-hands were rebelling. "We need a meeting," he said.

We sat down at the kitchen table. As a family we do this every so often when life throws us small or large wobblers. We lit a candle, everyone got a drink of something, and then sat in silence for a few minutes. The upshot of our meeting was as follows. By mid-December Sally has to come up to the following requirements:

1. No challenging of Jen.
2. No defecating or peeing inside the house.
3. No random unexplainable barking at unsociable hours.
4. Walk peacefully on the lead.

Colum wrote these out and fixed the list on the fridge door. We all felt much better. There is always something reassuring in having decided something. Made us feel as if we had a handle on the situation. Both Sam and I thought that Sal's fate was fixed; it was simply a matter of putting up with her mayhem until December. Colum said he felt he had definite markers to work towards with Sal.

"But to be fair to Sal," I said to Sam. "Both you and I really have to try to work with her. We can't just give up on her. We don't know if we will be able to rehome her and what kind of life she will have if we do. We may have a dog's life in our hands and we have to give it a serious go and try to help her."

Sam agreed he would try harder. He also said that his week at home on his own had given him a taste for getting his own place. He had loved the freedom of doing exactly what he wanted, being able to have his friends round and cook for them without asking us, making up his own timetable, shopping for himself, arranging the house as he wanted it, having doors open without having to think about dogs and generally just being in charge. So when we arrived home, not only did he have to contend with two parents who automatically resumed authority, but also have to put up with two dogs whose issues demanded that doors are shut and a firm regime is in place. In other words he is ready to fly the coop, and we can't completely blame

Sally for Sam's growing desire to stretch his wings. As a natural trajectory for a young man I can accept it – although miss him – but as a result of us rehoming a stressed dog, I will fight it totally. The dog will go out first.

So, on we went. The next hurdle to think through was the visit of our friends. We wanted to have Pádraig and Maureen and their kids over for a meal to thank them for their generosity to us. Without consulting the other, both Colum and I reached the same solution as to what to do with Sally.

"I was thinking we could move her crate upstairs to the spare room just for a few hours," I said. "We need to have some calm while Pádraig and Maureen are here, they've had enough stress recently."

"Exactly what I was thinking," grinned Colum.

"Oh, right, good."

And move the crate we did. Sal was quiet in her solitary space upstairs and we had a lovely afternoon and evening with our friends. At one point Colum asked Catriona if she would like to go upstairs with him and see Sally. Catriona's last encounter with Sal hadn't exactly been a good one and we wouldn't have blamed her if she had said it she was busy for the rest of her life. But being the gutsy wee lass she is, she agreed and trotted off with Colum. They appeared about twenty minutes later. I checked Catriona's face – no sign of worry. Good. Good. Colum said he was going to take Sal into the garden and this time Maureen asked if she could accompany him, curious as to how Sally was progressing.

Later in the evening when they had all driven away, I asked Colum how the garden session had gone.

"Pretty good. Sally showed off her stop/start thing and Maureen was impressed. You know we really have come a long way since their last visit."

I wondered to myself if it was more that we are slowly learning how we can cope with her. I thought back to that first epic afternoon when she had louped over our pathetic wee garden fence and stood quivering in the street. What unprepared twits we were.

We continued to keep the dogs separate for over a week; Sal continued her residence in the attic. Our initial plan was to bring her crate back down to the dining room once our friends had gone home. But it appeared that Sal liked her elevated status. Our attic was converted into two bedrooms some years before we moved into the house and, although rain and wind always sound ten times worse from this level, the pay-off is the distance from other noises in the building. There have been a number of nights when we hear our young neighbours revving up for a good-going teenage party which would make opportunity for a decent sleep rather slim, but which is do-able if Colum and I move into the spare room in the attic. Sal must have seen the potential of this room too as, when we went to check on her after our friends had left, she was stretched out on her side contentedly listening to some slumber-inducing symphony on Classic FM. She looked so snug that we left her crate there that night and the next day and the next. We soon began to call it "Sal's room". One afternoon as I came along the street I could hear muffled barking – Sal, letting the downstairs staff know that she would like her afternoon garden play.

"Where's that noise coming from?" asked a neighbour.

"Oh, it's just the mad dug in our attic," I replied smiling serenely.

The neighbour looked at me, thought she had heard wrongly, and then carried on pruning her roses.

Reintegration

And so we slowly edged forward. Jen and Sal lived total separate lives for over a week. Then, one evening, just as I was beginning to think about making dinner, Colum said he was going to let the dogs meet in the garden. I grabbed hold of the cast-iron excuse that I wanted to get on with the dinner. Colum said that was fine as it may be better to have Sam and his muscle power there.

I watched them from the viewing box of the sitting room window as Colum progressed down the path towards our garden. Sam was already in our garden with Jen off-lead. Sal gave a little wag to her tail when she saw Jen. Jen backed off a little but didn't cower. Colum came through the gate and let Sal off lead then went and sat with Sam on the bench, both of them appearing nonchalant, although I was certain they were on high alert for any sign of aggression from Sal. I couldn't see all that happened from my viewing point but it seemed to be ok. Then I saw the dogs begin to chase each other round the garden. They were playing. Colum looked up at me and gave me the thumbs up, a huge smile on his face. I went back into the kitchen, took one of our pottery goblets off the shelf and poured myself a good measure of red wine. There are some things you just have to celebrate.

When Sam came in later he described the re-union for me.

"It was as if Sal looked at Jen and Jen looked at Sal and thought "You're that dog that I don't like but actually I do, so…em…d'ye want to play?" and off they went. It was great."

Delighted as we were with the success of re-uniting the dogs, we thought the "ca' canny" approach was still the best one. Once back in the house we fed Sal and put her back in her crate in the attic. She was tired from the nervous effort of it all and from her charge about the garden. When I looked in ten minutes later she was on her side with her eyes closed. Over the next week we continued this softly softly strategy. The house still had too many corners that Sal could trap Jen in, if she wished, and we didn't want to give her the opportunity.

So each day they played together once, if not twice, in the garden. After their breakfast romp, both dogs were fed separately then Jen stayed in the sitting room, while Sal flitted about the kitchen and hall as we got our own breakfast. When I went to move towards my desk, I put her back in her crate and let Jen out. Jen slept on her bed mat in the hall. Mid-morning I took Jen around the hill – just a shortish circuit but enough to give her some time to do her downloads. She then went back in the sitting room. I then got Sally and took her to the garden where we played ball and practiced 'stop, start, change direction'. And so it went on. I began to wonder what people without dogs do with all their freedom.

Sometimes it all went really well, other times a feckin' cat appeared on the path which leads towards the garden and all hell broke loose. But I learned to just stand still and hold on to Sal's collar for dear life, trying to keep my pulse low, and then edged her towards the safety of the garden.

I wondered if we need a demystifier. When Sam was a toddler he had a fascination for plugs and sockets. We didn't want to keep yelling "No! No! *Dang..er..ous!*" to him so Colum hit on the idea of a demystifier. Onto the lid of a wooden box Colum fitted a socket and plug without wires. The box was painted in bright colours and attractive to a toddler's eye. Sam would sit for long stretches of time with the box between his crossed legs, breathing heavily with concentration and pulling the plug off the socket and then jamming it back on. He would lift the lid of the box and examine the back of the socket, then snap the lid down again and begin the whole process again. Eventually he got tired of the demystifier, and plugs and sockets never held any attraction for him again.

But stuffed cats aren't really a speciality of Colum's and it is open to question if Sal would then think that all cats can be grabbed and chewed without any harm to herself.

Hanging In

In early August I had begun my two-day-a-week job in the bookshop; this was making a huge difference in my life. Apart from being surrounded by books and being paid, there is the added bonus of the discussions, in which one gets involved with random customers, such as "Is a verb more important than a noun?" and "Is BSL a native language?" and "Do you think the Kindle will kill shops like this?" or the more extreme type of query such as "Do you have a book on Scots law that will tell me if I can legally shoot my neighbour's pigeons?'.

So it's not all sorting and stacking shelves, it's engagement with the reading culture of our town. And I get to wear clothes other than my dog gear. I do notice though that I miss having a "me" at home. The me who doesn't settle for only the everyday basic chores being done but adds on the watering of plants, the sweeping of stairs, the changing of bed linen, the cleaning out of a cupboard, the de-frosting of the fridge, the cleaning of windows, the constant tidying up and so on. My menfolk are great guys but whereas I might sort out washing while I prepare some lunch, they will schedule in the watching of the first half of a film. Good father-and-son time and all that but but but … you get the picture.

And my days at home, which are ostensibly supposed to be for writing, seem to be filled with endless rounds of dog care and catching up on jobs not done. One evening, tired from my day in the bookshop, I blew up about the stink from the sitting room carpet, the fact that our spare room was now a kennel, almost every door had serious scratch marks on it and every floor surface seemed to be covered in dog hair and said I was taking Sally back to the SSPCA. This squall passed over, mainly due to a conversation with two people who said the right thing at the right time.

Paula and Iain take their dogs to the same agility class as Jenna, and I had always admired their calm on my occasional visits to this class. A day after I had delivered my "I'm taking her back on Sunday morning" ultimatum, I went with Colum to the class. I don't attend this class very often. It's all a bit too frantic for me. But the day was sunny and warm and, as I had sustained a moody silence for the last twenty four hours, my higher self prompted me towards some communication with my partner. The walk along the cycle track to the class is a peaceful and pleasant and lends itself to meditative thoughts. I still hadn't reached a conclusion as to what I wanted to happen to Sally. My mind kept slipping to how much easier – and hygienic – our family life would be if she just wasn't around.

At the end of the class, after the dogs had exhausted themselves running through tunnels and over ramps, we moved outside and fell into conversation with Paula and Iain. They told us that both their dogs, who performed beautifully in the class, were rescue dogs and that it had been a long haul with both of them.

"Six months," said Paula. "At the very minimum, it takes six months to see a difference with a rescue dog. And, if I'm totally honest, around two years for them to really settle."

She then went on to tell us of their first rescue dog, Sam, who took it upon himself to be Paula's protector. If Paula had gone to bed and Iain wanted to join her, he had to wrap his arm in a thick towel, grab hold of Sam who had been lounging about their bedroom, and basically fend off Sam's ferocious growls and snaps with the aid of a rolled up newspaper.

"Any non-dog person would think we were mental!" laughed Paula. "But we persevered, because we just couldn't bear to think what might happen to Sam if we returned him."

This was all sounding rather familiar to me.

"And with Coll," their apparently placid Collie who was happily stretched out on the grass at her feet, "it took around three months before we could begin to start to work with him. He was so fearful of everyone." Paula went on to talk about how adaptable you have to be with rescue dogs. "If one way doesn't work, then you have to rethink and try it from a completely different angle and eventually you hit on the way the dog can cope with," she said.

Like me, there had been many times that she and Iain were on the verge of giving in and returning whichever dog. I told her how I was feeling and just how hard it all was.

"Sounds like Sally has found her way to a really good home. You guys are her best bet. I really hope you carry on. It will get better. Really it will."

While I was chatting to Paula, Colum had been talking with Iain on much the same lines. When we finally said good-bye and started on our way home I said, "Ok, Sally can stay for now, at least until December."

"Thanks," said Colum and did a wee dance of celebration.

What Sally Did Next

Had Sally known her fate was still undecided, I wonder if she would have then gone on to do what she did. It is useless to surmise of course. She did what she did and we once more had to cope with it.

Catherine had called to ask if I had any spare time to meet her for a walk as she felt the need of an old friend to chat to. She came over mid- morning and she, Jenna and I went off for a glen walk. The glen is always a balm to the soul. There have been many days when I have begun to batter around the wooded tracks up there, chewing over some tangled detail of life, only to become aware after some twenty minutes that my footsteps have slowed, my pulse has eased and I am content to stop and note how the colours of the trees blend together in a manner fashion designers will never be able to imitate, begin to hear the chirp of chaffinches high up in the branches, catch a glimpse of a soaring kestrel, watch how the mallard ducks make fan-like ripples as they swim around the far edge of the large pool, and how Jenna swims in a pretty lady-like manner as she pursues a floating stick. The glen did not fail us the morning. Catherine and I strolled around it and we returned to our house in a tranquil frame of mind ready for a cup of tea and a chewy bacon sandwich.

As we drove into our street I saw Colum at the parking bay outside our house. I flashed the lights at him and he waved then gave me the thumbs-down. I slowed the car, wound down my window and called "Is it Sally?" There was something about Colum's demeanour that spoke of Sally trouble.

"Yes, she's run off. Sam had her up the hill with Jimmy for a play and just as she going into Jimmy's garden, she hit on a scent and darted off. I don't know where she is. She's been gone about half an hour."

I parked, got out of the car then thrust the bag of crusty bread and other nice munchies we had picked up at the supermarket, on our way home from the glen, into Catherine's hand.

"Here, you go and get yourself some lunch and I'll help Colum look for Sal."

Just as I spoke we heard movement down the side of the house next door and a strange kind of anguished woof.

"Sally! Sally! Here, Sally!" I called. She appeared before us and I let out a gasp. She was shaking and holding up her left hind leg which was streaming with blood.

"Oh, Sally, Sally, what's happened to you?" I said.

I leaned forward and held onto her collar, and shouted to Colum who had moved off down the street that I had her. As he ran back to me, I was saying in a manic fashion, "Vet. Vet. Let's get her to the vet. Vet. Now."

We opened the boot of the car and Colum lifted Sally and climbed in with her. "I'll hold her. You drive."

Abandoning Catherine, who assured me she would link up with Sam, who had just appeared at the end of the road with Jenna, we drove off. There was a curious feeling of *déjà vu* about it all. When Jack had made his final exit I had driven the van to the vet with Colum in the boot holding our very sick dog and here we were again. I willed myself to be calm, 'to choose peace' as I had been advocating Catherine to do, and drove steadily to the vet.

Colum managed to phone ahead, so they were ready for us as we carried Sal in ten minutes later. The surgery was quiet and a white-coated vet soon appeared in the consulting room. My first thought was that his white coat was inadvisable, given the state Sal was in, but I presumed he didn't really care. As Colum held on to the quivering Sally and I gave sporadic detail about her. Sal's leg was in a terrible mess. The bone of her lower leg was exposed and there was lots of gunge hanging from it. The vet checked her eyes, manipulated her leg and felt all round her bowel area. I expected Sal to scream at some point but cradled in Colum's arms she just panted. Colum let out a sigh. I rubbed my hand over his shoulders, he seemed in need of pain relief as well as Sal.

The vet continued his probing and then said "Well, I can't feel anything broken and everything else feels ok, but that leg needs some serious attention. So we'll be keeping her in and operate on it this afternoon."

After checking our contact details, we said goodbye to Sal, as the vet lifted her up into his own arms. That white coat! I wondered if he knew that he would need to soak it in cold water to get the stains out. Maybe he would just throw it away. I hoped not. Looked like a good cotton to me.

Sinking into the front seats of the car, Colum and I both let out a long breath.

"Daft girl! Daft girl! Did you see her leg? It's horrible."

"But the incredible thing is that she came home," I said. "She actually came home."

With that glimmer of positivity we drove slowly home.

In our kitchen a short while later, we found Catherine at the stove, Sam munching a huge bacon sannie, a pot of tea on the table and, within seconds, another plate with a sannie for me.

"I was supposed to be consoling you," I said to Catherine "and making you lunch."

"Just sit down and eat," commanded Catherine. "You need it."

I acquiesced immediately.

"And you don't fool me for one minute. Despite all your protestations about the chaos this dog has brought you, when you saw Sally so hurt the look on your face was of utter love and compassion. Somehow that dog's found a way into your heart."

I couldn't answer as my throat seemed to have a huge lump in it that was nothing to do with the bacon sannie and my eyes were strangely out of focus.

They did manage to operate that afternoon and the vet – he of the white coat – phoned to give me a report later in the day. They had only been able to stitch the wound half way as the tension around the area was too great. Because of this he fully expected the wound to become infected but they would try and combat this with antibiotics. Meanwhile we had to keep her as quiet as we could, not allow her to play with Jen, keep her on the lead while in the garden, and bring her back to the surgery every two to three days to have her dressing changed and keep a close eye out for any sign of distress.

When I asked what the longer term prognosis was he said it was hard to tell. The fact that Sal was a young fit animal went in her favour but the deep tear to her leg was still a cause for concern and really only time would tell how it would heal.

We retrieved Sally from the surgery the next morning. A kennel nurse brought her out to us in the waiting area. Sal was now adorned with a pink lampshade and a stiff crepe bandage, also in pink, which was wound half way up her left hind leg.

"The team girlified her," said the nurse. "We thought she would like pink."

Personally I think Sal is more of a leopard spots kind of lass, but we let it go. The main thing was that she was standing before us, albeit a little lop-sided, but healthy enough to go home.

As Colum led Sal off to the car, having sent a volley of questions to the kennel nurse and an on-duty vet as to Sal's care and possible recovery, I remained to sort out the crucial issue of payment. A weighty bill was waiting for our credit card. As I slipped the card into the machine, I thanked the vital component of caution and common sense in our make-up which had guided us to take out insurance for Sal. My experience of our family Collies as I was growing up was that they rarely saw a vet and one was only called in when a dog was in dire straits. But the experience with the dogs — that Colum, Sam and I have shared together — is one that says you just never know the minute a dog will do something really daft and dangerous.

Once again I made a mental note to someday do a sponsored run for PDSA, so those poor sick dogs who haven't wealthy owners can get the treatment they need when they need it. Meanwhile I loaded the bill onto our credit card and gave the clerical assistant the insurance claim form. This was a time to pay up and shut up.

Sal was now seriously grounded. In some ways it gave legitimacy to our newly adopted regime of keeping her for long stretches in her crate while in the house. It was important that she rest and not stress her battered leg. And rest she did. The effect of the anaesthetic and the antibiotics must have kicked in as Sal seemed very happy to flop about on a mat for hours on end. We also had to go back to keeping Jen away from her. They might be fine on a pack level, but medically Sal wasn't up to jumping and tumbling with Jen. It's strange how some experiences, that have seemed rather tough and weird at the time, are actually preparing you for what has to come next. Had we not had practice in keeping the dogs isolated from each other while they were acting aggressively towards each other post-holiday, we would have found Sal's post-op days very awkward.

As it was we just swung back into pressing our lips to the crack in a slightly open door and yelling "Jen/Sal alert!", and waiting for the scurry of feet and claws and the welcome "Ok, come on through!" or as we began to say "Ok, you're free to land!"

And if we were not well versed in toileting Sal in the back garden and keeping her on a firm lead there and back again, we might have found the vet's injunction of "I know this will seem impossible, but you must keep her walking to a bare minimum," extremely difficult. In many ways it was just situation normal but with a slight added vigilance as to Sal's progress.

We had been given a list of symptoms to look out for which would suggest significant infection of her wound but fortunately, perhaps because of the rest she was getting, she seemed to be doing fine. Colum took her back to the vet two days later, to have her wound newly dressed, and then two days later again. The area was apparently still weeping but not deteriorating which was a good thing. Colum though found the visits frustrating.

"They all seem in such a rush and they don't really answer my questions about what the future holds for Sal and I keep seeing different vets all the time," he complained. "Today I actually felt as if the clerical assistant deliberately went to work through the back so she wouldn't have to speak to me."

As I listened to him I wondered if the problem was that it really hurt Colum that Sally was hurt. He needed assurance that she would fully recover and that she would learn from this experience and not do it again and so I wouldn't say she had to go. He had tried so hard to calm her down and integrate her into our family life, and so wanted it to work that this latest left-field challenge was completely exasperating him. There was therefore a lot more invested in his desire for a positive medical report than just improving health.

The Sketch in the Vet's

One morning around a week into her post-op phase, I offered to take Sal to the vet's. If I were writing a short story it would go like this...

It's Thursday morning, 9.05am, and I'm driving down our road towards the vet's. Sally, our rescue dog, who for reasons known to herself alone, badly tore her leg while running rampant off-lead last Tuesday, has to have her dressing changed. Colum, my long-suffering husband, has done the last two vet visits and come back a little frustrated each time as he feels that he can't get a direct answer to his question of how exactly Sal is doing. I have volunteered to take Sally today even though I don't really want to do it. There's always more than a modicum of possibility of chaos when out and about with Sal.

But fair's fair. I'm not doing my paid job today and Colum is. It makes practical sense that I do it. And I have an unsaid suspicion that a more softly softly approach might work for luring out a tentative prognosis than Colum's previous full-on interrogation of the on-duty vet. The old 'wise as a serpent, gentle as a dove' thing. I can do that. I'm quite calm today. I will wheedle out any info there is to be had on our Sal. I will. I am sure I will.

Half-way to the surgery Sal starts barking. The road is quite busy with relieved parents who have just deposited their offspring in the care of a school. As I slow up to wait at the traffic lights a bright yellow truck pulls up behind me. Sally jumps around the boot of our Berlingo. She has a bright pink lampshade around her neck and it keeps wacking off the triangular window of our van as she spins about looking for an opening. I wonder if the driver in the yellow truck can see her or is waving at her. I hope not. She seems nervy; I'm glad the drive to the vet is only ten minutes.

I put on Classic FM. We play this almost constantly for her while she rests in her crate at home. I'm hoping the subliminal message of familiar music = home = security will register on her excited brain. As she spins more furiously, I reckon it isn't working and switch to Radio Four which is what I wanted to listen to in the first place. The gravelly voice of Jenni Murray fills the van. She is giving an account of what will be on *Women's Hour* today. I haven't listened to that for ages. Makes me think of the pre-Sally days when I would drive up to the Gleniffer Country Park most mornings with our other dog, Jenna, and after a soul-enhancing stravaig about the glen, would tune into the second half of *Women's Hour* as I wound my way homeward. That was when life was calm. That was when owning a dog was simple, easy-peasy, lemon-squeezy. Now, as some comedian said somewhere, it was difficult, difficult, lemon difficult. We continue our merry way and arrive at the vet's. Good. It doesn't seem to be busy. Might turn out to be a peaceful experience.

I park the van and go round to get Sal out. It's always a bit tricky off-loading our pet. We had found out very early on that she had realised that the back door of a Berlingo van rises with a gentle slow ease, taking its time, no hurry at all. The person waiting outside has to step aside as the door comes up – unless you want a skint nose. This stepping aside affords a plentiful window of opportunity for a skittish dog to seize the moment and drop to the ground as its owner stands waiting for the door to finish its manoeuvre.

Having had a couple of mad chases after our newly rescued canine, we now have a method whereby the person stands to the side of the elevating door and when two to three inches of space opens up between said door and inside boot, an arm is extended into the boot and a quick grab of Sal's collar, leg, tail or whatever ensures her carefully-planned dreep to the ground is thwarted. Today my hand snatches her lampshade which surprises her as she can't quite see what is restraining her, and then I grab her lead which I deliberately left clipped onto her harness. Phew. I notice then that the protective plastic sock which we have been instructed to keep on her injured leg anytime she is outside of the house has come loose. Better fix it back on. I will look a complete numpty if I take her in without it. Busy holding her lead and securing her plastic sock on, I fail to notice another car pull up beside me and a man emerge carrying a ventilated box.

Plastic sock firmly on we make our way along the path and up the front steps. I stretch out my hand to open the glass-fronted door and my eyes fall on the figure inside. Oh, joy. A man and what is surely a cat. A cat in a box. Sally lifts her lampshade and begins to sniff. She's sussing it. I hover on the top step. The man is at the counter. The box is on the floor. I wonder if I should come back or should I wait a few minutes. But I can see that the rest of the waiting area is empty. It's just the man, the cat. Maybe he will get taken immediately. He doesn't. He goes and sits down. He puts the cat in the box beside him on the bench. I grit my teeth. Try to keep my pulse low – what did Amichien Julie say? … think peaceful, think calm … think peaceful, think calm … and open the door.

Sal clocks the cat immediately by scent or osmosis I'm not sure. What I do know is that I now have a mental dog to deal with. As Sal rears up on her hind legs – what this is doing to her sore leg is a question I haven't space to deal with – and let outs out a series of yowls. Three heads emerge from behind the counter as the clerical assistants perceive we have arrived. I lever my bum onto the nearest bit of the bench so to give me maximum pull-back, and call "*Cat issues!*" to the enquiring heads. The eldest head belonging to the substantial kind of woman that doesn't allow for disruption in her life, demands of me: "*Name?*"

I shout "*Sally*".

"*Daffy?*" questions the assertive head.

"*Sally!*" I yell again.

"*We don't have a Daffy surname on our books,*" shouts the head.

"*No! That's her name. My name is Scriven.*" I blast back. I now have my right hand on Sally's harness — designed to comfort and reassure the animal — and my left on her collar. She is still on two legs, dancing and squirming in her desperation to get over to the cat in the box.

"*Striven?*" shouts the head.

God, how hard can this be?

"*No. Scriven,*" I reply. Really, does it matter what the hell my name is? Can't this woman see I have other matters in hand. Literally.

The door at the far end opens. A vet appears.

"Sally?" she asks.

"*Yip!*" I shout. "*I'll try to come over but it could be a bit difficult.*"

The vet smiles, bless her, and walks calmly over to me. She places her hands inside Sal's lampshade and says "I remember you. You weren't like this last time."

"Welcome to my world," I think.

"I'll take her," she says. She obviously has me down as an inept owner.

"Good luck," I say.

She takes hold of Sal's lead as I let go of the harness and collar. Feeling the give of tension, Sally lunges towards the cat box. The owner shrinks backwards and pulls the box onto his knee.

"Woah girl, Woah!" says the vet who is now, I note, standing in text book horse restraining position.

I move around to the front of Sal, grab her harness again and the vet and I do a deft foxtrot out of the waiting area. We make it into the small narrow corridor. My shoulders sink a fraction.

"She has cat issues," I say lamely.

"Yes, so it would seem," says the vet who is sweating a little.

We go through to a consulting room. Sal is back on four legs.

"It's good she is putting her weight on her sore leg," pants the vet.

"Yes, it is."

"I'll take her to the treatment room. You can wait in the waiting room if you like."

If I like? I'm out of the room before she has finished the sentence. I wonder if the water fountain has anything other than water in it.

Back in the waiting room all is quiet. Man and cat has disappeared. The three heads have sunk behind the counter again. I need to use the momentary calm to check something with the clerical staff. They continue to ignore me. Stuff that. Time is precious.

"'Scuse me," I say in my most assertive manner, "but I need to sort something out before my dog gets back."

That seems to work. The middle head pops up. She is the youngest and newest of the team. She hasn't yet learned to nip at clients.

"Sure," she says.

I explain to her that our insurance claim doesn't seem to be being processed as yet and I just want to check that they have sent off the paperwork as one more bill will bust our bank account. She checks her computer and explains when the forms where posted. We both do mental calculations and decide that all is ok. I sink down on a seat. I have a few moments grace before Sal comes back. I could practice some deep breathing. It's good for menopausal women apparently.

The door into the street opens. A woman comes in carrying a fluffy ball.

"Aaaaaw," says the middle head. "How's he doing this week? Alfie! Alfie!"

The ball of fluff has a name? More *oooh*s and *aaah*s emit from the other heads. The woman sits down, the fluff ball bounces about her feet. The door opens again. A man and woman come in with a larger version of the fluff ball.

"Aaaaah, another Shih Tzu," says the second woman.

A whit? I would be embarrassed to go about saying I had one of those. They sit down near the first couple and begin Shih Tzu talk.

The man believes himself to be an authority on the breed. In rejoinder to whatever the owner of the pup says he answers "Yes, they do that".

There's obviously nothing that surprises him about these dogs. The older dog eyeballs me. I turn my gaze away. You're not intimidating me, wee guy. I've dealt with real dogs. There's no way a fluff ball with a clipped and combed fringe merits my attention.

The door opens again. A woman and a teenage girl come hesitatingly into the room.

"Em, we need to have our new dog checked out by the vet," says the woman.

The man perks up. A new owner. Excellent. Virgin territory for him to vent his vast knowledge on.

The woman and teenager walk over to the space on the bench near to the oldest Shih Tzu. The older Shih Tzu moves towards him and sniffs the wee terrier. The terrier snaps.

"Oh no!" says the terrier owner. "That's terrible behaviour."

"A real terrier," chuckles the man. "Ye see, the thing with those dogs is…"

But we don't learn the thing as two vets appear and the Shih Tzu pup and older Shit are taken off for examination. The room goes quiet. It's just me and the terrier folk.

"Ah'm that embarrassed," says the woman to her young girl. "We cannae huv him snapping at ither dogs, it's jist no on."

Should I bother? Can I be arsed? I pull myself out my lethargy. "Don't worry about it," I say. "It's just a pack thing."

"Aye, but that's no good. Our dug went for his."

"Actually it was the other dog's fault. He invaded your dog's space. Your dog was just telling him to back off," I reply. I'm not having a great wee terrier put down by a pampered shitty thing. They look uncertain. "It really is no big issue. Seriously. I've got a rescue dog and you'll see in a few minutes what a problem is."

They smile but they're not listening. Their world is revolving around their new arrivalt who looks perfectly normal and adjusted to me. I consider asking if they would like a swop.

The door to the small corridor opens again. My vet emerges holding Sal. She now has a bright blue bandage on her leg —Sal that is, not the vet — and seems a bit on edge.

"Did the dressing distress her?" I ask.

"No, that was fine but some twit came into the room carrying a cat. I told them to get the hell out," said the vet.

Sal sniffs the room. It must still smell of cat as she yowls again. The terrier people stiffen. I grab hold of Sal's harness as the vet tightens her grip on Sal's lead. Sal lets out another full throttle yowl.

"*She's doing fine!*" the vet yells, "*Healing well.*"

"*Great,*" I reply.

"*Bring her back on Tuesday.*"

"*Thanks,*" I shout, taking the lead from the vet who promptly disappears.

My plan of asking probing questions melts into dust. Something tells me I should just get home. But the gods have more amusement up their sleeves.

A door near the corner of the counter at the opposite end of the room opens. The man and the cat reappear and head towards the counter to settle up their bill. Streuth. The 'CAT!' switch in Sal's head flicks on. She goes ballistic. I stand in the middle of the room holding onto her, unable to move. I turn my head back towards the terrier people.

"*See what I mean?*" I shout. They don't reply. They are staring transfixed with their mouths open and their terrier has his paw raised in salute to Sal.

The man with the cat dithers. I gesture towards the door. He thinks I want him to go out. He goes towards the door.

"*No!*" I yell. "*I'm going out!*"

He stands on the doorstep holding onto his box which has gone curiously silent. He seems immobile. For God's sake this is no time to get the jitters. I'm the one with the mental dog. I switch to teacher-and-mum mode.

"*Come back in and right back into that corner!*" I shout. He does exactly as instructed.

I teeter towards the street door. Sal does a weird two-legged pantomime horse prance, her upper body turned to the cat while her hind legs follow my steps. I lever her out and stagger down the steps to the pavement. I don't look up at the window. I don't want to see the faces pressed against the glass. I stand in the street, holding onto Sally. Her whole body is shaking. I put my arms round her.

"It's ok. It's ok," I say. I'm actually talking to myself. She calms a little. Her catometer is sinking.

The gods then gleefully fling a final parthian shot. A fire engine which has quietly reversed out of the station next door puts on its klaxon.

WOOAWOOAWOOOAWOOOWAOOH!

Sally leaps for the sky. Cheers chaps. I bundle the shaking Sal into the car. Drive off. When I get home I remember I didn't pay.

The short story would end there but as you, good patient reader, will expect, the saga of Sally in reality continued. I phoned Colum when I got home and related the full epic to him. He didn't reply immediately and just as I was wondering if the connection had severed, I heard him take a breath as if he was about to speak but then give up the attempt and dissolve into wheezing laughter. I waited patiently for him to compose himself. I waited a full eight minutes.

"Oh that's brilliant," he finally spluttered. "Wait till I tell the guys this one."

And tell the guys he did, and any other unsuspecting captive audience he met over the next week or so. While glad to have provided so much entertainment, I did also announce that I wouldn't be taking Sal to the vet again – at least not on my own.

"Of course you could always do what I do when I go there," said Colum.

"What's that?" says I.

"Keep Sal in the car, go in and register, wait until the vet calls you and then go and get Sal and bring her in the side door and straight through to the consulting room."

"Oh right," I say. "Glad you told me that."

Baths and Bandages

But I didn't take Sal to the vet's again. There are some things that, if possible, one should leave to one's partner or husband and this, in my book, is one of them. So Colum and Sal trotted off to the vets every few days and finally one evening Sal hopped up the stairs still with lampshade on but no dressing. The wound had healed sufficiently to allow all bandaging to be taken off. Her leg looked skinny and vulnerable and there was a dark scar running down the inside of her left hind leg but the hair had begun to grow over the new skin and overall it looked pretty good. Things were moving the right way. But Sal, being Sal, didn't leave it at that.

The next evening found us phoning the emergency vet again. Despite her restricting lampshade Sal had managed to get to her wounded leg and worry at her scar which now looked red and sore. The vet, no doubt not really keen to drive to the surgery on a Sunday evening, advised us to wipe the scar with a medicated wipe, then pop a long sock over it and secure it somehow. We did this and sprinkled a few drops of Tea Tree essential oil over the sock for good measure. Dogs are not enamoured by Tea Tree and like neither the taste nor smell of it. This held Sal for the evening, but as we were still concerned by the look of the wound and the fact that she could obviously get to it, Colum took her back to the vet's the next evening.

When Sal returned home she was wearing an enormous lampshade – designed for a St. Bernard or Great Dane – but it was all the bemused vet could think of for our Sally Longshanks.

For the next couple of weeks Sal battered about the house working the massive lampshade like a satellite dish. I wondered if she could tune into the control tower at Glasgow Airport, but also worried that she wouldn't be able to reach her food and water dishes. Somehow though she managed and we got used to steering her up and down stairs, through doors and garden gates. The vet had advised us to still keep her walking and exercise to a complete minimum so to give the exposed wound a chance to heal. The crate we had inherited from Nan came into its own again and we continued our skilful dance of dog and room manoeuvres for the next fortnight. And then, in an attempt to get into the sympathy scene, Jenna decided to toss us a moment of concern.

Strolling around a park near my elder brother's flat one Sunday afternoon, Jen ran off in pursuit of a rabbit. We watched her circle around, crash through the undergrowth and belt round trees. Giving the game up as hopeless when the rabbit eluded her, she bounded back to us through some long grass. I heard a sound of cracking and then Jen appeared, still running, but with one paw smeared with blood. Colum and I ran to her.

"Oh no, no!" said Colum. "Not you as well!"

I held her collar as Colum squatted down to locate the source of the bleeding. It seemed to be coming from a deep puncture in her front right leg just above the paw. There was nothing sticking into it, no sign of glass or a sharp stick, or, God forbid, an old needle, but blood was still gurgling out.

Colum pressed his thumb to the area. "We need to keep pressure on it to stop it bleeding. Anyone got anything we can bind it with?"

I was already rummaging in my bag. All I could come up with was a plastic pooh bag, tissues and a sanitary towel. We could fashion a makeshift bandage out of all of this but we needed an elastic band or something to secure it. Both my brother's girlfriend and I automatically ran our hands through our hair and searched out pockets and bags looking for a band of some kind but not a one was to be found.

"We're just not girlie girls enough," I said. "Real girls wouldn't leave home without a scrunchie or so in case a pony-tail was required."

"I'll just tie the bag really tight," said Colum and proceeded to do so.

A good sign was that Jen didn't whimper as her leg was being bound up, but she didn't seem to think the wad of tissue and the black plastic bootee we constructed round her leg was a good look. As she seemed fine with putting weight on her leg we let her walk but it was slow progress. Every few steps she would stop have a sniff at the weird cumbersome bag on her leg, try to rip it off, be told not to, trot for another few yards then try to rip the bag off again.

Our plan that afternoon had been to stroll to the glass houses in the park and have a cup of tea but we abandoned this in favour of getting back to my brother's flat and checking Jen's paw out properly. The menfolk went ahead of us, saying they would carry Jen if she seemed distressed. Bridget and I followed on after stopping to check out a local store in the hope of buying some proper bandaging. All the store visit yielded was a box of fabric plasters and some more sanitary towels – as Bridget pointed out, they are designed to soak up blood, so we judged them possibly useful.

Colum was running a shallow bath for Jen when we got back to the flat, and Kenneth had found an old sheet which could be cut up into strips for bandages. Jenna was happily munching on wee bits of biscuit Kenneth was feeding her, so to distract her from her punctured leg. It all had a feeling of *déjà vu* for me, except this time a dash to the vet's didn't seem necessary as yet. Colum tipped some drops of ye wonderful Tea Tree into the bath so to disinfect the wound and then lowered a non-too-happy Jen into the water. Blood was still coming from her leg but it had slowed up and Colum managed to clean the area and check that there weren't any bits of glass or grit in the puncture. I then passed him strips of sheeting and he bound up Jen's leg and tied it by cutting a vent into the final strip and knotting it tightly. Jen still wasn't too pleased either with her dook in the bath or her new leg attire and was glad to escape the bathroom and trot into the living room where Bridget and Kenneth had laid out some tea. She got another biscuit for being a brave lass then slumped down on the carpet to have a good go and getting off her pesky bandage. Colum sat down beside her and pulled her into the crook of his legs.

"C'mon, wee girl," he said. "It'll be alright, just leave it alone and take five."

I said I thought we all needed to take five or twenty and slumped down into a chair as Bridget passed me a mug of tea.

"So now we have two hirpling dogs," I said. What fun.

To further complicate matters, Colum's mum was taken into hospital the next day, so, a little worried by her condition, Colum headed off down south for a few days. So I was once again head manager.

Just as I was girding up my wimpish spirit, Sam looked up from whatever computer game he was avidly playing and announced that he could help me. In fact, as his shop job had come to an end some weeks ago and his new job wasn't due to start for a week or so yet, he was free to help all I needed. Hurrah for wonderful sons!.

Over the days Colum was away there were a few times that I heard the words "bloody dogs" pass across Sam's lips over the days as he trudged past with a dog at 7 in the morning or 10 at night, but overall we did ok. And when Colum got home, now satisfied that his mum was well on the mend, we celebrated our success by removing Sally's huge lampshade collar. Sal has already indentified Colum as the one who deserves her devotion, so we gave the pleasure of the momentous "Taking off of the Collar" to my man.

As we sat around the kitchen table about to enjoy a welcome home cup of tea, Sal battered her way into the room.

"C'mon Sal. Let's get you out of that thing," said Colum.

Sal trotted over to him and sat patiently while Colum untied the straps and catches of the plastic contraption. As he stripped off the collar and Sally's head and neck emerged we all chorused "It's a dog!"

Sal gave herself a shake which seemed to ripple right through her body, then gave some wee skips. Colum ruffled her neck fur and Sal bent her neck into his hand to better enjoy the sensation. She then lifted up her injured leg and gave the area behind her ear a long long scratch. We could almost hear her say "*Ooooooooh*, that's *goooooood.*" After that she skipped out of the room and into the dining room where she proceeded to do five triumphal laps around the dining room table before coming back into the hall, finding a bone and tossing it into the air. One happy dog.

An hour later Colum thought we could try and accomplish yet another stage. Jen and Sal had been kept apart for six weeks. They had caught sight of each other at 'cross-over times', but we couldn't let them play for fear of further injury to Sal's leg. We presumed that their first meeting could therefore be a bit dodgy as we may have sent out unconscious signals that being together wasn't a good thing, so once again we decided to let them meet in the garden.

Sam took Jen down first and let her off lead and Colum followed a few minutes later with Sal. Once again I watched them go from the sitting room window. I saw Sal hunch into prey mode and my heart sank a little. But, coming closer to the garden gate, Sal began to wag her tail. Inside the gate I saw Jen wag hers. Sal and came through the gate and Colum let her off lead. Jen moved towards her, dropped into play bow stance and that was it, they were off. Charging around the garden, jumping on each other, chasing from one side to the next, skipping, dancing, happy happy mates. I found myself smiling.

"We did it," I thought. "Thus far, we did it."

A few days later, now that Sal's leg was well on the road to full strength, we let the girls meet and play together in the house. All went well for a few sessions then Sal started to annoy Jen and also urinated on the carpet twice. As I mopped up the soggy mess for the second time I found myself mentally framing an advert:

> Wanted: One compassionate home for highly-strung 2 year old female Collie. Former stray. Must be quiet adult but active household with very secure and accessible garden. No cats. Must be patient and willing to continue training in the Amichien method. Must understand about fixation of sunlight and shadows. Must tickle her behind her ears and leave Classic FM playing while left alone. Must give her a hollowed bone with butter once a week and good food twice a day for the rest of her life. Must try to love her.

I wondered where such a home could be found. As I put the disinfectant away and washed out the cloth and bucket, I heard a small voice in my head say "Here."

Swimming On

It is early December. Dusk falls around 3pm, the temperature averages just above freezing, the heating is turned up a few notches in our house, sensible people have taken to wearing woolly hats and several layers of clothing, I am finding it harder and harder to go for a run in the dark and cold, the first Christmas lights and trees are appearing in windows, people ask each other if 'you have started yet', the shops are getting busier, the pressure to get organised is on. But within our household peace, more or less, reigns.

As I write this Jenna is stretched out on the dining room carpet, her eyes tightly shut but her cute button nose twitches every few seconds – either to show that she is still on duty, or in accordance with her dream, I'm not sure which. Sally is out in the hall in what has become her basket. She is curled up in a loose ball, her head buried low, and cares not a whit about being on duty. She lazily opened one eye, when I padded past carrying washing for the machine; she opened it again as I took a cup of tea into the dining room and my desk, but judged neither actions as deserving of her input. Both she and Jenna are quite content and will not look for attention for another couple of hours at least. Six months on and life, as we once knew it with dogs, is re-emerging.

There has been no miracle. Sal still freaks if she sees a cat or fox, she still has the occasional accident in the house, she still doesn't really like the dark and still has spat every so often with Jenna. But there are now glimpses of light. Sally has begun to come back to us when off-lead. Well, I say 'we', I actually mean 'comes back to Colum' and there's a qualifying 'sort-of' entailed in the statement. I haven't actually been brave enough to try it yet and, on my rare walks alone with her, clip the double-ended lead firmly onto her harness and hold it with both hands. By contrast, Colum has managed to get Sally to the stage of playing up the hill with him and Jenna off-lead. Again I need to temper this statement in that Sal has a long rope still clipped to her but not clipped to Colum. He tried this method some weeks back and discovered that, provided there was a game happening, Sally was quite happy to dance around, trailing her long rope, and dash after a ball, ring, or frisbee and stay within range of Colum being able to step on the rope if she wouldn't come to him when called. This dance now happens at least twice a day and the result is two exercised and happy dogs. During one of the first sessions Colum took a video recording and texted the following to Julie in Edinburgh.

Hi Julie,

I thought you might like to watch the enclosed video of Sally to get an idea of where she is. I now take her up the hill and attach a long rope to her so that she can run freely and I can still catch her if necessary.

Best wishes,
Colum.

He received the reply:

To: Colum
Subject: Re: Sally progress update. Wow that is amazing, you must be delighted, I hope you are very proud of yourselves, I know it has not been easy and you need to have the patience of a saint! but it is well worth it to see such a happy relaxed dog. Thank you so much for sending me the clip I love it. Keep at it. I knew you could do it.

Stay calm and patient and you will all be fine. Thanks again
Julie

I however am not too great at playing football on a wind-swept muddy hill with a pack of dogs circulating me, with the off-chance that one of them will not come when called and a rugby-dive may be in order. So Colum has become the fun-meister of their morning and lunchtime romps and I accompany them only when a glen walk is scheduled.

And here we have another landmark to record. Sally can swim. She didn't know she could but the lure of sticks and Jen having fun in the water and the always attractive extra of being off-lead was enough for her to have a go. I have to say again that this was achieved by my wonderful man. He simply is much more adventurous than I am and a few Saturdays ago unclipped Sal as he threw sticks into a pool up the glen park. Sal apparently skittered around the edge for a bit then waded in. She was apparently totally surprised by all the wet stuff, how cold it was and more to the point,that the floor suddenly sloped away. She had to move her legs in a new way and some instinct inside of her told her how. After a few strokes she scampered back up on the bank, scooted off, Colum held his breath, and she re-appeared again and wanted to join in the stick game again.

On the next glen walk Colum tried it again and she did a few more strokes and again stayed within grabbing distance. She practised on subsequent walks and I went to spectate a few days ago. My whole being wanted to yell 'Nooooo!' when Colum unclipped her but I shut my mouth and watched. Jen was already in the water heading out for a stick when Colum threw in another. Sally barked a bit, skittered at the edge, then plunged in and swam out and out and out.

'Sally!' I shouted.

She heard me and turned and headed back to the bank. Incredible. Really incredible. Again my instinct was to quickly secure her, but Colum laughed and threw another stick and let her have a few more goes before quietly leaning over, when she came ashore, and clipping on the lead. Two tired, exhilarated and very clean dogs returned to the house.

What I have described here is, however, a good day. On other days, Sally just will not come back on the lead for any price – it always seems to happen, too, when we don't have another hour to muck about and entice her back, and when we finally manage to grab her, it is more a case of two against one, or as many people we can muster, rather than a dog happy to come back to its owners. And we return home, disillusioned and feeling back at square one. The bottom line, though, is that we haven't given up, we're still in there slugging it out, holding on to the belief that one day Sally will give up being frantic and make life easier for all of us.

And we're not totally alone in the effort either. There are other good -hearted people who have gifted us their wisdom and helped us work on some area of Sally's behaviour. I think of Nan, who taught Sally to eat slowly and quietly, who reminded us of the benefits of a crate and who offered us respite in the dark days of the first summer with her. I think of Val, who drove up from her snug coastal home one very very wet evening, when lesser spirits would have quailed, and showed us what T Touch had to offer stressed dogs and stressed owners. I think of the wonderful Katie, who took on a once-a -week walk of both Jenna and Sally without a murmur, and who copes with Jen's penchant for dining out on rabbit and deer, and copes with Sally just being Sally. Each of these excellent women have their own philosophies and belief systems where dogs are concerned. We don't agree with all of theirs and they don't agree with all of ours. What we do agree on though is that dogs are worth our efforts. And so we go on.

Decision

December 15th dawned. Our agreed decision day for Sal. I remember it happened quite simply. Colum and I were in the kitchen getting breakfast organised, Sam was in the shower. Something made me look at the calendar.

"Hey, it's December 15th," I said.

"Yip," said Colum "What d'ye reckon then?" He seemed to be holding his breath.

I walked over to the bathroom door, pulled it slightly open and called "Sam, December 15th, do you think Sal gets to stay or not?"

Without pausing in his ablutions, Sam replied "She's part of the scene Ma. It's ok with me."

Colum looked at me.

I sighed. "Ok. She can stay."

Colum bent down to Sal who was sniffing around her bowl in the hope of something going in it soon.

"Hear that girl? You're getting to stay!"

When he came in from work later that day he was carrying a bottle of bubbly.

A Year's Turning

It is Easter Monday. We have moved through a liturgical calendar year. The weather isn't as glorious as it was last April but the blossom is back on the trees and the light comes early and leaves later and later every day. Lacy salvia and delicate fritillaria have flowered in my newly-hoed and sorted bee-and-butterfly patch and the fennel and honeysuckle and clematis are stretching and opening up their stems. There is fresh nurturing compost on the border where we have planted crocosmia, rosemary, rhubarb and wild strawberry plants. The grass is still scant and grubby but around it the garden is coming back. I will go and potter in it later but for now I am sitting in our kitchen writing or, if truth be told, thinking.

Colum and I have been on holiday for the past four days, and have resolutely refused invitations to go and gather and gab elsewhere; instead we have chosen to take some time to be together, to walk, to do a local cycle ride, to sort the garden, to cook, to drink a glass or so of wine, to munch our Easter eggs, and to take stock of where we are. The house is quiet around me as I sit at the kitchen table. Sam is out working at his beloved IT shop – he landed this job a few months ago and so far it is feeding his soul. Colum is outside cleaning the bricks we rescued from a skip which are intended for a new path in the back garden. Jenna is snoozing upside down in her basket half way up the stairs.

And Sally? Sally is lying at my feet stretched out on her side with her eyes closed.

It would be great to now write 'which all goes to show that although it has been a tough year, it all paid off in the end', but that line belongs in a work of fiction and therefore not in this book. What then is nearer the truth? Well, by the very fact she lies spread out at my feet says that she is still with us. The fact that she is breathing says that she is alive. The fact that her eyes are closed but her ears are twitching, says that she is semi-relaxed. And that's roughly where we are with her – in 'semi' land, no definites, no massive achievements, no 'wow' moments to record. One year on from her coming home to live with us, she still freaks at the scent or sight of foxes, has recently taken umbrage to the returned roosting pigeons on our roof, still thinks cats an affront to civilization, and isn't thrilled by car journeys.

But, but, but…in that space of time (and this is my mantra when things don't seem to be progressing), she has learned her name, learned how to eat slowly, learned a handful of root words (bed / come / dinner / biscuit / play / walk / sit), and apart from a slip up on Christmas day when a friend knelt down beside the coffee table to sort a game of Scrabble and found his right knee smothered in fresh pooh, she has (touch wood, touch wood, touch wood) stopped down-loading in the house. And around 60% of her walk around the neighbourhood is frantic-free. We can have her off-lead if a game of footy is involved as well as a long trailing lead or rope – (note: I say we but I still mean Colum – chugging around a soggy hill with a ball just doesn't fill me with joy) and my occasional walks with her, amounting to fifteen minutes or so along the cycle track, still culminate in a sigh of relief when we reach the safe harbour of our front door. We also don't ask her to cope with large groups of visitors and make sure she is safely ensconced in her crate upstairs with an entertaining chew until the atmosphere is more settled. Neither do we try to have her with us if we are working or sitting in the garden as she prefers the comfort of her bed and the quiet and soothing sounds of Classic FM in our hall. She still isn't ready for our annual camping holiday which will happen in July but will stay at home with Sam – have to say this wasn't exactly on Sam's summer schedule, but he was seduced by our offer to pay him the amount we would a dog boarder. In other words we know our Sally better this year. We know what isn't a good plan and what should be. We are learning.

Arrival

Well we sincerely thought we were learning, but in hindsight – oh, that great enlightened perspective which pontificates a fraction too late to be of any use – we were still asking too much of Sally. What strikes me as I read back through this account of her arrival and first months with us, is just how incredibly naive we were, willing and well intentioned, yes, but going about it the wrong way none the less. There are so many instances of where we think up and try to follow through what I now view as insanely mad ideas – like taking her out for a good belt around the hill, seeing if she could run off lead up the local braes, letting visitors rush up to her to say hello, leaving her alone in the garden, taking her out in the car and other damaging impulses. Now, my Sally-experienced self shouts at my own narrative:

'Nooooo! Don't be so stupid! She can't cope with that! You can't cope with that. Don't do it! Don't! Don't! Don't! Oh ... you've done it. Jolly good. Now deal with that one. Twits!'

It took until Colum did the first part of the Amchien Bonding dog listening course for us to appreciate that we were still asking Sally to cope with a stage she wasn't ready for. Having watched numerous filmed scenarios of wolves in the wild, of stressed domestic dogs at home, listened and discussed the wisdom of the Amichien philosophy, Colum found himself seated beside the founder of the method, Jan Fennell, in the final session of the introductory course. Thinking that such a chance may never come again, Colum spoke very briefly to Jan about how Sally was still so nervous outside of the house and how difficult it was for me to walk her or to let her off the lead.

'Sounds as if you shouldn't be taking her out yet, poppet,' was Jan's answer.

A year on and Sally shouldn't be going out? Whit? When Colum got home and reported as much to me I felt like packing numerous suitcases and leaving. Thanks again to Sam and our lovely dog walker, Katie, who is a god-send for the dog owner ready to implode, I had only had to cope with two pulse-heightening struggles to the park and back, and so had got through the days Colum needed to be away. To now hear that Sal wasn't ready to go out – or do 'The Hunt' stage – sent me into complete bewilderment. Just what the hell were we to do then? Let her shit all over the house?

We needed Julie's help again. Jan obviously didn't know our house set up, couldn't see that we don't have a secure garden immediately accessible, but Julie did.

'How about taking her to the wee patch of grass just under your big tree outside the front door?'

The said patch of grass measures roughly two metres square. But it does have fairly good drainage and is two feet from the safe anchor of the front door. We tried it. Sally looked at us. We tried it again. She looked at us. We tried it again. She looked at us. We sighed and tried again. She did a pee! We texted Julie, exultant. Problem solved. We then found a pooh at the turn of the stairs, a pooh on the living room carpet, a pooh in the dining room. We texted Julie again.

'Ah, yes, you have to expect resistance,' she said, 'but keep going, she'll give in eventually.'

We employed the kitchen towel, disinfectant, incense, open windows and newspaper again and again and again. I wanted to leave. I dreamt of owning a one bed flat with cream coloured carpets or waxed wooden floors that were beautifully clean, a balcony with vibrant untrammeled plants in pots, and a life without dogs. We took Sal to the pee tree every opportunity we could, with me muttering 'This is stupid, this is really stupid'. She did a pooh there. We opened a bottle of wine. Drank too much, giggled at what the neighbours might think.

We went on holiday. Sam took Sal to the pee tree four or five times a day. Easy earnings for him. He phoned us on holiday and said "Sal is much better without Jen. We should only have one dog."

We suggested he might like to take Sal to live with him when he moves out. He didn't think that was a good idea. We didn't care. We were on holiday.

We got home. The dogs integrated fine. We stuck to taking Sal to the pee tree. Fortunately the summer was a wet one, helpful in washing away non-attractive scents. Had it been a scorcher, we might have had to do some serious explaining to sunbathing neighbours. As it was Sally had relative privacy for necessary downloads which we swiftly picked up and bagged. If our downstairs neighbour did witness what was going on she kindly refrained from comment.

We gave up on trying 'The Hunt' or walking Sally anywhere – that seemed a practice or routine belonging to other owners with other dogs and completely out of our immediate game plan. For the moment we settled on keeping her world very very small and refused to think too far ahead. By seriously narrowing in her world we simultaneously removed ourselves from tension arising from attempting to walk her. We neared something like happiness.

In other words we did the shift. We thought we had done it months ago. I now see were just dabbling in the shallows of the method. We hadn't. And I also came to realise that there was a huge amount of psychological residue from our previous twelve years of owning dogs which made desperate attempts to negate our new *modus operandi*. Although I could see the positive effect our new regime was having on Sally and on us, there were days when I worried how other people would judge us. On other days however when my fiesty self was in ascendancy I argued back to these unseen critics: 'Stuff you, we're dealing with a demented rescue dog, when you take on such an animal, then we'll talk.'

In the late autumn Colum completed the second stage of the Amichien Bonding course. Instead of stressing as to how I would cope with Sal while he was away, life was calm and most do-able. Sal spent most of her day lolling in her basket in the hall idly watching the curious behaviour of the human inhabitants around her. Once or twice a day she roused herself to run twenty laps round the dining room table followed by a five minute cool down tussle with Jen. She went out to the tree at regular and irregular intervals depending on when Sam and I thought about it, and off-loaded whatever she wanted to off-load. I swore I could almost hear her humming to herself.

And it wasn't just Sal who was finding her place in the scheme of things. You know when you see someone awakening to something that they were born to do? That's what I saw when I met Colum coming home very late one evening from the second residential part of the Amichien course. As he came up to where I was standing waiting with Jenna where our road meets the station path, streetlight fell across his face but I saw that there was no need for any artificial assistance for it was already lit up, happy and totally alive. Sometimes in life we perhaps need a nudge, a shove or the experience of re-homing a deranged rescue dog to remind us of our unique self and what we should be doing with that self. The apparently insurmountable problem, Sally, had indeed proved to be the way through.

Acceptance

It's mid-November now. Light fades around four o'clock, most of the leaves are off the trees, it was deeply misty in our street last night, people are once again talking of getting organized for Christmas and in the Scriven household we are gearing up to celebrate Sam's 21st birthday in a week's time. He hasn't yet moved out despite making lots of rumblings about it but I expect he will soon and it will be because it's what young men do rather than because a crazy dog is making home life untenable. Like all of us, he now laughs when Sally does something daft – such as when Sally got into his room and swallowed his ear-plugs and poohed them out at the pee tree, intact, some hours later. And he still swears when he experiments and attempts to walk Sally up in the street or down the back garden – an optimism often rewarded with a materialisation of her former mental self and a swift return to the house. But, like the rest of us, he views Sally as part of what happens now. She has been factored in.

It still isn't totally easy. It would be nice if she was chilled enough to cope with the outside world. It would be amazing if we could walk her over the park with Jenna, let her romp around the glen, canter about with other dogs, take her on holiday with us, stretch her long limbs along gull-strewn seashores and swim in cool rivers. But such is the stuff of dreams. Maybe it will happen, maybe it won't. And whether it takes another month, another six months, another year or another five years to see her at peace with whatever perceived dangers she imagines to be lurking out there, it matters not. For now, she seems happy in her limited life. And we are happy to let her progress at her own pace. We have, in other words, arrived at the point of beginning. As T S Eliot appreciated (he, the estimable chap, whom I mentioned long syne who liked constant tea while writing) sometimes in life we suddenly awake to a new understanding of the place we have always been in.

After almost two years of wondering when Sally will settle and behave as other dogs do, we have given that up as a futile conjecture and instead find ourselves accepting her as she is, listening to what she's telling us and being aware of what she is bringing us. How long she has had to wait.

Lightning Source UK Ltd.
Milton Keynes UK
UKOW06f2350101116
287404UK00017B/514/P